P9-AQZ-956

Evil

A Historical and Theological Perspective

Hans Schwarz

Translated by Mark W. Worthing

Fortress Press   Minneapolis

EVIL
A Historical and Theological Perspective

Copyright © 1995 Augsburg Fortress. All rights reserved. Except for brief quotations in critical articles or reviews, no part of this book may be reproduced in any manner without prior written permission from the publisher. Write to: Permissions, Augsburg Fortress, 426 S. Fifth St., Box 1209, Minneapolis, MN 55440.

Scripture quotations unless otherwise noted are from the New Revised Standard Version of the Bible, copyright © 1989 by the Division of Christian Education of the National Council of the Churches of Christ in the United States.

Interior design: ediType
Cover design: Brad Norr

Library of Congress Cataloging-in-Publication Data

Schwarz, Hans, 1939–
  Evil : a historical and theological perspective / Hans Schwarz ;
translated by Mark Worthing.
    p.   cm.
  Includes bibliographical references and index.
  ISBN 0-8006-2857-8 (alk. paper)
    1. Good and evil.   2. Good and evil—Comparative studies.   3. Good
and evil—Biblical teaching.   4. Good and evil—History of
doctrines.   5. Theodicy—History of doctrines.   I. Title.
BJ1401.S42   1995
231'.8—dc20   94-31474
                                                             CIP

The paper used in this publication meets the minimum requirements of American National Standard for Information Sciences—Permanence of Paper for Printed Library Materials, ANSI Z329.48-1984.   ∞™

Manufactured in the U.S.A.   AF 1-2857

99 98 97 96 95   1   2   3   4   5   6   7   8   9   10

OMEN.ST
3J
140
942
1995

Contents

Abbreviations

ACW   *Ancient Christian Writers*. Westminster, Md.: Newman, 1946–.

ANF   *The Ante-Nicene Fathers: Translations of the Writings of the Fathers down to A.D. 325*. 10 vols. Grand Rapids, Mich.: Eerdmans, 1950–51.

BHH   *Biblisch-historisches Handwörterbuch*. Edited by Bo Reicke and Leonhard Rost. Göttingen: Vandenhoeck and Ruprecht, 1962.

ER   *The Encyclopedia of Religion*. Edited by Mircea Eliade. 16 vols. New York: Macmillan, 1986.

FC   *The Fathers of the Church*. A New Translation. Washington, D.C.: Catholic University of America Press, 1947–.

HDT   *Handbuch der Dogmen- und Theologiegeschichte*. Edited by Carl Andresen. Göttingen: Vandenhoeck and Ruprecht, 1982.

LW   *Luther's Works*. Edited by Jaroslav Pelikan and Helmut T. Lehmann. 46 vols. St. Louis: Concordia; Philadelphia: Fortress Press, 1955–86.

NPNF   *A Select Library of the Nicene and Post-Nicene Fathers of the Christian Church*. 14 vols. First Series. Grand Rapids, Mich.: Eerdmans, 1956.

NTD   *Das Neue Testament Deutsch*. Edited by Peter Stuhlmacher. 11 vols. Göttingen: Vandenhoeck and Ruprecht, 1981ff.

TDNT   *Theological Dictionary of the New Testament*. Edited by Gerhard Kittel. Translated by G. W. Bromiley. 10 vols. Grand Rapids, Mich.: Eerdmans, 1964–76.

TDOT   *Theological Dictionary of the Old Testament.* Edited by
           G. Johannes Botterweck and Helmer Ringgren. Translated
           by David E. Green. Grand Rapids, Mich.: Eerdmans,
           1980–.

TWAT   *Theologisches Wörterbuch zum Alten Testament.* Edited
           by G. Johannes Botterweck and Helmer Ringgren.
           Stuttgart: Kohlhammer, 1973–.

TRE   *Theologische Realenzyklopädie.* Edited by Gerhard
           Krause and Gerhard Müller. Berlin: Walter de Gruyter,
           1977–.

Preface

The East-West conflict has finally been overcome. What was once "the evil empire," as former U.S. president Ronald Reagan once termed the former USSR, has now been transformed into several independent nations, most of which are seeking friendly relations with the West. A new world order has emerged. But the world has not become more peaceful. Instead of the East-West stand-off we now have numerous local clashes. Nations like the former Yugoslavia disintegrate, and formerly peaceful neighbors suddenly turn into vengeful enemies who threaten one another with extinction. Then there is the senseless killing that takes place in our (own) metropolitan areas. It makes the national news only if something really nightmarish happens, as for instance when someone using a semiautomatic weapon kills a dozen innocent children who were playing in the school yard during their lunch break. Environmental problems also haunt us. The ozone layer protecting life on this planet is getting thinner every year, and the ozone hole is no longer a periodical phenomenon above distant Antarctica but now also exists closer to home over the North Pole. As the second millennium comes to a close, we do not seem to be on the path toward peace and security but rather on the road leading to destruction. Especially in Germany, but also in such an optimistically geared country as the United States, one gets the feeling that we are living in the worst of times with even worse still to come. While "radical evil has always existed; it now threatens to overwhelm us entirely," as a recent author on evil concluded.[1]

In this situation it is important to not lose sight of reality. First of all, is it really true that things are getting progressively worse,

---

1. Jeffrey Burton Russell, *The Prince of Darkness: Radical Evil and the Power of Good in History* (Ithaca, N.Y.: Cornell Univ. Press, 1988), 273.

or are there certain areas in which we manage to do quite well? Furthermore, how far does evil reach as far as our destiny and that of the world around us are concerned? Are we heading for an inevitable apocalypse, or is there something else for us in store? While I did not want to write a book on the interpretation of history, the human involvement with evil cannot be explained without reference to our historical context. It is therefore shortsighted to treat this topic without reference to the life sciences that decisively contribute to the interpretation and understanding of evil. I would also contend that theodicy, the question of why God allows evil, provides a rather narrow focus because it usually fails to show the depth of human depravity. While evil is God's very own problem, it is also our problem. This problem has a specific cause in the antigodly, in that which stands against God and the goodness of the created. Evil is neither a primeval decree nor an inescapable fate, but has its origin in a power that always denies or negates. While we are all caught in the dragnet of evil, we are not helpless victims, as if evil were simply an impervious "it." We can fight evil and indeed should do so.

At the conclusion of this preface I would like to express my thanks for various suggestions and helpful criticisms I have received in working on this topic. Primarily I would like to mention here Verena Grüter, Jens Colditz, and especially Mark Worthing, who also translated this manuscript into English. Hildegard Ferme, who helped with many angles of the production of this manuscript, also deserves many thanks. I remain, of course, responsible for any shortcomings that the text might still contain.

Introduction

Encounters with phenomena that are perceived as being negative belong to the most fundamental of human experiences. While experiences that are judged to be positive are generally and understandably accepted without further reflection, negative experiences, especially in the form of evil or sin, pose for many people a seemingly inexplicable problem. What do we actually mean by saying that something is "evil" or "sinful"? Designations such as "evil," "bad luck," or "sin" are often used interchangeably. We frequently speak of something being "bad" when it does not exhibit the characteristics that we prefer. In other instances we often actually mean to say that a particular act or situation is evil or sinful, though still calling it just "bad." When discussing a person guilty of some crime we may tend to speak of sinful structures when what we really have in mind are inadequate social structures.

Underlying this semantic confusion is the fact that the theological concept of "sin" has largely disappeared from our everyday vocabulary. We do not want to offend anybody by calling something or someone sinful because in our secular society we tend to shy away from a more penetrating religious evaluation and remain instead with a religiously neutral surface view. Sin, as a fundamentally religious concept, usually designates an offense against a religious taboo or cultic law. If one violates, for instance, one of the Ten Commandments, then one has sinned. Moral "evil" overlaps considerably with that which is generally called sin. As a rule, however, evil is understood as the opposite of that which we hold to be good. Thus evil has a patently ethical character because it is at variance with the intended or expected behavior. The word "evil" can also signify that which has been maliciously brought about. Yet it describes just as easily a negative event that virtually assumes the character of an impersonal fate. Finally, "guilt" designates one's own entanglement in that which is negative. It is through guilt that one bears the burden of what others experience as negative.

Although one may view that which is negative simply as the opposite of that which is experienced as positive, the initial identification of that which is negative, or evil, is far from simple. It is we ourselves who categorize a thing or event as negative, evaluating it as having a "not good" character. In this way that which is contrary to our perceived needs, interests, or wishes is often labeled as negative. This can be seen most poignantly in those instances in which images of the enemy are erected that deny that which is good in the "other," portraying them at the same time as the incarnation of all that is evil. Such subjective defamation can be found in both private and public life, and all too often in the realm of international politics as well. Hence other human beings are made to appear devilish and their right to existence denied. Nevertheless, it would be shortsighted to speak only of a subjective characterization of negative experiences as if objective evidence of the perversion of positive experiences was lacking.

Of course that which one portrays as evil, similarly to that which is portrayed as good, is subjugated to a multitude of transformations. Despite all of this semantic maneuvering, however, the undisputed phenomenon of that which is concretely negative looms before us. Every human society testifies at least indirectly to the existence of this phenomenon. Each has developed a system of laws and regulations based upon the insight that people do not always conduct themselves in a manner that society at large deems appropriate. Similarly, all religious worship, whether monotheistic, polytheistic, or of some other form, witnesses to the fact that people have become alienated from their own essence. Therefore, the spirits, or gods, are to be appeased for human misbehavior through various religious practices. Even the very concept of redemption implies the acceptance of the fact that we are entangled in something that does not belong to our essential nature. Consequently, we encounter everywhere the idea of a basic evil that contradicts our fundamental orientation and our true self. That which is negative certainly has a subjective aspect, yet it also transcends the merely subjective.

The experience of the negative necessarily gives rise to the question, Why? Why is life on this earth characterized by the fact that humans make life miserable for each other? Why are even the "best" people, apart from any human interference, visited by serious diseases and other evils? Is there a force within and yet transcending humanity that functions, as it were, as a *diabolos* or as a "distorter," continually detracting from the experience of the good in our lives and turning it instead into something negative? It is precisely this problem of evil, a problem that daily affects us and others, confronting us through newspaper, television, and drama, that has occupied the human mind through the ages. Because this is not only a religious but also a general human problem, we will begin our look at evil with a theological foray into behavioral research and psychoanalysis.

Chapter 1

So-called Evil in the Light of Behavioral Research

The Ambivalence of Aggression • Lorenz

In his book *On Aggression,* Konrad Lorenz sought to illumine through research in animal behavior that aspect of evil identified with aggressive behavior. He took up the theory of natural selection developed by Charles Darwin, which is built upon the recognition of a significant overproduction of descendants among animals and plants and the postulation of a corresponding reduction in descendants through the struggle for survival. According to this view, only those able to demonstrate their superiority can reproduce and succeed in this struggle. This struggle for existence has a certain survival value inasmuch as it provides an advantage for the future of a species whenever the stronger of two rivals wins the territory or fought-over female and brings its specific, advantageous characteristic into the reproduction pool. Hence such aggressive behavior is judged to be positive.

When one applies, however, this intraspecific aggression, that is, the aggression within a particular living species, to our contemporary cultural-historical and technological situation, Lorenz arrives at an entirely different conclusion, considering it "the greatest of all dangers."[1] Yet our prospects of successfully confronting this danger will not be improved so much by regarding it as something metaphysical and inevitable as by examining the natural causes in the chain of aggressive behavior. Lorenz maintains that the aggression instinct "has been derailed" by the living conditions of our

---

1. For this and the following citation see Konrad Lorenz, *On Aggression,* trans. Marjorie Latzke (London: Methuen, 1966), 23.

modern civilization. Yet this instinct, as argued already by Darwin, has natural causes. The aim of this aggression is not the annihilation of fellow members of one's own species, although this can occasionally come about through an unfortunate accident. Rather, it is a part of the life-preserving organization within all life-forms (38f.). Lorenz, unlike Darwin, does not limit the positive contributions of aggressive behavior to selection through fighting between rivals, but rather points out that aggression also contributes to the distribution of members of the same species within available living space, to the defense of offspring, and even to the protection of weaker members of a group, as well as to other positive effects. Even "blossoms of personal friendship and love" (39) can sprout forth out of aggression.

For what reason, then, does aggression, which in the instance of animals and plants is valued as something positive, become the root of all evil in the case of humanity? Konrad Lorenz believed that in all probability hereditary aggression, which remains with us to this day as a "bad" inheritance, is caused through the process of intraspecific natural selection, which through many thousands of years, especially through the entire Paleolithic period, has left its imprint upon us (34). By developing weapons, clothing, and social organization, humanity was able, to a certain degree, to stave off the external threats of starvation, freezing, and being eaten by large predatory animals. But then the selective drive led to the evolution of wars that drove neighboring tribes against one another as enemies. Thus developed an intense cultivation of all the so-called virtues of the art of war, many of which continue to be viewed by large segments of modern humanity as desirable ideals.

Lorenz identifies this phase of transition into humanity with the development of abstract thought, which led humans to a dialogical and questioning interaction with their environment.[2] In this phase, according to Lorenz, humans no longer followed without reflection their instincts as in paradise, where they acted or failed to act based solely upon their desires. Humanity discovered its first tools: the hand axe and fire. The human "quickly learned to use these tools to kill his brother and to roast him, as the discovery in the dwelling places of Peking Man demonstrates: Alongside the first evidences of the use of fire lay broken and clearly burned human

---

2. For the following see Lorenz, *On Aggression*, 205–36.

bones."[3] Conceptual thought made possible human dominion over
the other varieties of life; within the human species, however, it
led to an exaggerated aggression drive from which we continue to
suffer to this day.

Conceptual thinking enabled humans to develop a culture and
to transfer knowledge acquired by one group to other humans.
This produced such radical and rapid changes in living conditions
that human instincts were unable to adapt. One could easily imagine the corresponding result in the case of various animals and
birds if they were suddenly given new tools, for instance, the chim-
panzee a hammer and the dove the beak of a bird of prey. The
results, in all probability, would be devastating, for the naturally
proven balance between the ability to kill and the instinctive inhibition against killing would be destroyed. In the prehistory of
the human species, according to Lorenz, no special, highly developed inhibition was necessary to prevent a sudden, fatal assault
because such an assault was not yet possible. "The attacker could,
in any event, only by means of scratching, biting, and strangling
succeed in killing his victim who, for this reason, had ample opportunity to appeal to the sympathy instinct of the attacker through
demonstrations of submission and cries of fear." Through the discovery of artificial weapons, however, there arose the possibility
of killing with a single strike. The previously existing balance between the relatively weak inhibition against aggression and the
ability to kill members of one's own species was thereby destroyed.
Conceptual thought, however, not only led to the development of
culture but also made possible the rational responsibility of human
beings, who could now ask and answer questions concerning the
consequences of their actions.

If aggression is no longer directed toward the nonhuman world,
which has been largely domesticated by humans, but is rather expressed only between members of the human family, then it can
only lead to the most peculiar and inappropriate aberrations. Especially problematic today is the aggression drive, inasmuch as it
finds no appropriate outlet in contemporary civilization. For this
reason Lorenz pleads for a reorientation of aggression in order

---

3. The English translation (205, 207) of this and the next quotation is quite
liberal and in places only partial; thus the German original (319f., 323) has
here been followed. See Lorenz, *Das sogenannte Böse: Zur Naturgeschichte der
Aggression,* 33d ed. (Vienna: G. Borotha Schoeler, 1973).

to steer it in a more peaceable direction.[4] This can take place in part through athletic competition between individuals and nations, inasmuch as such competition is an important cultural achievement of humanity and makes possible a culturally ritualized form of combat. A person must, therefore, learn that inherited inclinations cannot be blindly followed, but must rather be controlled and their consequences scrutinized with far-sighted and responsible self-examination. Lorenz comes, therefore, to the conclusion that "man is not so evil from his youth, he is simply not quite good enough for the demands of life in modern society."[5]

Despite these hints of optimism, however, Lorenz is so negatively disposed toward our modern society that he can even speak of the "deadly sins of civilized humanity."[6] On the basis of seven specific cultural changes Lorenz shows that behavioral mechanisms that were originally developed to help preserve the human species were disturbed, thereby bringing about dysfunctional disturbances that can only be regarded as pathological.[7] These changes are: (1) the overpopulation of the earth, which, through the overabundance of social contacts, forces each of us to isolate ourselves in a fundamentally antihuman way, and additionally, the crowding of many persons within a limited space, which provokes aggression; (2) the destruction of our natural habitat; (3) the rat race of humanity against itself; (4) the disappearance of all strong emotions and passions through pampering; (5) genetic deterioration through deficient selection pressure on development and the lack of preservation of the norms of social behavior; (6) the breakdown of tradition; and (7) the increasing susceptibility of humans to indoctrination. Consequently, we are faced not only with the negation and undoing of the creation process, through which humanity evolved from animals, but also with an active hostility against that which we hold to be upright and good.

Lorenz reaches the conclusion that this socially devious behavior· is a phenomenon "that makes many religions believe in an adversary of God. When we consider all that has happened and

---

4. Lorenz, *On Aggression,* 240f.

5. Lorenz, *Das sogenannte Böse,* 333. The English translation, *On Aggression,* 216, translates this passage somewhat liberally as: "The imagination of man's heart is not really evil from his youth, as the book of Genesis asserts."

6. For the following see Konrad Lorenz's *Civilized Man's Eight Deadly Sins,* trans. Marjorie Kerr Wilson (New York: Harcourt Brace Jovanovich, 1974).

7. See Lorenz, *Civilized Man's Eight Deadly Sins,* 5.

is happening in the world today, it is difficult to argue with those who believe that we are living in the days of an anti-Christ" (59). Lorenz does not wish to represent humanity as the instinct-poor beings he once did, but rather, he now contends that the human being has available more instinctive drives than any animal (see 6). Many of these drives, however, are so distorted that we are confronted with human self-destruction. Lorenz no longer concerns himself so much with aggressive behavior per se, as in his book *On Aggression;* rather, he directs his arguments against that which he describes as a false development of civilization. He thereby rejects the biblical affirmation that a person is evil from youth (Gen. 8:21).

According to Lorenz, the average person follows the Ten Commandments in his conduct among personal friends out of natural inclination. "One does not lie to a friend or steal from a friend, one does not covet a friend's wife; least of all does one kill a friend."[8] Although within a small group of friends the Ten Commandments would be followed, the genetically programmed inclinations of the human being are not sufficient to make equitable the social requirements of a modern society composed of millions of individuals. The individual is not genetically programmed to show responsibility toward an anonymous and personally unknown member of mass society in the same way as toward acquaintances and close friends.

Nevertheless, a system of prescriptions and prohibitions has evolved in the course of the development of civilization that continually compels us to do violence to our inborn behavioral programs. Along with other members of society we are placed in the perpetual straightjacket of cultural norms for our behavior. According to Lorenz, the tension between natural human inclination and cultural demands increases proportional to the development of a civilization (128). In today's industrial societies there already exist a dangerously high number of people who can no longer cope with this tension and become either antisocial or neurotic. In other words, they either suffer alone or cause suffering in society at large. The natural disposition of the human is consequently no longer suited to the conditions of our contemporary culture. Under these circumstances cultural as well as

---

8. Konrad Lorenz, *The Waning of Humaneness,* trans. Robert Warren Kickert (Boston: Little, Brown and Co., 1987), 126.

genetically programmed norms, which until recently were seen as virtues, lead to negative consequences. In regard to these conditions Lorenz has in mind especially a technocratic system that leads to an overorganization and incapacitation of humanity. Nevertheless, Lorenz is ultimately optimistic and believes that humanity will be successfully recovered because the ability to love and establish friendships, with all the accompanying emotions, originated in the course of the development of the human tribe precisely in the same manner as the ability to measure and count. "*Both* kinds of phenomena draw upon and relate to *the same* reality, a reality to which a feeling and experiencing fellow human belongs just as well as those things that are measurable and countable" (236f.).

If we now wish to present a brief summary of Konrad Lorenz's understanding of evil, we must remember that for Lorenz there is no such thing as general evil in a strictly definable sense. Evil is closely bound with humanity becoming human. It cannot, however, be equated with the phenomenon of being human, but rather arises from the possibilities opened up by human existence. Evil does not attack persons like an inescapable fate, even if it is not yet known whether humanity and the whole creation can actually escape the consequences of evil. Although evil is perpetrated by individual persons, it must always be seen within the context of society as a whole, in which it manifests itself. Evil actions always have a social aspect. Finally, it must be pointed out that the Ten Commandments were not introduced by God as a supernatural impediment to evil, but as that which is natural and appropriate to the just conduct of the human species. Konrad Lorenz, therefore, does not deny the existence of evil, but rather shows how in various ways evil is bound to the development of humanity. In so doing, Lorenz seeks to limit the damage done through evil by appealing to human responsibility.

Self-Endangered Humanity • Wickler, Wilson, Eibl-Eibesfeldt, Hassenstein

Wolfgang Wickler demonstrates in his book *The Biology of the Ten Commandments* that animals cannot avoid what appears to be morally analogous behavior, whereas humans, on the other hand, know that they are capable of immoral action.[9] The risk to humans is to be found in the fact that they desire to do more than they are able and that they are able to do more than they ought (1). The human is aware of its capability to endanger itself and is therefore called to be responsible. Nevertheless, Wickler, even as a pupil of Konrad Lorenz, rejects the claim that aggression is a genuine instinct with its own endogenous production of arousal and corresponding appetite-satisfying behavior (109f.). For this reason he rejects the thesis that one can deduce psychological and sociological data relevant to human aggression from the observation of animal behavior.

Although Edward Wilson, with reference to Lorenz's book *On Aggression,* rejects the view that aggression is an instinct continually in search of an outlet, he readily admits that human beings are aggressive from birth.[10] Still, he points out that in each species aggression is comprised of various types of responses, each of which has separate controls within the nervous system. Wilson lists no fewer than seven categories of aggression, several of which had already been mentioned by Lorenz. He would disagree with Lorenz, however, that we are among the most aggressive of species. For Wilson, human aggression is neither a bestial instinct nor a dark fate nor a pathological symptom stemming from an upbringing in a cruel environment.[11]

According to Wilson, humans tend to defend themselves against external threats with unreasonable hate, thereby allowing animosity to escalate to such an extent that they react to the cause of the threat with excessive force. In other words, their actions far overshoot what would have been sufficient to defend themselves against the threat. Because we are no longer hunters or gatherers who settle our disputes with spears, arrows, and stone axes, the learning of violent aggression has become anachronistic. For this reason Wilson believes that we must come to the point in our psychological development in which we are able to master and reduce our deeply rooted tendency to learn violence. Only in this way, in the interests of human well-being, can this aspect of our nature once more be put on a leash. The human being

---

9. Wolfgang Wickler, *The Biology of the Ten Commandments,* trans. David Smith (New York: McGraw-Hill, 1972), 56.

10. Edward O. Wilson, *On Human Nature* (Cambridge, Mass.: Harvard Univ. Press, 1978), 101 and 99.

11. For this and the following see Wilson, *On Human Nature,* 119f.

appears, therefore, according to Wilson, to exhibit through over-reaction an inappropriate level of violence and is thus required to become aware of this overreaction in order to once more bring it under control. Hence Wilson concedes that humans possess a certain amount of aggression, but he seeks to limit the excesses of this aggression.

Irenäus Eibl-Eibesfeldt, the successor to Konrad Lorenz in human ethology at the Max Planck Institute in Seewiesen, Germany, did not just want to limit the excesses of aggression as suggested by Wilson. As a behavioral researcher he saw that intraspecific aggressive conflicts exist among vertebrate and invertebrate alike and that the human species is no exception to this rule. Similar to Lorenz and Wilson, he did not wish simply and sweepingly to equate aggression with evil. In so doing, the question of a possible aptitude-promoting function of aggressive behavior would be neglected from the very beginning and the path to a rational discussion of the problem obstructed.[12] Eibl-Eibesfeldt limits his discussion to intraspecific aggression because this is interesting for intrahuman behavior and because the majority of all vertebrates fight within their own species. Aggression is assigned here to the category of adversarial behavior, to which also belong defensive behavior, subjugation, and fleeing. According to Eibl-Eibesfeldt, however, one must distinguish between two classes of members of the same species: those who belong to a specific group—between the members of which aggression is effectively contained through a sort of trust relationship—and those who do not belong to the group.

Against outsiders of one's group, social inhibitions in hostile disputes, in the case of animals as well as humans, are so reduced that the conflict can go as far as murder; indeed, killing can even be the declared goal. Whoever does not belong to the group is treated almost as if belonging to another species, whereby, especially in the case of war, one is able to describe the enemy as inhuman or inferior. In this way any lingering inhibitions toward the enemy based upon sympathy are eliminated. This type of destructive group-aggression that is found in war is clearly to be differentiated from the aggressive disputes between members of

---

12. For the following see Irenäus Eibl-Eibesfeldt, *Der Mensch—Das riskierte Wesen: Zur Naturgeschichte menschlicher Unvernunft* (Munich: Piper, 1988), 205ff.

the same group, as for example in the fight over rank. This latter type of aggression serves the process of socialization, not that of exclusion.

Eibl-Eibesfeldt rejects the view that aggression is handed down exclusively through social models, as is more or less assumed by the learned-behavior theory of aggression, or that it is a purely reactionary response to frustration. Frustration, of course, can trigger aggression, as in the case of children who easily get into fights on the way home from school if they have been regularly restricted in their need for movement during the school day. Likewise, aggression can be learned from social models. Thus children can learn that an enraged father strikes the mother when they themselves experience frequently such behavior. Still, there exists an aggressive social experimentation through which a person learns what is allowed and what is forbidden. When, for example, one enters a new stage of development and must adapt to a new group or community, one seeks to test the limits of one's freedom of action. In this way social pecking orders are also redefined.

This sort of aggressive behavior between individual persons has very little to do with the destructive and strategically planned societal aggression of war. Such aggressive encounters between individuals are a cultural inheritance through which ethnologic adaptations are passed down. War, as a form of strategically planned aggression that is carried out in enemy territory and with the help of lethal weapons, aims for the annihilation of the opponent and is a product of cultural evolution. The implementation of war requires that aggression-stimulating mechanisms be used and aggression-inhibiting mechanisms suppressed. Although this insight alone is insufficient to help eliminate war, Eibl-Eibesfeldt leaves no doubt that warlike aggression is neither ethnologically necessary nor genetically unavoidable. Thus Eibl-Eibesfeldt distinguishes an aggression that is beneficial and necessary for intraspecific coexistence from a type of aggression that, especially as directed against outsiders and facilitated with modern means, leads directly to self-destruction.

Bernhard Hassenstein, a zoologist from the University of Freiburg, Germany, recognizes as well that aggressiveness in the case of animals occurs in a variety of situations. A self-generating aggressiveness that leads to combat and that must periodically be satisfied cannot, however, according to Hassenstein, be postulated for either humans or animals on the basis of current research.[13] One can recognize aggression with certainty only as it occurs in the service of other biological functions. In the case of combat between members of the same species, annihilation as well as the sparing of the opponent can occur. Thus one cannot conclude that animals of the same species that are capable of fighting do not in fact kill one another. Rather, it appears much more to be the case that animals capable of combat that live within some sort of social structure have no inhibition against killing members of their own species that do not belong to their own particular social unit. This applies to humans as well. We possess, in all probability, a biological inhibition against killing known members of our own social group. Whether the same applies to those foreign to our own group remains, however, an open question.

Hassenstein points out that the decision over the killing of other persons falls within the realm of culture and that a possible natural aptitude for such decisions provides no guidelines. He concedes, however, that people can be motivated to mass aggression, a fact very probably the result of natural conditioning, because such infectious aggression corresponds to the attack upon a group's enemy. Hassenstein nevertheless writes: "The individual can, to the extent that his volition dominates, mold his actions to correspond to the results of his reflections. Then he is as free in his actions as he is in his thoughts" (82). In a relaxed environment the human being is capable of making free decisions after weighing and considering various possibilities. The human is also capable of mobilizing forces against the natural, instinctive drive that produces mass aggression and shaping his or her actions, after a conscious weighing of the possibilities, in a more humane fashion. In this way Hassenstein demonstrates that we are not simply victims of our drives or of genetic determinism, but are instead capable of responsible action to such an extent that this responsibility is not lessened through external, manipulative pressures. Nevertheless, Hassenstein likewise indicates that we are inclined, through our natural drives, to endanger other persons.

We can consult behavioral researchers of various specializations and will get the same answer: humans are indeed not a morally

---

13. See Bernhard Hassenstein, "Das spezifisch Menschliche nach den Resultaten der Verhaltensforschung," in *Neue Anthropologie,* ed. Hans-Georg Gadamer and Paul Vogler, vol. 2 (Stuttgart: Georg Thieme, 1972), 82–96.

deficient species, but in our humanity and personhood we remain continually at risk. Each person has a capacity for good as well as for evil, whereby both capacities, through human cultural development, have exponentially multiplied. The human being must not, therefore, become simply a victim of his or her own evolution. Nevertheless, humanity, through this very evolution that has also provided many new developmental possibilities, is threatened as never before. Although even Konrad Lorenz indicated clearly several faulty developments of human culture, he does, nevertheless, not wish to be seen as a cultural pessimist. He hopes that ominous constellations on the human horizon can be diffused and even replaced through insight and new adaptations. Behavioral research, then, sees humanity as being actually endangered, a circumstance that for individuals and for the population as a whole continues, to a certain extent, to produce negative consequences. Hence evil is neither declared to be a biological given nor viewed as an inescapable fate. Evil is a reality that surrounds us and decisively influences our lives. It is precisely this reality, however, that we can and must confront, without knowing in advance whether it will overcome us or be overcome by us.

Chapter 2

Psychoanalytic View
of the Human Predicament

Konrad Lorenz himself pointed out that the consequences of aggression were often to be equated with what Freud understood as
a death instinct. Thus we turn from the behavioral to the psychoanalytic view of the human predicament.[1] Here, alongside of such
classical representatives of psychoanalysis as Sigmund Freud, Carl
Gustav Jung, and Erich Fromm, we will also consider the work
of Eugen Drewermann, whose comprehensive treatment of the
structures of evil has, at least for a time, created something of a
sensation.

An Inborn Inclination for Evil • Freud

Sigmund Freud, the founder of modern psychoanalysis, recognized, as did Lorenz after him, an aggression drive in humanity.
This recognition, however, did not come easily for Freud. For
twenty years, Freud, in his analysis of human behavior, resisted
recognizing an independent aggression drive that would be equated
with destruction.[2] Only through the impact of World War I was he
ready to accept the existence of an aggression drive. Thus he wrote
in his 1915 work "Thoughts for the Times on War and Death"

---

1. See Konrad Lorenz, *On Aggression,* trans. Marjorie Latzke (London:
Methuen, 1966), ix–x. See also Wolfhart Pannenberg, *Anthropology in Theological Perspective,* trans. Matthew O'Connell (Philadelphia: Westminster, 1985),
142f.

2. So Helmut Nolte, "Über gesellschaftstheoretische Implikationen des Aggres-
sionsbegriffs," in Wolf Lepenies and Helmut Nolte, *Kritik der Anthropologie:
Marx und Freud, Gehlen und Habermas über Aggression* (Munich: Hanser,
1971), 104f.

that evil could not be eradicated. "Psychological—or, more strictly speaking, pyscho-analytic—investigation shows instead that the deepest essence of human nature consists of instinctual impulses which are of an elementary nature, which are similar in all men and which aim at the satisfaction of certain primal needs."[3] To be sure, these primitive impulses can be culturally transformed so that they lose their effective reality. It must, nevertheless, be admitted that "our unconscious is just as inaccessible to the idea of our own death, just as murderously inclined towards a stranger, just as divided (that is, ambivalent) towards those we love, as was primaeval man" (299). Through war the cultural transformations are stripped away, and primitive humanity, which encountered the foreigner with murderous intent, comes once again to light. Instinctive drives, though inherently neither good nor bad, contain hidden within them the potential for evil, which repeatedly breaks out into the open.

In *Beyond the Pleasure Principle* (1920) Freud presents the aggression drive as the externally oriented, secondarily autonomous variant of the self-destruction drive. Important in this regard is the concept of narcissism. Wrote Freud in 1925: "The ethical narcissism of humanity should rest content with the knowledge that the fact of distortion in dreams, as well as the existence of anxiety dreams and punishment dreams, afford just as clear evidence of his moral nature as dream interpretation gives of the existence and strength of his evil nature."[4] According to Freud, human behavior is largely determined through sexuality, which consists of both good and bad tendencies. Alongside of *eros,* the drive that supports the living substance and embraces ever greater numbers of individual units, there exists another, opposing drive: the death instinct. Unlike the eros instinct, the death instinct breaks apart the individual units and is bent upon returning them to their primordial, inorganic condition.[5] In the cooperation and opposition of these two instincts Freud sought to explain the phenomena of life.

---

3. Sigmund Freud, "Thoughts for the Times on War and Death" (1915), in *The Standard Edition of the Complete Psychological Works of Sigmund Freud,* ed. James Strachey (London: Hogarth, 1957), 14:281.

4. Freud, "Moral Responsibility for the Content of Dreams" (1925), in *Collected Papers,* ed. James Strachey (London: Hogarth, 1950), 5:157. A good introduction to Freud's interpretation of the human condition and the Christian understanding of original sin is offered by Sharon MacIsaac, *Freud and Original Sin* (New York: Paulist, 1974).

5. For this and the following see Freud, *Civilization and Its Discontents*

In this collaboration the two instincts seldom appear in isolation from one another, but have varying levels of intensity and are often intermingled with each other so that from our perspective they are indistinguishable.

Freud admits that in the beginning he advocated the existence of these two instincts only hesitantly and tentatively, but then became increasingly convinced of their reality. That he also encountered opposition regarding this view he indicated when he wrote: "For 'little children do not like it' when there is talk of the inborn inclination to 'badness,' to aggressiveness, and destructiveness, and so to cruelty as well" (120). Freud establishes that the inclination toward aggression "is an original, self-subsisting instinctual disposition in man" (122) that finds in civilization its strongest impediment. Civilization is a process in the service of eros that seeks to gather together not only isolated human individuals but also families, tribes, peoples, and nations into a great union in order to bind them to one another through their libidos, thereby resisting the natural aggression drive of humans in which the hostility of the one is directed against the whole and that of the whole against the one. The aggressive instinct "is the derivative and the main representative of the death instinct which we have found alongside of Eros and which shares world-dominion with it" (122).

The battle between eros and death, between the drives toward life and destruction, is, according to Freud, the essential content of life and is indicative of human struggle for survival. We are not dealing here, however, with a simple dualism, for "it is very rarely that an action is the work of a *single* instinctual impulse (which must in itself be compounded of Eros and destructiveness). In order to make an action possible there must be as a rule a combination of such compounded motives."[6] For this reason it is difficult to isolate the two instincts in their manifestations. Moreover, the destruction drive only becomes such in that the death instinct "is used against the objects with the help of special external organs. The lifeform protects its own life, so to speak, through the destruction of that which is foreign." But a part of the death instinct remains always active within a living being and shows itself in

---

(1930), ed. James Strachey, trans. Joan Riveriere, in *The Standard Edition* (1961), 21:119.

6. For this and the following quote see Freud, "Why War?" (1932), in *The Standard Edition* (1964), 22:210.

normal as well as in pathological phenomena. Nevertheless, the external expression of these destructive, driving forces is judged to be exculpable and beneficial. The human and the human community are therefore seriously jeopardized. Yet in order to fathom fully the human predicament, we must, along with Freud, distinguish between the id, the ego, and the superego.

The foundation of all psychic life is the id, which consists primarily of chaotic and unconscious drives. Prominent among these drives is the reproduction drive, or libido. But in all affirmations of life the libido is mixed with the death wish, the goal of which is to once more achieve a state of lifelessness. In conformity with its source and development the libido is closely bound to the body, in which it strides forward from the oral phase of nursing and the anal phase, which has to do with the control of the excretion organs—both of which phases are known as pregenital—to the Oedipus phase, which is characterized by the death wish against the father and incest wish toward the mother.[7] Connected with the libido is the threatening power of the death instinct, which is primarily directed against humanity itself.

If humans do not wish to destroy themselves, they must direct the death instinct to the outside in the form of aggression or destruction. In this regard Freud said: "It really seems as though it is necessary for us to destroy some other thing or person in order not to destroy ourselves, in order to guard against the impulsion to self-destruction."[8] Yet it would be wrong to describe the death wish as something entirely negative, for together with the libido it serves life. It leads the eros to be in control of the objects of its pleasure and helps us to achieve control over nature. But the death wish can erupt at any time in its naked power as aggression and destruction and endanger the culture that was made possible through the libido. Freud acknowledges that "in consequence of this primary mutual hostility of human beings, civilized society is perpetually threatened with disintegration."[9]

To comprehend the entire structure of being, however, we must

---

7. Freud, "Two Encyclopedia Articles" (1923), in *The Standard Edition* (1973), 18:242ff.

8. Freud, *New Introductory Lectures on Psychoanalysis* (1933), in *The Complete Introductory Lectures on Psychoanalysis,* trans. and ed. James Strachey (New York: W. W. Norton, 1966), 569.

9. Freud, *Civilization and Its Discontents,* trans. and ed. James Strachey (New York: W. W. Norton, 1962), 59.

go beyond the id and turn to the ego. The ego emerges from the id as that part of the id that is oriented toward the external world. It functions in such a manner that it recognizes internal and external stimuli, orders them, and initiates reactions to these stimuli. Thus the task of the ego can be described as that of a mediator. This does not rule out, however, that the ego also pursues its own interests. Freud alludes to this when he says: even if the death instinct "emerges without any sexual purpose, in the blindest fury of destructiveness, we cannot fail to recognize that the satisfaction of the instinct is accompanied by an extraordinarily high degree of narcissistic enjoyment, owing to its presenting the ego with a fulfillment of the latter's old wishes for omnipotence" (68). But the ego must also represent the demands of the external world over against those of the id. This corrective function of the ego is facilitated by the superego.

The superego originates through the internalization of external authority, by means of which one is able to identify with this authority. This is especially important for humans as social creatures. According to Freud, the ideals and laws of a society are nothing other than a collective superego (89). The superego of the individual is formed through education by the collective superego and becomes the "vehicle of tradition and of all the time-resisting judgments of value which have propagated themselves in this manner from generation to generation."[10] The superego binds together families and societies through the submission of the interests of the individual to those of the parents and of society. Yet the superego also has its negative side. It can assume cruel and demonic features that drive one to neurosis, melancholy, and even death. The "conscience" of the superego can lead to a sense of guilt or to aggression or even to suicide.

Regardless of the direction in which we look, we notice that humanity is continually struggling to find its way between life and death, between the creation and protection of life and its destruction. One is, therefore, practically forced to the conclusion that Freud presents a dualistic understanding of humanity that is torn "between the life and death instincts."[11] Yet it is not only within individuals that these instincts are to be seen. Every culture is

---

10. Freud, *New Introductory Lectures,* 531.
11. See Freud, "Beyond the Pleasure Principle" (1920), in *The Standard Edition* (1955), 18:53.

also torn between life and death.[12] Freud broadens even wider his perspective when he says:

> And now, I think, the meaning of the evolution of civilization is no longer obscure to us. It must present the struggle between Eros and Death, between the instinct of life and the instinct of destruction, as it works itself out in the human species. This struggle is what all life essentially consists of, and the evolution of civilization may therefore be simply described as the struggle for life of the human species.[13]

If this dichotomy is so all-pervading, one could conclude that it is not possible "to transcend the limits of the human condition or to change the psychological structural conditions that make humanity possible."[14] This is precisely, however, the limit of psychoanalysis. As Ernest Becker has convincingly shown, "Psychoanalysis failed therapeutically where it fetishized the causes of human unhappiness as sexuality, and where it pretended

---

12. See Paul Ricoeur's detailed analysis of Freud in *Freud and Philosophy: An Essay on Interpretation* (New Haven: Yale Univ. Press, 1970), 302ff.

13. Freud, *Civilization* (n. 9 above), 69. This would mean that Freud does not accept a (destructive) death instinct in humanity, but rather, he describes the intrinsically human awareness of finitude and the resulting effort to overcome this finitude. Muzafer and Carolyn W. Sherif, "Motivation and Intergroup Aggression: A Persistent Problem in Levels of Analysis," in *Development and Evolution of Behavior,* ed. Lester L. Aronson et al. (San Francisco: W. H. Freeman, 1970), 566, are only partly correct when they assert that Freud's concept of a death instinct is not scientifically justified. While we reject along with them the simple idea of a death instinct, Freud's concept is more complex and more true to reality than they assume.

14. So Ernest Becker, *The Denial of Death* (New York: Free Press, 1973), 277. In his convincing book Ernest Becker follows largely the thought of Freud by means of a heavy reliance upon Otto Rank, a student of Freud, and he shows that the human fear of death provides the primary stimulus for human actions. In a posthumously published book, *Escape from Evil* (New York: Free Press, 1975), a sequel to *The Denial of Death,* Becker attempts to demonstrate that "man's natural and inevitable urges to deny mortality and achieve a heroic self-image are the root causes of human evil" (xvii). In other words: the attempt of humanity to become like God and deny its finitude are not only the stimulus to heroic acts but also the cause of all evil. Of course one must ask whether our activities are really only a reflection of our fundamental denial of what we are not, namely, God, or whether these activities can and should be understood as an attempt on our part to desire to live as we ought to live, as representatives of God. The Pauline recognition, for example, that humanity knows what is good, but does what is evil, indicates that human actions cannot be simply attributed to a single stimulus. When Becker in the final analysis expresses a hope for "that minute measure of reason to balance destruction" (*Escape from Evil,* 170), he seems implicitly to admit this because "reason" can serve as a means of self-preservation or as something that allows humans to live as they ought to live.

to be a total world-view in itself."[15] Carl Gustav Jung has here blazed a path different from that of Freud in which he deviates from Freud's primary subject of analysis, namely, human sexuality, and breaks through to a more comprehensive and differentiating view of humanity.

The Integration of Evil • Jung

Jung distinguishes between the conscious and the unconscious aspects of the human psyche. The conscious is oriented toward the external world and has as its center the ego. The unconscious part of the human psyche is divided into two distinct realms, the personal and the collective unconscious. The personal unconscious contains that which one has forgotten, suppressed, unconsciously perceived, thought, and felt, providing that these things reveal a close relationship to the experiences of the individual.[16] The collective unconscious consists of the collective memory of humanity, as for example conditions and situations indicative of human nature such as anxiety, danger, struggle against insurmountable odds, relationships between the sexes, attitudes toward father and mother figures, experiences of the powers of light and darkness, and others.[17]

Jung discovered the collective unconscious in his work with patients whose dreams contained picture motifs that were not related to any concrete life experiences of the patients.[18] These motifs, however, were related to religious symbols that were not consciously known to the patients. Jung called these potent picture motifs of the collective unconscious archetypes. "The archetype is, so to speak, an 'eternal' presence, and it is only a question of whether it is perceived by consciousness or not."[19] Similar to

---

15. Becker, *Denial of Death,* 194.

16. Carl Gustav Jung, *Psychological Types* (1921), trans. H. G. Baynes, rev. R. F. C. Hull, in *The Collected Works of C. G. Jung,* ed. W. McGuire, 2d ed. (Princeton, N.J.: Princeton Univ. Press, 1971), 6:377 (625). See also Helmut Harsch, *Das Schuldproblem in Theologie und Tiefenpsychologie* (Heidelberg: Quelle and Meyer, 1965), 115.

17. See Jolande Jacobi, *The Psychology of C. G. Jung,* trans. R. Manheim (New Haven: Yale Univ. Press, 1962), 34f.

18. For the following see Harsch, *Das Schuldproblem,* 116.

19. Jung, *Psychology and Alchemy* (1935–36), in *Collected Works,* trans. R. F. C. Hull (New York: Pantheon Books, 1953), 12:211 (329) (references to *Collected Works* in the following notes are to this series of volumes unless 2d ed. is noted); see also 11f. (12ff.), where Jung points out that it is important,

Freud's id, the archetypes have a unique, ambivalent aspect. According to Jung, this is already to be seen in the picture of the serpent in Genesis 3 when it becomes the picture of either the tempter or the savior. Similarly, the great mother can be either the threatening Tiamat or Mary, the saving queen of heaven. Also, the image of the father is divided between that of the violent, castrating demon, and the benevolent sage who leads us to the realm of the spirit.

In contrast to Freud, Jung does not dwell so exclusively upon the negative side of the collective unconscious, but emphasizes its positive powers that give new impulses to life.[20] While in the collective unconscious the antitheses are not yet distinguished from one another, the situation is different when the ego emerges and these things move into the realm of consciousness. The paradise of primordial unity and wholeness is then irrevocably lost. Thus Jung believes that "there is deep doctrine in the legend of the fall: it is the expression of a dim presentiment that the emancipation of ego-consciousness was a Luciferian deed."[21] As the ego seeks to achieve cognition it encounters insurmountable antitheses and is torn between opposing forces such as spirit and matter, male and female, good and evil, life and death. Although we cannot return to the primordial unity, we are able to overcome the inner strife through individuation. This means that we become "a single, homogeneous being, and, insofar as 'individuality' embraces our innermost, last, and incomparable uniqueness, it also implies becoming one's own self."[22] Individuation is therefore equated with "coming to selfhood" or "self-realization." This process of individuation is guided by what Jung calls the archetype of the self. The individual now comes to its self as well as to the collective self because in its wholeness the individual also reflects the cosmos.

especially for Christians, to bring the archetype into harmony with the conscious mind, lest the Christian faith become simply an external, religious veneer and the inner person remain unchanged.

20. See Jung's criticism of Freud when he says that Freud overemphasizes "the pathological aspect of life" and interprets "man too exclusively in the light of his defects." So Jung, "Freud and Jung: Contrasts" (1929), in *Collected Works* (1961), 4:335 (773).

21. Jung, "The Phenomenology of the Spirit in Fairytales" (1948), in *Collected Works* (1959), 9/1:230 (420). Jung continues his comments on the fall when he perceptively says: "Man's whole history consists from the very beginning in a conflict between his feeling of inferiority and his arrogance."

22. Jung, *The Relations between the Ego and the Unconscious* (1916), in *Collected Works* (1953), 7:171 (266).

"The individuated ego senses itself as the object of an unknown and superordinate subject" (238 [405]). Does this mean that we finally come to a point at which the dichotomy is overcome and ego-consciousness ceases?

If we wish to determine to what extent we can achieve wholeness, we must accompany Jung one step further in his analysis of the person, for he distinguishes still another aspect from the ego that is directed toward the external world and that he calls *persona*. The *persona* can be understood similarly to a mask in Greek theater, for through it we play a role in society, and it filters out everything that does not belong to this role. What the ego considers to be irreconcilable with its *persona* is relegated to the unconscious as a "shadow" (see 138f. [225] and 156 [246]). Thus the shadow contains the undeveloped, the inferior, and the suppressed, as well as wild drives, the immoral, the evil, and the destructive. Jung desires to achieve an integration of the shadow as a part of the individuation process because "mere suppression of the shadow is as little of a remedy as beheading would be for headache."[23] We should rather love our shadow, just as Jesus called us to love our enemies.[24] Similar to the way in which God integrates in some ways his own shadow, evil, we are summoned to overcome moral suffering through the integration of our shadow.[25] Of course Jung realizes that we cannot overcome evil by ourselves, but "we hope to put our trust in the higher powers."[26] The attempt at self-redemption wins humanity nothing.

---

23. Jung, *Psychology and Religion* (1938), in *Collected Works* (1971, 2d ed.), 11:77.

24. See Jung, "Psychotherapists or the Clergy?" (1932), in *Collected Works,* 11:340f. (522f.).

25. Jung, "A Psychological Approach to the Dogma of the Trinity" (1942–48), in *Collected Works,* 11:196ff. (290ff.). Because Jung wants to maintain human responsibility for evil, he is careful not "to impute all evil to God." He is even convinced that "through the intervention of the Holy Spirit, however, man is included in the divine process, and this means that the principle of separateness and autonomy over against God—which is personified in Lucifer as the God-opposing will—is included in it too." We must ask, however, whether the biblical promise that God will be all in all may be interpreted as to indicate a hope in a possible unification of good and evil. The eschatological hope of the New Testament shows that evil is beyond integration and can only be overcome through elimination.

26. Jung, "Good and Evil in Analytical Psychology" (1959), in *Collected Works* (1964), 10:467 (883); see also 465 (879), where Jung, in reference to evil, or the devil, says: "I personally find it hard to believe the idea of the *privatio boni* still holds water"; that is, evil is not simply a deficiency of the good, as Augustine supposed.

Clearly, Jung goes beyond Freud's dualistic picture of humanity. While Freud saw a deep chasm within humanity between good and evil, Jung admits that there are evil traits within and beyond us that are sometimes not reconcilable with one another. But Jung insists that everything ultimately serves the good. This is to be seen most clearly when Jung suggests that the "shadow" of God will be taken up into the Trinity, making it a Quaternity. This positive relationship to evil in Jung is to be explained by the fact that his view of the biblical portrayal of evil is highly idiosyncratic.

Jung is "indeed convinced that evil is as positive a factor as good."[27] According to Jung, it would be a logical contradiction for a quality to be able to exist without its opposite. When something is good, then there must also exist something bad, for one cannot maintain that something is good when it cannot be distinguished from something that is its opposite. The same applies to the affirmation of the existence of good. Thus one cannot identify the good with being and evil with a deficiency of being. When something is good and a little evil is added to it, say 5 percent, one could not for this reason reduce its existence to 95 percent, so that the 5 percent simply vanishes. Jung believed that the classical Christian definition of evil as a *privatio boni,* that is, as a diminution of the good or a deficiency of being, is to be accounted for by the desire to avoid the introduction of a dualism. The *privatio boni* theory, however, is in itself contradictory. According to this theory, even the devil, as evil incarnate, must be good inasmuch as he exists. Because, however, he is evil through and through, he simply has no business existing.

In the conflict between the early church and the Gnostics, God and Christ could have only a single meaning, which they hold to this day, namely, that they are good without qualification.[28] In order to escape any hint of dualism Christ must not possess a shadow side that actually belongs to him. When one begins with the premise that God is the *summum bonum,* that is, the highest good, one could never reach the conclusion that he created evil (52f. [94–97]). He simply created that which is good and that which is less good, whereby the latter is seen as the worse of the two. Jung believes, however, that this type of argumentation is

---

27. Jung, "Answer 5," in H. L. Philp, *Jung and the Problem of Evil* (New York: Robert M. McBride, 1959), 18. For the following see 18ff. in the same work.

28. See Jung, *Aion* (1951), in *Collected Works* (1959), 9/2:44f. (79f.).

dangerous, for there are things that, seen from a certain perspective, are so evil that one can be deluded with such arguments into a false security. Also, in human nature there are things that are so dangerous that they simply cannot be explained with the concept of a *privatio boni*. "Human nature is capable of an infinite amount of evil, and the evil deeds are as real as the good ones so far as the psyche judges and differentiates between them" (53 [97]). Only in the unconscious does there exist no differentiation between good and evil. Therefore it is important that the danger of evil not be overlooked.

Jung summarizes his misgivings to the effect that the doctrine of evil as a *privatio boni,* or a deficiency of the good, provides an overly optimistic view of evil in human nature and an overly pessimistic view of the human soul. In order to counter evil, early Christianity balanced Christ against the Antichrist because one cannot speak about height if there is no depth, or about good if there is no evil. Together with Christ, therefore, the devil comes into the world as the adversary of God. In early Christian circles, according to Jung, Satan was even viewed as the older brother of Christ (61 [113f.]). Along with the doctrine of evil as a deficiency of good another danger made its appearance in the early church, for evil appeared to exist only as an omission that one could effectively deal with by a change of attitude. This psychological interpretation of evil, however, attributes an ominous power to the psyche or soul because God himself must intervene to deliver humanity from the curse of evil.

For Jung, as psychologist, the Christ symbol is of highest importance, for it is probably the most highly developed and differentiated symbol of the self.[29] While one encounters within one's own self an amazing unity of contrasts, Christ, on the other hand, represents only the good, and the devil, as his adversary, only the evil. This opposition, according to Jung, is the real problem of the world, which remains to this day unresolved. The reality of evil and its incompatibility with the good keep the two opposites apart and lead unavoidably to the crucifixion and neutralization of everything living. Jung even understands Gnosticism in a positive manner when he says: "The dualism of the Gnostic systems makes sense, because they at least try to do justice to the real meaning of

---

29. So Jung, "Introduction to the Religious and Psychological Problems of Alchemy," in *Collected Works* (1953), 12:19 (22).

evil. They have also done us the supreme service of having gone very thoroughly into the question of where evil comes from."[30] Jung rightly notes that in this regard the biblical tradition, as well as the early church, says very little.

In a monotheistic religion, according to Jung, everything that turns against God must ultimately be traced back to him. Moreover, it is difficult, within a trinitarian understanding, to make a place for the devil. As the antagonist of Christ, for instance, he would have to receive an appropriate, opposing position as a son of God. But this would lead to a gnostic view in which, according to Jung, the devil, or "Satanael," is called the first son of God, and Christ the second. A logical result of the incorporation of Satan would then be the expansion of the Trinity to a Quaternity, which has been, however, already strongly attacked by the church fathers. Jung, on the other hand, seems to have no problem with a Quaternity, because even in the Old Testament, Satan was one of the sons of God. Of course, it is strange for us to imagine that in God both good and evil could be united, or that God could even perhaps desire such a thing. Yet for Jung the legend of Lucifer is just as little an absurd fairy tale as the story of the serpent in the garden of Eden.[31] Life as an energy process needs opposites, without which there would be no energy. Good and evil are, therefore, simply moral aspects of a natural polarity.

In the story of Job one finds a very clear association of evil with God. It is remarkable, according to Jung, how quickly Yahweh gives in to the proposals of Satan.[32] Neither does God bring Satan to account when Job's innocence is proven. One must, therefore, assume that Yahweh plays along with Satan. His willingness, according to Jung, to deliver Job into the murderous hands of Satan shows that his own tendency toward unfaithfulness is projected onto Job as a "scapegoat." Jung writes:

> We have plenty of evidence in the Old Testament that Jahwe is moral and immoral at the same time, and Rabbinic theology is fully aware of this fact. Jahwe behaves very much like an immoral being, though He is a guardian of law and order. He is unjust and unreliable according to the Old Testament. Even the God of the

---

30. Jung, "A Psychological Approach," 169 (249).
31. For this and the following see Jung, "A Psychological Approach," 196f. (291).
32. See Jung, *Answer to Job* (1952–67), in *Collected Works* (1958), 11:390 (616).

New Testament is still irascible and vengeful to such a degree that He needs the self-sacrifice of His son to quench His wrath. Christian theology has never denied the identity of the God of the Old Testament with that of the New Testament.[33]

Yet Jung does not simply equate the Old and New Testaments in this matter, for he notices a curious metaphysical phenomenon that Christ points to: he saw Satan fall from heaven like lightning.[34] In this vision, according to Jung, a metaphysical event becomes temporal, the final separation of Yahweh from his son of darkness. Satan was banned from heaven and no longer had the opportunity to drag his father into questionable enterprises. He therefore also no longer had a relationship of personal trust with Yahweh. He was deprived of the affections of his father and sent into exile. Jung finds the explanation for this punishment in the fact that the story of Job had, for Satan, finally reached its conclusion, even if in a strangely limited form. He had, indeed, no longer access to the heavenly household, but continued to exercise dominion over the earth. Only at the end of time will he be made forever powerless. Yet he cannot be blamed for Christ's death, for this sacrificial death was decreed by Yahweh.

As a result of the partial neutralization of Satan, Yahweh identified himself with his luminous side and became the good God and loving father. "He has not lost his wrath and can still mete out punishment, but he does it with justice. Cases like the Job tragedy are apparently no longer to be expected. He proves himself benevolent and gracious. He shows mercy to the sinful children of men and is defined as Love itself." Although Christ had the full trust of his father and felt himself one with him, he nevertheless included in the Lord's Prayer the petition: "And lead us not into temptation but deliver us from evil." With this petition he asks God not to drag us into evil, but to deliver us from it. This means, therefore, that the possibility still exists that Yahweh might revert back to his earlier ways, and that we must guard ourselves against this possibility. For this reason Christ wishes to make his father aware of this destructive tendency and asks him to refrain from it.

While Jung seeks to recognize a development within God, we will, in contrast, when the question of evil is taken up from the

---

33. Jung, "Answer 5," 19f.

34. For this and the following see Jung, *Answer to Job,* 410 (650f.), and for the following citation see 410 (651).

perspective of the biblical witness, point out that the actual change is not to be found in God but in our understanding of God. To be sure, Jung is correct when he says that "the God of the Old Testament is both good and evil."[35] We must disagree with him, however, when he continues by saying that God "is just as much the father or creator of Satan as of Christ." Jung comes to his answer concerning the mystery of evil in the contemporary world through his lifelong work with patients and from his own experience. In this way he came to recognize that God, too, had a dark side.[36] We must agree with Jung that evil cannot be restricted to a simple *privatio boni*. But even Augustine, as we shall see, had not done this. The alternative to a *privatio boni,* however, is not to be found in the localization of evil in God. Neither is it to be found in the manifestation of evil in humanity itself, for God's creation includes more than just humans. This means, then, that the power that aligns itself against God cannot be located in the human consciousness.[37]

As can be seen in his *Answer to Job,* Jung has projected a great deal into the biblical tradition that the texts themselves do not justify. This is because Jung sought to solve the mystery of evil with these projections, a mystery that is described but not solved in the Christian tradition. Whether he does justice thereby to the Judeo-Christian tradition, with the exception of its fringes, is doubtful. For Jung, the attribute of holiness in relation to God plays almost no role. Had he emphasized this more, much, if not all, that he attributes to the subjective, evil actions of God would have been explainable. The holiness of God requires, for example, when God does not wish to stop being God, that everyone who opposes him be correspondingly punished. This makes God, however, neither a wrathful demon nor unpredictable. Rather, God expects that the honor due him be given without hesitation or ulterior motives. Precisely with regard to the holiness of God, however, it is to be seen that humans themselves wish very much to be in God's place.

---

35. Jung, "Answer 5," 20.

36. So also Wallace B. Clift, *Jung and Christianity: The Challenge of Reconciliation* (New York: Crossroad, 1988), 131.

37. Thus rightly Clift, *Jung and Christianity,* 145, who points here to the "angelic world" in a broad sense, thereby referring to Paul Tillich, among others, as supporter of this view.

The Tragedy of Evil • Fromm

In Erich Fromm we notice a compassionate concern for the unfolding of life,[38] which is deeply influenced by the psychoanalysis of Freud and Jung as well as by evolutionary thought. Fromm claims that "the growing process of the emergence of the individual from his original ties, a process which we may call 'individuation,' seems to have reached its peak in modern history in the centuries between the Reformation and the present."[39] Of course, the beginning of modernity is not the cause of all our problems, although it did magnify them because the existence of humanity itself has become a problem.[40]

Whereas animals, living completely within nature, are guided by instinctive behavior, humans have lost such instinctive mechanisms. Although living within nature, they at the same time transcend it and are conscious of themselves. In setting themselves over against nature they have lost their unity and feel unbearably alone, lost, and powerless. This same process can be seen in the development of individual human beings. Each of us initially feels at one with our environment, but then becomes gradually more aware of our individuality. Fromm determines, therefore, that "on the one side of the growing process of individuation is the growth of self-strength," but on the other side of this process is a "growing aloneness."[41] Human existence implies "freedom from instinctual determination of...actions," which is prerequisite for the development of human culture. The troubling fact, however, is that the two sides of this development, growing power and increasing individuation, are not balanced. Consequently, the history of humanity is littered with conflict and strife, and "each step in the direction of growing individuation [has] threatened people with new insecurities."

---

38. See Edward S. Tauber and Bernard Landis, "On Erich Fromm," in *In the Name of Life: Essays in Honor of Erich Fromm,* ed. Bernard Landis and Edward Tauber (New York: Holt, Rinehart and Winston, 1971), 1. In this collection we find excellent essays on various aspects of Fromm's work as well as a selective bibliography of his writings.

39. Erich Fromm, *Escape from Freedom* (1941) (New York: Holt, Rinehart and Winston, 1960), 24.

40. For this and the following see Erich Fromm, "Psychoanalysis and Zen Buddhism," in D. T. Suzuki, Erich Fromm, and Richard De Martino, *Zen Buddhism and Psychoanalysis* (New York: Harper, 1960), 86f.

41. This and the following citations are taken from Fromm, *Escape from Freedom,* 29, 32, and 36.

If the human being is self-conscious, maintains Fromm, "he realizes his powerlessness and the limitations of his existence. He visualizes his own end: death."[42] Yet we cannot go back to the prehuman state of harmony with nature without giving up our humanity. Fromm claims, therefore, that a human being "must proceed to develop his reason until he becomes the master of nature, and of himself." But can a human being really achieve this? Fromm appears to give a partial answer when he admits that the short life span of humans does not allow, "under even the most favorable conditions," the full development of their potential.[43] Furthermore, instead of responding to their freedom with dedication and work in solidarity with nature, humans often seek to escape from their freedom through a sadistic domination of, or a masochistic submission to, the object to which they are supposed to relate. Or perhaps they attempt to rid themselves of the object through its destruction.[44] Yet according to Fromm, "The intensity of destructive strivings by no means implies that they are invincible or even dominant."[45]

According to Fromm, evil is a specifically human phenomenon. It manifests itself in the "syndrome of decay," which consists of the love of death, narcissism, and symbiotic fixation upon incest. It prompts people to destroy for destruction's sake and to hate for hatred's sake. Yet this decay syndrome, which is symbolic of regression, is countered by a growth syndrome that is symbolic of progress and expresses itself in the love of life, humanity, and independence.

While Fromm admits that the human heart can become hardened and inhumane, he contends that it can never become nonhuman. "It always remains a man's heart."[46] Even the followers of

---

42. Erich Fromm, *Man for Himself: An Inquiry into the Psychology of Ethics* (1947) (New York: Holt, Rinehart and Winston, 1959), 40; for the following quotes see 31 and 32.

43. Don S. Browning, in his book *Generative Man: Psychoanalytic Perspectives* (Philadelphia: Westminster, 1973), 115f., provides a helpful guide to the anthropology of the important contemporary psychoanalysts and rightly warns that in light of such statements it is hardly fair to accuse Fromm of "glib utopianism and perfectionism."

44. Fromm, *Escape from Freedom,* 173, 179.

45. For this quote and the information in the following paragraph see Fromm, *The Heart of Man: Its Genius for Good and Evil* (New York: Harper, 1964), 22f.

46. For this and the following see Fromm, *Heart of Man,* 150 (quote), 138, 120f., 48, 45, and 50 (quote).

Hitler or Stalin, Fromm insists, began their lives with the chance to become good people. Human nature in its essence is neither good nor evil, although a contradiction is rooted within the very condition of human existence. This conflict requires a resolution, for which there are only two possibilities: either to regress or to progress. Even if these possibilities create new contradictions, humans should be able to resolve these problems either progressively or regressively. In the struggle between the love for life (biophilia) and the love of death (necrophilia), neither tendency is ever present in its pure form, that is, holiness or insanity. In most cases there is to be found a mixture of both forms of love, and our spirit orients itself toward whichever one dominates. For Fromm, of course, the question of which form will ultimately gain the upper hand is largely settled because unlike Freud, he contends that there is an inherent, qualitative predisposition toward life to be found in all living substances. Thus he labels the "death instinct" as "a *malignant* phenomenon which grows and takes over to the extent to which the Eros does not unfold."

In contrast, for instance, to Konrad Lorenz, Fromm desires to show that the problem of human life does not lie in a reduction of instinctive reactions, but rather, that human aggression is conditioned by society and works in collaboration with the biological necessities of humanity.[47] As the writings of Fromm repeatedly show, the fundamental problem of humanity is indeed grounded in its character, but not in (deficiently) instinctive behavior. This is also to be seen in Fromm's denial of the existence of original sin.[48] "The Bible leaves no doubt that it does not consider man as either good or evil, but endowed with both tendencies.... Yet it is very significant that in the story of the 'fall' the Bible never calls Adam's act a sin."[49] What Adam can be reprimanded for, however, according to Fromm, is his disobedience. If, therefore, disobedience is sin, admits Fromm, then Adam and Eve sinned. Yet for Fromm disobedience is virtually a liberating act:

> The act of disobedience set Adam and Eve free and opened their eyes. They recognized each other as strangers and the world out-

---

47. See "Erich Fromm: Some Biographical Notes," in *In the Name of Life*, xiv.

48. See the extensive treatment by Ramon Xirau, "Erich Fromm: What Is Man's Struggle?" in *In the Name of Life*, 152.

49. So Fromm, *You Shall Be as Gods: A Radical Interpretation of the Old Testament and Its Traditions* (New York: Holt, Rinehart and Winston, 1966), 159.

side them as strange and even hostile. Their act of disobedience broke the primary bond with nature and made them individuals. "Original sin," far from corrupting man, set him free; it was the beginning of history. Man had to leave the Garden of Eden in order to learn to rely on his own powers and to become fully human.[50]

Fromm offers with these comments an idealistic interpretation of the fall that leaves no place for the concept of original sin. He believes he is supported in this interpretation by the Old Testament tradition because even the prophets confirm the idea that humans have a right to be disobedient. Only after their disobedience can human beings establish a harmony between themselves, other persons, and nature through the forces of reason and love. Fromm even believes that humanity, through new acts of disobedience, has progressed in its development. This applies to humans' spiritual as well as intellectual development because they liberate themselves from authorities that would not tolerate any new thoughts or any new freedoms for the individual.

For Fromm the biblical witness portrays a humanity that is not sinful and in its very nature depraved, but rather a humanity that simply has evil inclinations and therefore a tendency toward evil. One must consequently take into account that while "the Bible acknowledges the fact of man's 'evil imaginings,' it also believes in his inherent capacity for good."[51] Thus, for example, Israel is called a holy nation. Fromm, however, does not overlook the fact that the Israelites, together with their kings, sinned. According to the Jewish understanding of humanity, all people are born with the capacity to sin, but are able to change their ways, rediscover themselves, and through their own efforts, apart from any gracious act of God, redeem themselves. "Man, in the biblical and post-biblical view, is given the choice between his 'good and evil drives'" (162). Because humans have, in many ways, the freedom of choice, they can sometimes go too far and forfeit this freedom. This can be seen, for instance, in the story of the exodus from Egypt, in which, according to the biblical understanding, God hardened the heart of Pharaoh. Also in the prophetic writings, according to Fromm, it is emphasized that humans can lose their ability to choose. For this reason the prophets pressed the people so often to exercise

---

50. For this and the following see Fromm, *On Disobedience and Other Essays* (London: Routledge and Kegan Paul, 1981), 1f.
51. Fromm, *You Shall Be as Gods,* 161.

their ability to choose and not to fall into the misfortune of a lost freedom of choice (see 165).

According to Fromm, we do not need any self-accusation or penance in order to be accepted by God after we have sinned. According to the Jewish view, a person is free and independent. When we sin, thereby straying from the right path, we can always again show remorse, which means that we are returning to the right path.[52] In our changes and conversions we are not dependent upon God, for our sin is our own sin and our repentance is our own repentance. There is, therefore, no ground for a self-accusing submission. There is also no collective or original sin, rather, we all share a common human nature. "Because we all share in the same humanity, there is nothing inhuman in sinning, hence nothing to be ashamed of, or to be despised for. Our inclination to sin is as human as our inclination to do good and as our capacity to 'return'" (175f.). As human beings we stand on our own two feet and need neither a savior nor a God who shows us grace.

As we now seek to summarize Fromm's position, it is to be noticed that the antagonistic conflict that Freud found within humanity is interpreted by Fromm as a positive possibility for life. Does this mean that for Fromm no radical evil exists, either internal or external to humanity? We receive from him no direct answer to this question. Fromm characterizes evil as the human being's loss of the self *"through the tragic attempt to rid himself of the burden of his humanity."*[53] Therefore we are confronted here with something tragic that could well be identified with that which is fateful, and thereby, also with something for which humanity is not ultimately responsible. This unaccountability cannot be undone by the fact that Fromm speaks within the same context of a lesser and a greater evil, in which the greater evil is always directed against life itself, whereas the less significant evil merely reveals a deficiency. The fateful character of evil is also addressed by Fromm when he argues that one needs a "rational faith in man's capacity to extricate himself from what seems the fatal web of circumstances that he has created."[54]

Within human life Fromm observes that which is fateful. Yet he does not feel comfortable with identifying anything external

---

52. For this and the following see Fromm, *You Shall Be as Gods*, 169.

53. Fromm, *Heart of Man*, 148.

54. Erich Fromm, *The Anatomy of Human Destructiveness* (New York: Holt, Rinehart and Winston, 1973), 438.

to humanity from which evil summons its threatening power. It is, however, doubtful whether his hope will prove correct that we can turn back from this fate in order to build a society "in which no one is threatened: not the child by the parent; not the parent by the superior; no social class by another; no nation by a super-power" (435). This, however, is also not a "rational faith," but rather wishful thinking that has up to now not been fulfilled. Thus, on the one hand, we must affirm that humanity, as Fromm demonstrates, possesses a potential for life. Yet, on the other hand, we must not forget that which is essentially evil, that is, that which threatens to destroy the potential for life. While we welcome and affirm Fromm's passion for life, we must at the same time point out that the realization of this passion in humanity is inadequately grounded.

Evil as the Consequence of Alienation from God • Drewermann

The controversial Roman Catholic theologian and psychologist Eugen Drewermann, in his broad-ranging work *Strukturen des Bösen* (Structures of Evil), a best-seller in Germany, offers an interpretation of the Yahwistic primeval history from an exegetical, psychoanalytical, and philosophical perspective. On the basis of his exegetical investigations Drewermann sees a central theme of the Yahwistic primeval history in the knowledge of good and evil.[55] If the communion with God is abandoned, that which God had created as good and which in his presence *is* good is transformed into something negative. Thus a requalification of the fundamental structures of human existence occurs, which appears in the form of curse and punishment for the sins of humanity. When humans separate themselves from God, they fall back onto their naked creatureliness and discover what they really are apart from God. Yet human beings continue to strive after the goal for which they had originally been destined. Because this goal, however, is attainable only in community with God, these continuing efforts to reach the goal alone only increase the alienation from God. Therefore, according to Drewermann, in the final analysis, "the sin, as well as the attempt to change our lost being in or with

---

55. Eugen Drewermann, *Strukturen des Bösen*, pt. 1: *Die jahwistische Urgeschichte in exegetischer Sicht,* 6th ed. (Paderborn: Schöningh, 1987), 313.

God into a being-as-God, is really the attempt to recover the lost God through the divinization of humanity" (314).

Drewermann does not wish to understand this desire to be as God as pride, arrogance, or Titanism, but rather, he views sin from its very origin as an intertwined network of uncertainty, anxiety, defensiveness, rebellion, and finite self-empowerment. From this perspective, then, Drewermann suggests a psychological interpretation of sin. Out of the strife with God arises the strife of humans among themselves; out of the angst for God arises the human angst for one another, which is capable of escalating to murder, and out of the fear of murder arises the instrumentation of death, which serves as a deterrent. In reaction to this arises the human attempt to divinize the natural vitality of life. Because humans have lost their unity with God, they strive to achieve this unity through the divinization of humanity. "The result, however, is the autocratization of each individual and the atomization of humanity into monads of reciprocal incomprehensibility" (315).

In his exegesis of Genesis 2 and 3, Drewermann emphasizes that humanity remained human throughout the process of its alienation from God. One encounters, however, a new meaning and significance of being human in the transformation of blessing into punishment.[56] Sin contains already within itself its own punishment, for when it achieves that which it intended or desired, it transforms this into its opposite. Humans are pulled into a continuous battle with evil, and while they believe they can defeat evil, they are in danger of being defeated by it. The Genesis narratives are silent, however, as to the question from whence evil comes. Evil appears here much more "as a potentiality within God's creation." That it comes to fruition rests entirely with humanity. At the beginning of this process stands the mistrust through which humanity falls away from God and falls back onto its basic creatureliness and nakedness. It is significant "that the human is naked as a creation of God, and that after its alienation from God must be ashamed of this nakedness." Through the alienation from God, the essential purposes of man and woman are altered and deprived of their original quality.

The fundamental distinguishing characteristic of life without God is existence in the face of death. It is a part of the nature

---

56. For this and the following quotes see Drewermann, *Strukturen des Bösen,* pt. 1, 106–9.

of sin "that the human, who out of angst falls into sin, has an even greater angst for God after and in sin." Sin is not a stride toward knowledge: it brings no advancement in knowledge, as one might infer from the words of the snake. Drewermann, rather, characterizes sin "as an orientation which is not only original within humanity but for which humanity itself is also responsible." Before God, human life need not be what it now is, as it stands under the sign of alienation from God and banishment. "That God has his life within himself, but that humans in their sin are banished from the source of their life, delineates the irreconcilable difference between God and humanity and is the reason for the humiliation which sin brings over humanity."

Evil remains, therefore, exegetically inexplicable for Drewermann. Theologically, evil brings about the separation between God and humanity, including the distancing from and rebellion against God on the part of humanity, so that from it are produced the crisis and futility of human conduct. Interesting in Drewermann's understanding of sin, however, is that while he emphasizes the nakedness of humanity as constitutive for sin, he emphasizes also that angst drives humanity toward sin. Drewermann is not satisfied, however, to remain simply with these exegetical findings; he seeks, rather, to illuminate them through the findings of psychoanalysis. This approach, then, produces some very interesting results.

Drewermann reaches the conclusion that the structure of the Yahwistic primeval history reveals a very high degree of thematic correspondence with the psychogenesis of the individual. In this regard there is no reason to doubt that ontogenesis provides the model for the Yahwistic primeval history. In other words, this means that the Yahwistic primeval history "rests upon the course of development of the individual up to the individual's entrance into full maturity and uses the ontogenetic schema in the sequence of the individual's developmental phases as the outline of its own theologically motivated series of statements." Drewermann even goes beyond this conclusion when he claims that the ontogenetic conditions of consciousness repeat the early history of humanity, which, as he believes, is a speculative but nevertheless justifiable assumption:

> Enough evidence is accessible today in the study of prehistory, paleoanthropology, ethnology, and the history of civilization to

show that humans evidently lived in former times much as a child in our own time lives. The feeling of guilt, which ice age hunters overcame in the killing of animals which they honored as divine, and the sorrow of early farmers at the harvest of the fruits of the field, find parallels in the guilt feelings and sorrow of the child who, on the basis of its oral ambivalence, is separated from its mother. Thus also the phallic rites and practices of the fertility religions find their counterpart in the importance that the child, upon the first awakenings of its sexuality, accords its reproduction and child-bearing organs.[57]

Drewermann appeals here to Jung when he determines that it appears "as if the biogenetic fundamental law of the recapitulation of phylogenesis into ontogenesis has validity not only for the development of the physical body but also for that of the soul." Drewermann does not notice, however, that with the so-called biogenetic fundamental law he takes up a claim of the once popular German Darwinist Ernst Haeckel (1834–1919) that is today rejected by most biologists. Yet according to Drewermann, the developmental history of each individual mirrors that of humanity, in regard to not only the body but also the soul. The subjects of oral, anal, and genital phases go far back into the history of human evolution and find their theological interpretation in the primeval history of Genesis.

When Drewermann comes to speak of Genesis 2 and 3 he understands the sojourn in paradise ontogenetically as memories of the time before and after birth, in which the child passes through the phases of autoeroticism and narcissism "until it is capable of its first pre-ambivalent oral object possession. This time of the mother-child dyad is in fact a time of paradisiacal security. On the thematic level paradise is a symbol of the unity with one's self and an expression of the wholeness of the soul."[58] The primeval unity with the mother, according to Drewermann, finds its necessary end "in the ambivalence conflicts of the oral-sadistic phase, in which the child falls into the conflict of having to destroy that which it loves and that from which it lives. The resultant weaning counts as punishment for the violation of the eating ban; the introjection

---

57. For this and the above see Drewermann, *Strukturen des Bösen*, pt. 2: *Die jahwistische Urgeschichte in psychoanalytischer Sicht* (Paderborn: Schöningh, 1985), 549ff.; for the following quote see 549.

58. For this and the following quotes see Drewermann, *Strukturen des Bösen*, pt. 2, 236f.

of the lost object leads to the unavoidable establishment of feelings of guilt."

Drewermann finds the basis for the oedipal conflict in the oral problematic, which in the phallic phase likewise leads to ambivalence of feelings, to the relinquishing of the object (castration), to the introjection of this same object, and to the establishment of a concentrated authority in the ego. The perception of nakedness and shame is understood by Drewermann analytically as an indication of something lacking (the castration motif). He interprets the punishment resulting from the fall as "portrayals of the five paleoanthropological primal fears." The whole of human existence is transformed into angst through the fall, through which originates a depressive fear of death, and reactive to it, a yearning for death. The angst for the loss of the object leads to the emergence of guilt feelings and self-debasement. "The punishment of the serpent (Gen. 3:15) appears on the object level as a castrative tendency toward revenge emanating from the woman, which is correspondingly opposite to the woman's punishment of subordination under the man (Gen. 3:16)."

The images from Genesis 3 have, in Drewermann's opinion, human-oriented significance and teach us to understand human fears as natural matters of fact, as an evolutionary dowry. With this perspective, however, arises also the question of the free responsibility of humans. Drewermann directs his attention to these problems in the third volume of his investigation within the framework of the philosophical formulation of the question. More important for us here, however, is Drewermann's acceptance of Freudian categories, for with this comes the danger, as he himself recognizes, that as with Freud, religion and infantilism become collapsed into one so that through the maturing of the human being religion will become just as superfluous as a theological interpretation of Genesis 2 and 3. Must it then be the case, asks Drewermann, as with Freud, that "religion can only assert itself when it binds intrinsic emotions and instinctive energies of human nature to the imaginations of childhood and thus keeps humanity childlike"?[59] Drewermann disagrees with the thrust of this thesis, for the point of his psychoanalytical interpretation is to set out the evidence that humans can find themselves only when they become

---

59. For this and the following quotes see Drewermann, *Strukturen des Bösen*, pt. 2, 241f.

children, theologically speaking, and God stands over against them as absolute Person, as "Father."

When humans know and accept themselves in every part and aspect of their creaturely existence, they can overcome the angst that hinders them from becoming genuine selves. Because human freedom finds in God its support and orientation, humans are able to decide for independence and freedom. "Only when people theologically become 'children' can they psychologically cease to remain children and stop transferring their yearning after father and mother to human authorities or attempting to make themselves God." Hence for Drewermann, God, according to the Yahwist, is the person "from whose source humans alone can allay the angst of their own freedom, order the chaos of their impulses, work through the unconsciousness of their existence, and give hope to the wretched hopelessness of their being." Humans can therefore live humanly only when God is not lost to them in their existential anxiety, but rather becomes their father. With this, however, the question that Drewermann raises, of whether religion and infantilism are the same, is not answered. Alongside of the Freudian claim that the two are to be identified Drewermann places the contention of their dissimilarity.

When one, along with Drewermann and in agreement with Freud, parallels the human phylogenesis with the human ontogenesis, that means that the history of humanity is paralleled in that of the individual; and when one also, with Drewermann, seeks to read these developmental phases out of the Yahwistic primeval history, then even his positive statements concerning the conquest of primal fears through trust in God that are based upon this groundwork no longer make sense. Drewermann's project suffers from two inadequacies: (1) He wishes to shed light upon the fundamental theological statements of Genesis on creation, fall, and evil through use of Freudian psychoanalysis. In so doing, however, he overlooks the fact that the structures of parallelism between phylogenesis and ontogenesis that he has in mind are highly controversial in the field of biology. (2) The phenomenon of angst holds an unduly high status with Drewermann. We can agree with him that the result of the disturbed relationship with God is a disturbed existential relationship to one's self and other beings, which results in angst. Yet angst is not that which drives people to sin. Volume 3 of Drewermann's work shows that he is heavily influenced by Kierkegaard's concept of angst. Thus it appears once more that an inappropriate principle prejudices his exegesis, instead of the converse, in which the exegetical investigation questions the principles of interpretation. Drewermann's attempt to trace the structures of evil is, to be sure, a noteworthy achievement that brings together much diverse material. In the final analysis, however, he allows himself to be guided by external criteria that detract from the sources he seeks to interpret.

Chapter 3

The Phenomenon of Evil from the Perspective of the Old Testament

If one wishes to do justice to the phenomenon of evil in the Old Testament, one cannot simply interpret the usage of certain words used to describe evil but must also examine the related phenomenon of sin. Moreover, the question of the origin of evil is introduced through the creation stories. Finally, in regard to the Old Testament, evil as an occurrence is to be distinguished from the evil one, whereby the concept of Satan and related phenomena emerge.

The Negative in Light of the Old Testament

Evil or wickedness, called *ra* or *raah* in Hebrew, is rendered in Greek as *kakos* or *poneros* and stands in opposition to the good or the divine.[1] Thus *ra* and *raa* denote in the first instance something negative and then also something that is God-opposing. That which is negative can refer simply to the experience of natural events or objects. Thus we read in the Old Testament of a bad, that is, brackish, water (2 Kings 2:19). Or the Israelites complain to Moses and Aaron that they have led them to an evil, that is, miserable, place that is "no place for grain, or figs, or vines, or pomegranates" (Num. 20:5). Additionally, we read in the story of Joseph of the seven fat and seven poor, very ugly, and thin, that is, bad, cows (Gen. 41:19). Evil can mean bad in the sense of inferior or not useful, but it also denotes something that is unsuitable

---

1. So Alfons S. Geyser, "Böse, Bosheit," in *BHH* 1:268.

for cultic use. In this sense fruits and nourishments, the land, or even people (1 Sam. 25:3) can be evil or bad.[2] Also, a wild animal is called an "evil animal" (Gen. 37:20). Finally, there is mention of a person's bad or evil reputation (Neh. 6:13; Deut. 22:19). Evil is simply that which is bad and which could, therefore, be better, without regard to whether it has to do with human conduct, natural givens, or valuations.

When one looks at humanity, evil takes on a moral dimension. Thus the Psalmist calls out to God, asking him to protect him "from those . . . who plan evil things in their minds" (Ps. 140:2f.). In connection with the flood narrative it is said of humans "that every inclination of the thoughts of their hearts was only evil continually" (Gen. 6:5). The lawbreaker who must be purged is evil (Deut. 17:7). An evil person is characterized by pride (Job 35:12) and a deficient fear of God (Prov. 8:13). Men, women, children, neighbors, and the entire Israelite community (Num. 14:27) can be wicked or evil. Even the ways of humanity are sometimes evil and reprehensible (Jer. 18:11), as well as bad or evil abominations (Ezek. 8:9), or malicious deeds of humans (Deut. 28:20). Evil stands in contrast to the good (2 Sam. 13:22), so that the conceptual pair good and evil can represent totality, hence everything from good to evil.[3]

When evil denotes a human act or attitude, it stands in opposition to God and his will.[4] Misery and calamity are the punishment of God for the evil that Israel has done as it turned to other gods (Deut. 31:17f.). We read in the apocryphal Wisdom of Solomon (14:27) that the worship of anonymous idols is the beginning, cause, and end of every evil. The punishment of God for individuals or the entire people when they deviate from God's ways is that which is perceived as evil or calamity. Similarly, we read in the prophet Jeremiah the word of the Lord: "Hear, O earth; I am going to bring disaster [evil] on this people, the fruit of their schemes" (Jer. 6:19). Thus the Psalmist can also conversely say: "Even though I walk through the valley of the shadow of death,

---

2. For this and the following see Günther Harder, "Poneros (The Old Testament and Later Judaism)," in *TDNT* 6:549f.

3. See also Herbert Haag, *Vor dem Bösen ratlos?* (Munich: Piper, 1978), 51, with regard to the primeval history.

4. From the following it will be clear that in contradiction to Harder's view (551), evil is not always "characterized through its opposition to God and his will."

I fear no evil; for you are with me" (Ps. 23:4). Yet the path of alienation from God leads to destruction for the individual as well as for the entire people. In the wisdom literature, especially in the Old Testament proverbs, humans are warned to abandon evil and, with the help of wisdom, to take hold of the good and turn away from the bad. Thus we read in Prov. 14:22: "Do they not err that plan evil? Those who plan good find loyalty and faithfulness." Similarly, the Psalmist warns: "You who love the Lord hate evil; he guards the lives of his faithful; he rescues them from the hand of the wicked" (Ps. 97:10). This action-consequence connection, however, is not always carried through. This fact is already clearly noted in the Old Testament when it is made known that God sends evil and also delivers from it.

Before we can pursue the question as to the origin of evil, we must first observe that evil, especially in its ethical dimension, is directly bound to sin. As the wife of Potiphar, the Egyptian captain of the guard, attempted to seduce Joseph, he recognized immediately the connection between moral evil and sin and asked: "How then could I do this great wickedness, and sin against God?" (Gen. 39:9). David reacted similarly when the prophet Nathan confronted him with his reprehensible conduct in regard to Bathsheba and her husband, Uriah. He does not simply confess: I have behaved wrongly toward Uriah, but rather: "I have sinned against the Lord" (2 Sam. 12:13). The evil that a person does not only is borne in the interpersonal realm but is also always behavior that is against God; that is, it is sinful. The phenomenon of sin, therefore, cannot be ignored in any discussion of the concept of evil in the Old Testament.

There are several words for sin in the Hebrew language. The most frequently used of these is *chattat,* or *chet.* What is denoted thereby is to be seen in Judg. 20:16, where we read that among the men of Benjamin were seven hundred elite fighters "who were left-handed; every one could sling a stone at a hair, and not *miss.*" "Missing the target" or "straying from the path" are in profane Hebrew represented by the word "sin."[5] While this purely profane

---

5. See Rolf Knierim, *Die Hauptbegriffe für Sünde im Alten Testament* (Gütersloh: Bertelsmann, 1965), 56. Klaus Koch, "Chata," in *TDOT* 4:311, however, questions whether the four texts given by Knierim (Judg. 20:16; Prov. 8:35f.; 19:2; Job 5:24) suggest at all a carnal, that is, profane, meaning, or whether they do not more likely contain a "metaphorical" usage. But even at that, one must observe that the theological usage of the concept of sin is heavily predominant.

use of the word is rare, it nevertheless poignantly illustrates the basic religious meaning of the word. Sin is a failure, it is a shooting past or a missing of the target.

Interesting for the understanding of sin in the preexilic period is the story of Abimelech, king of Gerar, and Sarah, Abraham's wife (Genesis 20). Out of fear that he would be killed because of his attractive wife, Abraham passes Sarah off as his sister. As a result the king takes her as his wife. God appears to Abimelech in a dream and reveals to him the true state of affairs. Also, God informs him that "it was I who kept you from sinning against me" (Gen. 20:6). The next morning Abimelech confronts Abraham with what he has done and lavishes gifts upon him to compensate for the injustice. Only after Abraham intercedes to God on behalf of the king are he and his household healed from the infertility that had come upon them as a curse. Sin is here not defined over against the norm of an express law or commandment of God. But it is, as everywhere in the Old Testament, an offense against God. Humans do not sin against their nature, against other people, or against some norm, but rather always against God. Sin, in the action-consequence connection that for the Israelites was obvious, is not only an evil act but also a corresponding result of this act. The crime latches itself unseen onto the perpetrator and remains near to him or her so that it affects him or her ominously. Sin awakens the wrath of God and unleashes God's personal reaction, providing a third party does not vicariously intervene and turn aside this reaction.

As we see in the case of King Jeroboam, sin is able to destroy not only the perpetrator himself but also his household (1 Kings 13:34). Thus laments the Psalmist to Yahweh that he wishes him to hide his face from human sins (Ps. 51:9). Also, the Psalmist asks God to "wash me thoroughly from my iniquity, and cleanse me from my sin" (v. 2) and "to purge me . . . and I shall be clean" (v. 7). With the comment, "I was born guilty, a sinner when my mother conceived me" (v. 5), the way is not cleared for a traducian doctrine of original sin, that is, the belief that sin is "inherited" through the act of procreation. Rather, this text shows an awareness of an entanglement in a sphere of sin that exists "even before birth, through family solidarity."[6] Thus a distinction is made between the sin of the individual, which can be atoned, and the sin that transcends generations, for which an atonement can appar-

---

6. So Koch, "Chata," 4:314.

ently not be expected. On the basis of this context of sin it became the primary task of the writing prophets to hold up before Israel its sins and offenses (Mic. 3:8). Also, the rebuked generation is not the first to have sinned (see Jer. 3:25). Yet not only humans but also the entire land is profaned through sin and idolatry (Jer. 16:18). On account of sin, rain and harvest are withheld from Israel (Jer. 5:25), and even Israel's enemies could assault it because it had sinned against the Lord (Jer. 50:7). Therefore King Nebuchadrezzar's captain of the guard, after the conquest of Jerusalem (585/586) by the Babylonians, concludes logically: "The Lord your God threatened this place with this disaster; and now the Lord has brought it about, and has done as he said, because all of you sinned against the Lord and did not obey his voice. Therefore this thing has come upon you" (Jer. 40:2f.).

Although the prophets announce the coming day of Yahweh, "cruel, with wrath and fierce anger, to make the earth a desolation, and to destroy its sinners from it" (Isa. 13:9), they nevertheless take into account a final, positive change. This can, however, only originate from Yahweh because he helps humanity obtain a new orientation. "I will forgive their iniquity, and remember their sin no more" (Jer. 31:34). Deutero-Isaiah also speaks of an atoning servant of God who bore the sin of many and interceded for transgressors (Isa. 53:12). A similar concept is expressed in the ritual offering of a sacrifice for sin. But it must here be noted that Yahweh does not receive the sin offering in order to pacify his wrath, but rather Yahweh himself is "the subject of an act that is performed in his name by the priests."[7]

The second Hebrew word for the concept of sin, the noun *avon,* is taken up in the prophetic and cultic literature of the exilic and postexilic period as the primary term for human guilt and disaster.[8] The basic meaning of the word includes the concepts of deviation, reversal, confusion, bending, turning, and offense, all of which appear mostly in metaphorical application in reference to theologically significant facts or actions that are objectively disqualified with the aid of this metaphor.[9] This root meaning of the word can still be detected in Ps. 38:6 where the Psalmist says: "I am utterly bowed down and prostrate; all day long I go around mourning."

---

7. So Koch, "Chata," 4:316.
8. So Klaus Koch, "Awon," in *TWAT* 5:1160.
9. So Knierim, *Die Hauptbegriffe,* 238.

The guilt of sin, as *avon* can also be translated, arises through crimes such as the fratricide of Cain (Gen. 4:13), the unfaithfulness of a servant to his king, as in the case of David's relationship with Saul (1 Sam. 20:1), or the blasphemy of the sons of Eli (1 Sam. 3:13). Guilt hangs upon one as a reified substance, and the sinful offense leads to one's disastrous undoing. Although in many cases no direct relationship to God is indicated in regard to an offense, for the Israelites the connection between destructive conduct and destructive consequence is obvious. The atonement for sin can be accomplished on earth through institutions such as the monarchy (2 Sam. 19:20f.). Yet the king, too, can so load himself down with sin that the only option that remains for sinners seeking to avert the weight of guilt from themselves is to turn toward God (2 Sam. 24:10).

Similar to sin, the disaster of guilt grows out of idolatry (Ezek. 14:3f.), a lack of concern for the poor (Ezek. 16:49), dishonest behavior (Ezek. 18:8), and other offenses that fill the land with bloodshed and injustice (Ezek. 9:9). As biblical citations in the preceding sentence indicate, the term *avon* is frequently employed by Ezekiel because for him guilt constitutes the greatest problem upon which life revolves. The one who has committed sin and become burdened with guilt wastes away and is doomed to ruin (Lev. 26:39). The one, however, who is free from guilt can live freely (Num. 5:31). For this reason the entire guilt of the people shall be transferred on the day of atonement onto a scapegoat who carries it out into the wilderness (Lev. 16:21f.). The possibility exists, however, that the Israelites humble themselves before God and confess their sin so that God once more remembers his covenant with them (Lev. 26:40ff.). The guilt of sin, in the final analysis, always has to do with God because God alone can grant forgiveness.

Finally, we must take into account still a third concept in connection with the sin complex, the Hebrew noun *pesha*. In its verbal form the word can be translated as "to break with," as well as "to lay hand upon," or "to misappropriate, or desecrate."[10] Used as a substantive it indicates an "offense" or "crime" and all phenomena that point to a concrete form of offense, such as property theft, embezzlement, misappropriation, rebellion, heinous acts, or

---

10. For a full description of the word's meaning see Knierim, *Die Hauptbegriffe,* 178f.

misdeeds. The basic meaning of this term is inferred from the story of Jacob and Laban, when Jacob is accused by Laban of having stolen his idols. Jacob, who was not aware of any injustice, answered Laban: "What is my offense [*pesha*]? What is my sin, that you have hotly pursued me?" (Gen. 31:36). For further clarification of the meaning of this term Prov. 28:24 is useful: "Anyone who robs father or mother and says, 'That is no crime [*pesha*],' is partner to a thug." Once more the word here describes an outrageous instance of criminal conduct. Finally, in Amos 1:3—2:8 this term is used to denote an entire series of offenses to which God will put a stop and bring to justice.

A crime or offense, as denoted by *pesha,* does not have to do with some trivial offense but with a legal violation that is especially outrageous or provocative. "Pesha is therefore an outrageous, unclean, activity of both small and great measure of destructiveness to the community which can take on a great causticity in the legal realm, in the realm of international law, and particularly in relationship to JHWH as the God who molds Israel as his people."[11] The one who commits an offense not only rebels against Yahweh but also breaks away from him, takes away that which belongs to Yahweh, and in turn plunders and desecrates it. Thus *pesha* denotes more a criminal act than a criminal thought or attitude.

It is not surprising that this term frequently occurs in parallel relationship to *chattat* (Ps. 32:1) or to *avon* (1 Sam. 25:28) or to both together, as in Ezek. 21:24, where Yahweh says: "Because you have brought your guilt to remembrance, in that your transgressions are uncovered, so that in all your deeds your sins appear—because you have come to remembrance, you shall be taken captive." The offenses of the individual and of the people provoke the action of Yahweh. Yet the goal of this action is not destruction. Thus in the name of Yahweh the comforting promise is given to the exiled survivors of the people: "I, I am He who blots out your transgressions for my own sake, and I will not remember your sins" (Isa. 43:25). Although Israel has offended Yahweh with the worst sins, all offenses are dismissed through the catastrophe of the exile. Likewise, in the previously mentioned ritual of the scapegoat the texts speak not only about sins but also about putting off or setting aside (*peshaim*). God is thereby understood as *both* punishing *and* forgiving.

---

11. Horst Seebass, "Paescha," in *TWAT* 6:801.

The various terms used for the entire complex of sin and evil in the Old Testament reveal that the human missing-of-the-mark is a presupposed fact and is an intrinsic part of being human.[12] The continuing threat of humanity is indicated through the variety of dangers arising from being human and from humanness. There is, however, hardly any distinction made between what we term sin and crime. As creator and sustainer God strives against sin and thereby evil as well. This is to be seen symptomatically in the flood story of Genesis 6–9 where God in fact carries out judgment for the excessive and deeply rooted sins of humanity, but in the end declares solemnly that such annihilation shall never be repeated (Gen. 8:21). At the end of the flood the creator reaffirms the preservation of the human race despite the human tendency toward evil. God does not intervene with punishment in each instance of an evil act by an individual or by a group, rather, he can also endure these actions without bringing about a new judgment against them. Thus Yahweh says: "I will never again curse the ground because of humankind, for the inclination of the human heart is evil from youth" (Gen. 8:21).

The situation is entirely different in regard to the people of God. To be sure, the usual human shortcomings and evil acts are also to be seen here. Yet every evil deed is preceded by the good that Israel has learned from its God. Likewise, it is preceded by the "yes" of God's people to remain faithful to their God. For this reason disobedience, shortcoming, and forgetting what God has done for Israel are spoken of in an entirely different sense. Sin, guilt, and evil are not spoken of as if they were inevitable, but one remembers, rather, that in the beginning a good and unbroken relationship existed between God and his people. But how did this grave transformation occur? How is that to be explained which has now befallen humanity and which humanity itself confirms through its evil actions? Is the answer to be found in a hereditary factor, a genetic defect, or even perhaps in an intentional change in humanity brought about by God?

---

12. For this and the following see Claus Westermann, *Elements of Old Testament Theology,* trans. Douglas W. Stott (Atlanta: John Knox, 1982), 118f.

The Mysterious Cause of Evil

When considering the cause of evil, one thinks instinctively of the story of the fall in Genesis 3. Yet nowhere in the Old Testament is a "doctrine" of the fall spoken of,[13] for the story of the fall in Genesis 3 is quite remarkably isolated from the rest of the Old Testament.[14] The story is taken up neither by the Psalmist nor by the prophets nor by any other Old Testament writer.[15] The story, however, is not to be understood as the expression of an isolated event. The Yahwistic primeval history in Genesis 3 is distinguished through an entire series of sin stories: after Genesis 3, chapter 4 reports the fratricide of Cain and Lamech's unrestrained threats of revenge. In Genesis 6, we encounter the marital union with angels, upon which, in the same chapter, the flood follows (Genesis 6–8). Finally, the primeval history concludes with the story of the tower of Babel (Genesis 11). Each of these accounts sheds light in its own unique way on the mysterious breach between God and humanity as well as God's response to this breach.[16] Among these stories the incident that is portrayed in Genesis 3 is not simply one among many but the very first sinful incident that occurs with the first woman and the first man, whose name Adam (the Hebrew word for man or humanity) comes to be understood in the latter part of Genesis 3 as a proper name. In speaking of Adam as a particular person, the Yahwist seeks to make the archetypical character of this event known. The sin that is committed in Genesis 3 is not simply a violation of God's command not to eat from the tree of the knowledge of good and evil. Rather, the human mistrust of God is much more central to the story. The original basis of life, as sketched in the Yahwistic creation narrative, is characterized by innocence, "as living in a pure childlike relationship to God. This is a life which is also reflected in the relationship of man and woman." But now, however, the harmony between God

---

13. See Walther Zimmerli, *Old Testament Theology in Outline,* trans. David E. Green (Edinburgh: T. and T. Clark, 1978), 168.

14. Nevertheless, it is not quite accurate when Ludwig Köhler, *Old Testament Theology,* trans. A. S. Todd (Philadelphia: Westminster, 1957), 178, says that "the priestly writer knows nothing of paradise, the fall or the cursed ground." While the priestly writer knew no story of the fall as such, the flood story elevates the appearance of sin not just to an individual but to a global level. For a discussion with Köhler on this point see Zimmerli, *Old Testament Theology,* 173.

15. So Gerhard von Rad, *Genesis: A Commentary,* rev. ed., orig. trans. J. H. Marks (Philadelphia: Westminster, 1972), 102.

16. For this and the following see Zimmerli, *Old Testament Theology,* 168.

and humanity is destroyed.[17] The Yahwist's effort to bind creation and fall so closely together is not intended to show how the once good creation allegedly became so bad, for even after the fall, the world, including humanity, remains God's good creation. The Yahwist, rather, is much more interested in demonstrating the reason for the present fate of humanity.

It is often claimed that the disruption of the original harmony was advantageous because it led to a realization of human possibilities. Hegel, for example, understood sin as logically necessary for recognizing the good, for if a person "has no knowledge of evil, he has no knowledge of good either."[18] He claims that "the phase of negation is, indeed, a necessary element in human development." Friedrich Schiller thought similarly and wrote concerning the fall: "This instinctive fall of humanity brought, to be sure, moral evil into the creation, but only in order to make the morally good possible. Hence the fall is without a doubt the most fortunate and greatest occurrence in human history. From this moment on humanity realized its freedom; here also was laid the first remote cornerstone of human morality."[19] This idealistic conception of human sinfulness is also affirmed by many psychoanalysts. Thus Erich Fromm, 175 years after Schiller, claimed that "this first act of disobedience is man's first step toward freedom." The human is driven out of paradise and is now able "to make his own history, to develop his human powers, and to attain a new harmony with man and nature as a fully developed individual instead of the former harmony in which he was *not yet* an individual."[20] Carl Gustav Jung was somewhat more cautious when he wrote: "There is a deep doctrine in the legend of the fall: it is the expression of a dim presentiment that the emancipation of the ego-consciousness was a Luciferian deed."[21] Inasmuch as Teilhard de Chardin described the same facts, he likewise came close to an idealistic view

---

17. Theodorus C. Vriezen, *An Outline of Old Testament Theology,* 2d ed. (Oxford: Blackwell, 1970), 414.

18. Georg Wilhelm Friedrich Hegel, *Lectures on the Philosophy of Religion,* trans. E. B. Spies and J. B. Sanderson (New York: Humanities Press, 1962), 1:276; and idem, *The Philosophy of History,* trans. J. Sibree (New York: Dover, 1956), 407.

19. Friedrich Schiller, *Etwas über die erste Menschengesellschaft: Übergang des Menschen zur Freiheit und Humanität* (1789), in *Gesammelte Werke,* ed. Reinhold Netolitzky (Gütersloh: Bertelsmann, 1959), 4:103.

20. Erich Fromm, *The Heart of Man: Its Genius for Good and Evil* (New York: Harper, 1966), 20.

21. Carl Gustav Jung, "The Phenomenology of the Spirit in Fairytales," in

and claimed that evil was a necessary by-product of evolution, by means of which nature, through many errors and trials, moves upward in its evolutionary path.[22]

An evolutionary model forms the basis of the idealistic interpretation of the fall in which the later stages are characterized as more highly developed and therefore better. Against this view, however, two objections must be raised. First, it is difficult to prove that an evolutionary development to a higher level is necessarily better. From the perspective of biology, for instance, humans are not "better" than reptiles, although they represent an evolutionary higher development of life than reptiles. Something similar to this can be argued in regard to cultural development among humans. A more highly developed culture is not necessarily qualitatively better than a "more primitive" culture, even if one differentiates between these from a moral point of view to facilitate better classification. Second, one must take into consideration the fact that the story of the fall would seem incompatible with evolutionary theories, even if this does not hold true for each evolutionary interpretation. This is made clear in two ways. First, the origin of sin in Genesis 3 cannot be causally deduced from the good creation of God.[23] When Adam was questioned by God concerning his behavior, he sought to make such a deduction and said: "The woman whom you gave to be with me, she gave me the fruit from the tree and I ate" (Gen. 3:12). In this way he attempted to justify himself by ascribing the cause of evil to God. The woman attempted to make a similar causal deduction, although not quite as daring a one, when she responded to God's reproach by saying: "The serpent tricked me, and I ate" (Gen. 3:13). In both instances it is suggested, with apologetic intent, that the cause of evil is to be found externally. But neither of these attempts is able, before God, to excuse the seriousness of the situation. Second, there exists no

---

Collected Works, trans. R. F. C. Hull (New York: Pantheon Books, 1959), 9/1:230 (420).

22. See Pierre Teilhard de Chardin, *The Phenomenon of Man* (New York: Harper, 1959), 301f., where he says: "The involuting universe...proceeds step by step by dint of a billion-fold trial and error. It is this process of groping, combined with the two-fold mechanism of reproduction and heredity..., which gives rise to the...tree of life." See also 310, where he makes use of the same terminology when he speaks of the "evil of disorder and failure" as a necessity in the evolutionary process.

23. For the following see the instructive comments of Zimmerli, *Old Testament Theology,* 168f.

causal connection between these first sins and the appearance of subsequent sins. To be sure, the Yahwist illustrates in drastic manner the rapid growth of evil, which spreads like a wild fire. But nowhere is the appearance of a new sin tied to the commission of a previous sin so that the burden of guilt of later sins might be reduced.

Evil came through the appearance in the world of the first man and the first woman, and it continues to reveal itself in conjunction with the appearance of humans. One might call to remembrance here what behavioral psychology determined concerning the phenomenon of aggression. In a variety of forms aggressive drives are already to be found among animals. These drives normally serve, however, to facilitate the survival of a species and not to jeopardize it. This applies likewise to aggression directed toward other species, as in the case of defense or hunting; and even within species, as in the establishment of hierarchies, defensive behavior, or the selection of mates. As human beings appeared, however, and began to exercise dominion over one another and their environment and to develop increasingly sophisticated tools and weapons, the aggressive drives became increasingly ambivalent. They increased the potential for good as well as for evil. Thus many animal species were annihilated and others domesticated, parts of humanity destroyed and others forcefully merged through "worldwide" civilizations. As psychoanalysis shows, the activities of humans are highly ambivalent; they comprise the drive for life while at the same time spreading fear and death.

The appearance of evil cannot be compared to a disastrous stroke of fate against which humanity was helpless. We must not overlook the fact that it is not the man or woman but rather the snake who appears as the tempter in the account of the fall. Yet we would overstep the limits of the interpretation of the temptation story to claim that the woman had a more direct access to the dark side of life than the man because she was first tempted and then becomes the temptress.[24] It is nevertheless emphasized that humanity was not sinful from the very beginning, but that the temptation originated externally. The cause of evil, however, is not some God-opposing principle external to God's creation, even though this view was held within Gnosticism. The snake, which

---

24. Von Rad, *Genesis*, 90, offers this interpretation in his exegesis of Gen. 3:6.

becomes the tempter, is described as an animal and thereby as part of God's creation but not as a part of the heavenly court.[25]

Still, the primeval history gives no answer to the fundamental question of where evil comes from. Along with the rest of the Old Testament, not the slightest attempt is made to take refuge in either a dualistic or pluralistic worldview. It is beyond the interests of the Yahwist why a part of God's good creation became the tempter, because the answer to this question would not contribute to the description of human sinfulness. The guilt, in all its severity, is allowed to stand as unexplained guilt. Still, there are two additional facts that require further clarification, namely, what provoked humankind to sin and what were the consequences for humans after they had fallen into sin.

The first human pair was tempted to become like God, that is, to know good and evil. Yet it is difficult to accept that God would have created a creature capable of becoming his potential challenger, so that the first human being "is potentially God."[26] While for the Yahwist it is absurd that anyone could equal Yahweh, it is not incredible for him to propose that a human would desire to be equal to the divine being Elohim.[27] Yet the stimulus to sin goes beyond the human aspiration to be like God. As humans were tempted to recognize good and evil, they wanted to be aware not only of the difference between good and evil but also of everything, that is, the totality of all things from good to evil.[28] The human temptation at that time consisted of, and continues to consist of, the desire to know everything and to know it better than our human or divine "opponent." This arrogant stance threatened God and neighbor and every harmonious relationship to them. Yet this stance must not be confused with the inquisitive human spirit, for the goal of its efforts is not the egoistic "knowing better," but rather the analytical, measuring knowing concerned with the relationship between things. Sinful knowing-it-all consists of the destructive wish of humanity not to recognize a "You" that

---

25. See Johannes Fichtner, "Ophis (Gen 3)," in *TDNT* 5:573, who emphasizes the created nature of the serpent.

26. This view is expressed by Erich Fromm, *You Shall Be as Gods: A Radical Interpretation of the Old Testament and Its Traditions* (New York: Holt, Rinehart and Winston, 1966), 23.

27. Similarly, von Rad, *Genesis,* 88f., in his exegesis of Gen. 3:4f.

28. See von Rad, *Genesis,* 88f.; and Henricus Renckens, *Israel's Concept of the Beginning: The Theology of Genesis 1–3* (New York: Herder and Herder, 1964), 274f.

possesses its own sphere, but rather to regard it as an "It" that is not allowed to have any secrets. This human hubris destroys fundamentally the relationship to God as well as to neighbor and also damages the created character of nature inasmuch as it regards nature as a thing to be possessed by humans.

God does not react to the sinful pride of humanity as an offended tyrant. Yet the harmonious unity with God was severed and the first human pair expelled from the garden. But the threat that Adam and Eve would die on the day on which they ate from the tree of knowledge of good and evil (Gen. 2:17) was not realized through their sin. They were only once reminded that they would return to dust, from which they were formed (Gen. 2:7; 3:19). Indeed, almost as if to hold the original threat in contempt Adam now ventures to name his wife "Eve," that is, the mother of all living.[29] Even the obligation to work cannot be understood as an actual curse resulting from the fall because Adam was already supposed to tend the garden (Gen. 2:15). As the harmonious relationship with God was broken, however, the harmonious relationship between humanity and nature as well as between man and woman also disappeared. The Yahwist acknowledges thereby that life is difficult, filled with hatred and passion and permeated by a yearning after harmony. But life did not cease, for "the Lord God made garments of skins for the man and for his wife, and clothed them" (Gen. 3:21). Instead of lamenting evil, the Yahwist points to signs of grace that were given the first human pair on their journey through life: garments of skins and God's assistance in dressing.[30] This merciful act of God might be understood as a better foreshadowing of the gospel than Gen. 3:15, the text usually referred to as the "Protoevangelium" or protogospel that speaks of the lasting enmity that will hold sway between the serpent and humanity.[31]

When we leave the Genesis account of the fall and seek to determine the cause of evil from other Old Testament sources, our task becomes even more difficult.[32] For example, we find in Amos

---

29. See Zimmerli, *Old Testament Theology,* 172.

30. So correctly Vriezen, *An Outline,* 415.

31. For an interpretation of Gen. 3:15 see Fichtner, "Ophis (Gen 3)," 574f. At this point there exists no hint that the enmity between humanity and the serpent will be overcome. But such enmity will no longer exist in the messianic age, because the original harmony will then be reestablished.

32. See for this and the following Vriezen, *An Outline,* 304, who also notices the difficulty of introducing evil into a monotheistic religion without associating it directly with God.

that Yahweh asks his people: "Does disaster [that is, evil] befall a city, unless the Lord has done it?" (Amos 3:6). God stands behind the evil and the good. After Job is seized by misfortune, he is convinced of this omnipotence and says to his wife: "Shall we receive good at the hand of God, and shall we not receive the bad?" (Job 2:10). His wife, however, appears to take no comfort in this, for she wants her husband to renounce and even to curse God because he is the cause of all the evil that has befallen Job. In Deutero-Isaiah the pressing question of whether God is the cause of evil is likewise answered in the affirmative, for there we hear the Lord say: "I form light and create darkness, I make weal and create woe, I the Lord do all these things" (Isa. 45:7). In other texts we discover that the Lord can even incite one person against another (see 1 Sam. 26:19).

God is the only God who knows good and evil, and everything depends upon him. But then we also learn that there is a spirit of evil that is to be distinguished from Yahweh and that afflicts the people (1 Sam. 16:14f.). But such a statement does not diminish the understanding that God is the only genuine power, for it is God who sends the evil spirit.[33] It would be tempting to speak here of a demonic god, in light of whose actions no one can be secure. Or to assume that the Israelites ascribed good and evil to Yahweh in order to preserve a monotheistic understanding of God. These attempts at a solution, however, fail. God is not a demon, and his works are always directed toward the triumph of his kingdom and the advance of his plan of redemption. Thus the Psalmist is correct when he confesses: "For his anger is but for a moment; his favor is for a lifetime" (Ps. 30:5). Israel was nevertheless also convinced that Yahweh ordains for individuals as well as the entire people tests, afflictions, or even judgment, and in this sense does "evil."[34] From this perspective one can understand the story of Job, who was afflicted by God and was led thereby to a deeper understanding of God. God is never, however, understood as a capricious God before whose deeds one must fear but rather as a holy God before whom one dare not appear as if an equal or in a demanding manner. Behind the statements of the incomparable circumspection of a God who creates good and evil stands the recognition of

---

33. See Werner Foerster, "Daimon," in *TDNT* 2:11, who, in reference to this text, writes: "OT monotheism is thus maintained, since no power to which man might turn in any matter is outside the one God of Israel."

34. See Haag, *Vor dem Bösen ratlos?* 23.

the absolute sovereignty of God over life and death, fortune and misfortune, well-being and calamity.

In the case of God's activity the opposite of good is not moral evil but rather misfortune or divine judgment, as that which normally results from the evil actions of humanity. "Thus says the Lord of hosts, the God of Israel: You yourselves have seen all the disaster that I have brought upon Jerusalem and all the towns of Judah...because of the wickedness that they committed" (Jer. 44:2f.). When humans abandon their evil actions, God can avert the misfortune that he had intended for them. The inhabitants of Nineveh learned this as they pursued a path of moral repentance. "When God saw what they did, how they turned from their evil ways, God changed his mind about the calamity that he had said he would bring upon them; and he did not do it" (Jon. 3:10). Yet the ways of God are not always easy to fathom. One must recognize the incomparable sovereignty of the God who says, "My thoughts are not your thoughts, nor are your ways my ways" (Isa. 55:8).

But how should one respond when one reads, for instance, in 1 Sam. 16:14: "Now the spirit of the Lord departed from Saul, and an evil spirit from the Lord tormented him," or similarly in Judg. 9:23: "God sent an evil spirit between Abimelech and the lords of Shechem; and the lords of Shechem dealt treacherously with Abimelech"? Or when one reads of the sons of the high priest Eli: "But they would not listen to the voice of their father; for it was the will of the Lord to kill them" (1 Sam. 2:25)? Do we not encounter here a demonic, sinister, treacherous, and unpredictable God? Thus the prophet Isaiah receives the command from Yahweh to go to his people and harden their hearts so that they hear, but do not understand; see, but do not recognize (Isa. 6:9f.). Up to and including the time of the great writing prophets like Isaiah, God is viewed as an absolutely sovereign God from whom comes good and evil. The question of theodicy, or of how a just God can also cause evil without thereby himself becoming evil, is not posed in this form. The emphasis, in fact, is upon God's sovereignty, since only because he is sovereign can one expect from him the mighty acts that show him to be the Lord of history. Consequently, all the effects of life, the dark as well as the light, the frightening as well as the cheerful, the threatening as well as the saving, are transferred to Yahweh. He is the final ground of all things and the sole causality of life.

Yet already in the book of Ecclesiastes (ca. 230 B.C.) it is emphasized that "God made human beings straightforward, but they have devised many schemes" (Eccl. 7:29). The wickedness of humanity does not find its origin in God but rather in humanity alone. Still more clearly, we read in the apocryphal book of Sirach (ca. 180 B.C.) that God is not a party to the sins of humans: "Do not say, 'It was the Lord's doing that I fell away'; for he does not do what he hates. Do not say, 'It was he who led me astray'; for he has no need of the sinful. The Lord hates all abominations; such things are not loved by those who fear him. It was he who created humankind in the beginning, and he left them in the power of their own free choice" (Sir. 15:11-14). To be sure, we also read in Sirach that "good things and bad, life and death, poverty and wealth, come from the Lord" (Sir. 11:14), yet it is held at the same time to be true that "all the works of the Lord are very good" (Sir. 39:16). The author of Sirach points out here that one cannot blame God for evil. Although God sovereignly created good and evil, all of his works are so good that one cannot, as the first human pair attempted, diffuse or deflect evil as something inflicted upon humans from outside themselves. In addition, Sirach indicates that the works of God "will be done at the appointed time" (Sir. 39:16). God has organized everything in accordance with his goal, including that which, at the present time, does not seem recognizable as such. As a result, therefore, one can here conclude that "humanity, and not some power external to it, creates evil; and even in those instances in which Yahweh appears as the author of misfortune, humanity is not excused from its own responsibility."[35]

As one could no longer look back upon the great acts of God through a presumed direct lineage, and as one increasingly saw oneself within the broadening historical context as a pawn of historical world powers, it was no longer so easy to attribute everything to God and continue, nevertheless, to hold fast to his promises of salvation. If God was to remain in the future the one upon whom salvation ultimately depended, then he could not continue to be understood as the author of both good and evil. Evil was, so to speak, excluded from God, without falling into a dualism in the process. Thus one comes to a distinction between evil

---

35. Haag, *Vor dem Bösen ratlos?* 61. Yet when Haag maintains that this holds true for the Old Testament from its earliest to its latest writings, one must disagree, for there developed an increasingly strong impression that an external power must be at least co-responsible for evil.

as an act or thing and its underlying causal force that is distinct from God.

The Exclusion of Evil

When one views evil as a causal force distinct from God, mythological imagery can be employed in which an unequivocal identification of evil is not important. One can also comprehend evil through a more personally related understanding that recalls, for instance, persons involved in court proceedings. In the mythical imagery of the poetic writings and also of the prophets, Leviathan, a multiheaded, largely mythical primal creature, becomes the embodiment of evil. According to the view of the Old Testament, Leviathan was killed by the creator of the cosmos (Ps. 74:13f.) or has been abidingly subdued (Ps. 104:26f.). The most disparate symbols and identifications are to be found in Leviathan. As a creation of Yahweh, Leviathan is roughly comparable with the crocodile as a large, dangerous creature (Job 41:1ff.), yet on the other hand it becomes the embodiment of the power that opposes God (Isa. 27:1). The prophet expresses the hope that in the last days God will usher in the new creation, whereby the chaotic force Leviathan, also called the twisting serpent and dragon, will be decisively defeated. A similar and perhaps even identical chaotic force is "Rahab," who was likewise defeated by the creator in primordial times (Isa. 51:9; Job 26:12f.). Metaphorically, the threatening power Rahab can be identified with Egypt (Isa. 30:7). The God-opposing power introduced with these various images resists God's plan of redemption. These images point no doubt to Babylonian influences and primeval myths. These were combined with the Israelite conception of the correspondence between end time and primordial time, for one expected in "the end times a new assault of the chaos dragon against God and a new victory of God over him."[36] Important here is that evil and the God-opposing power in their symbolic form resist both the creation and the final deliverance through Yahweh and desire to bring both to naught, but will, however, themselves be defeated.

In an entirely different manner, much less mythological and almost profane, another external-to-God causal force is encountered

---

36. Haag, *Vor dem Bösen ratlos?* 96. See also in this regard Gerhard Schmitt, "Rahab," in *BHH* 3:1547f.; and Marie-Louise Henry, "Leviathan," in *BHH* 2:1076f.

in the Old Testament, the figure of Satan. The term "Satan" has the original meaning in its verbal form of "to be at enmity with, to persecute, and more specifically, to demonstrate enmity through accusation."[37] This means that this term belongs initially to the realm of the profane and only gradually took on theological significance. As a substantive the term "Satan" in the Old Testament can also be used to designate an enemy. For example, the leaders of the Philistines feared that David could become their adversary (Satan) in battle (1 Sam. 29:4).[38] Often the adversary (Satan) is an enemy of Israel who accuses Israel in the name of Yahweh and points to the evil that Israel has done (1 Kings 11:14, 23).[39] The ancient passage concerning Balaam and his ass shows us that even Satan can be identified with someone who is a part of God's heavenly court. Because Balaam unconsciously does something against God's will, God himself becomes the adversary, blocks his way, and hinders him from carrying out his own will (Num. 22:22ff.).[40]

In the book of Job the function of Satan as the accuser is portrayed with particular clarity. In the opening chapters Satan, as a member of God's heavenly court, questions whether Job is really so blameless and upright as he appears. Because Satan is not understood as a demonic power but as one of the sons of God, he needs God's permission in order to test the integrity of Job.[41] Consequently, it is ultimately God who tests Job. It is, however, difficult to understand Satan as the accuser in analogy to a legal trial. Against such a view one might mention the fact that there were many other life-threatening powers that worked against Job, such as disease, death, theft, and the devastating forces of nature. The "cause of the evil," however, takes place in conjunction with God and not in opposition to him, whereas the temptation by the serpent in the fall narrative takes place "behind God's back." Nevertheless, Satan functions in the story of Job as a heavenly op-

---

37. So Kurt Lüthi, *Gott und das Böse: Eine biblisch-theologische und systematische These zur Lehre vom Bösen, entworfen in Auseinandersetzung mit Schelling und Karl Barth* (Zürich and Stuttgart: Theologischer Verlag Zürich, 1961), 116.

38. For this and the following see the investigation by Rivkah Schärf Kluger, *Satan in the Old Testament,* trans. H. Nagel (Evanston, Ill.: Northwestern Univ. Press, 1967), esp. 34ff.

39. See Gerhard von Rad, "Diabolos (The Old Testament View of Satan)," in *TDNT* 2:73.

40. Von Rad, "Diabolos," 2:74.

41. For more details see Kluger, *Satan,* 73ff.

ponent of a peaceful life and earthly comfort.[42] The result of his activity, however, is not the destruction of Job, as one might fear, for Job achieves a deeper piety and surrenders himself fully to God as a result of the fateful blows dealt him.

In the fourth vision of the prophet Zechariah the accusing function of Satan is once more made clear. Yet he is no longer viewed as a son of God but rather as the accuser who stands at the right side of the accused high priest Joshua as both appear before the angel of the Lord (Zech. 3:1ff.). Satan continues to seek to show the evil side of humanity, in this instance in the evil deeds of the high priest during the exile. It is no longer clear, however, that he acts with the intention of advancing the kingdom of God. God finally intervenes in the case through an angel in order to allow the high priest to receive grace and forgiveness (Zech. 3:4).[43]

In 1 Chronicles 21 Satan's position as independent from God is advanced still further.[44] This is the only text in the Old Testament in which Satan is used as a proper name. In 2 Sam. 24:1 we read: "The anger of the Lord was kindled against Israel, and he incited David against them, saying, 'Go, count the people of Israel and Judah.' " The Chronicler, however, reports the same event with the following words: "Satan stood up against Israel, and incited David to count the people of Israel" (1 Chron. 21:1). When we compare here the Old with the New Testament, we notice a similar shift. In Hos. 11:10, God is compared to a roaring lion, while in 1 Pet. 5:8 it is the devil who is called a "roaring lion." The statement that God could incite David to sin was probably regarded as objectionable at the time of the writing of Chronicles. In both versions, however, that of the Chronicler and that of the book of Samuel, we read that God decrees the punishment for David's sin. Nowhere in the Old Testament does Satan achieve the status of a dualistic opponent of God who restricts God to serving

---

42. For this and the following see von Rad, "Diabolos," 2:73.

43. See Herbert Haag, *Teufelsglaube,* with contributions by Katharine Elliger, Bernhard Lang, and Meinrad Limbeck (Tübingen: Katzmann, 1974), 200; see also Lars Gösta Rignell, *Die Nachtgesichte der Sacharja: Eine exegetische Studie* (Lund: Gleerup, 1950), 101. Kluger, *Satan,* 142, comments in the vein of Jung: "In Zech. 3:1ff. the differentiation process has advanced further. *The separation of Satan, the dark side of God, is followed by the corresponding release of God's light side.*"

44. Relative to this paragraph see von Rad, "Diabolos," 2:74f.; see also Kluger, *Satan,* 161. Haag, *Teufelsglaube,* 213f., comments here correctly that in 1 Chron. 21:1 Satan does not replace Yahweh, but rather his wrath that was kindled against Israel.

as the principle of the good. Finally, even the satanic temptations must further God's redemptive plan. This is also to be seen in the above cited account concerning David. Because his royal power was diminished through the punishment of God, he became more receptive to the will of God.

In this passage it is again evident that God was originally understood without exception as the source of both good and evil. Yet the tendency arose to see God's function in reference to the cause of evil only in his judging of humanity for its sinful behavior. This means that the cause of the activation of evil in humanity must be found outside of God: first the temptation by someone out of God's good creation, then in the image of the heavenly accuser, and finally in the increasingly independent figure of a malevolent Satan. But we can hardly agree with the otherwise very instructive work of Rivkah Schärf Kluger when this author says that in the case of the "figure of Satan we have to do with the result of a developmental process within God."[45] It is not, however, the divine person that had developed, but rather the Israelite conception of God that had gradually become clearer. This process of clarification is continued with increased vigor in the New Testament. We must, however, recall once more to memory a decisive point: regardless of to whom the cause of evil in an event is attributed, the Old Testament contends that the existence of an evil tempter external to humans does not decrease their responsibility for their own actions. Even when the temptation appears irresistible, the responsibility of humans for their actions endures unchanged.[46] We can read this clearly in the Chronicler's version of the temptation of David, for there he confesses: "Was it not I who gave the com-

---

45. Kluger, *Satan,* 79. It is also questionable whether Haag, *Teufelsglaube,* 217, is correct when he maintains that the coming to prominence of Satan in the Old Testament is the result of an ever stronger inclination to prevent the clouding of the transcendence and holiness of God by unclean elements. We must agree that there exists without doubt a conspicuous development in the Old Testament understanding of God. This would seem, however, to be accounted for much more by the nature of the (political) reality that stood in increasing disharmony with the expectations of salvation, as the exile became a part of the past and nothing decisive was achieved toward the reestablishment of the Jewish kingdom. In the event one wished to continue to believe in the realization of God's salvation history one had to assume obstructing factors external to God and humanity. Regarding the problem of the gradual clarification of the concept of God see Hans Schwarz, *The Search for God* (Minneapolis: Augsburg, 1975), chap. 6: "From a Tribal God to the Savior of Mankind," 158–78.

46. So Zimmerli, *Old Testament Theology,* 150.

mand to count the people? It is I who have sinned and done very wickedly" (1 Chron. 21:17).

In order to fully understand the figure of Satan we must look beyond the Old Testament and turn, at least briefly, to the extra-biblical and intertestamental material, which was also influential for the sources of the New Testament. Because the principal references to Satan (Zech. 3:1; Job 1f.) appear first in the early postexilic period,[47] Babylonian and Iranian influences could have easily contributed to the Israelite conception of Satan. In fact, there exists a close parallel between the biblical book of Job and the so-called Babylonian Job, or "Poem of the Righteous Sufferer."[48] This poem tells of a persecutor who brings diseases upon a righteous man. While this Babylonian persecutor, or disease demon, has similarities with the tempting function of Satan, this function in the biblical book of Job is only a single characteristic of Satan. Additionally, the Babylonian disease demon will be ultimately defeated by a good god, whereas according to the book of Job, Satan does not oppose God, but rather acts with his permission. Therefore, the righteous Babylonian man attributes his suffering to the accuser while Job ascribes his predicament to God. Although definite textual parallels are to be recognized between the Babylonian and the biblical narratives, the theological reasoning at decisive points runs in opposing directions.

There is, however, another aspect in which the Babylonian conception becomes important for the biblical understanding of Satan. When the dealings of Satan are described in the Old Testament, they often resemble in their course the court ceremonial, as it is transmitted from the Babylonian account. According to Babylonian mythology, the relationship between God and humanity resembles that of the court ceremonial. God is the judge and humans seek justice. In the ceremonial appears an accuser, a royal official, who travels throughout the land and represents the "eyes

---

47. So Georg Fohrer, *History of Israelite Religion,* trans. David E. Green (Nashville: Abingdon, 1972), 375.

48. For the following see Kluger, *Satan,* 87ff. and 133. See also Georg Fohrer, *Das Buch Hiob,* in *Kommentar zum Alten Testament* (Gütersloh: Bertelsmann, 1963), 16:44, for a brief description of this text. Fohrer does not, however, mention Satan in this connection. For a translation of the Babylonian Job see " 'I Will Praise the Lord of Wisdom' ('Poem of the Righteous Sufferer')," trans. Robert H. Pfeiffer, in *Ancient Near Eastern Texts relating to the Old Testament,* ed. James B. Pritchard (Princeton, N.J.: Princeton Univ. Press, 1950), 434–37.

of the king."[49] The concept of the "eyes of the king" is likewise known in Media, Persia, and Egypt. Because this image is so widespread, we should not be surprised to find traces of it in the accusing function of Satan in Job 1f. and Zech. 3:1ff.

Of much greater significance than these Babylonian parallels is the influence of Zoroastrian doctrine upon the Old Testament conception of Satan.[50] At the center of Zoroaster's teaching stands Ahura Mazda, the one high god who determines the entire development of the world (Yasna 31:8). Because Zoroaster (Zarathustra according to the Persian transcription) excludes evil from his conception of Ahura Mazda, he can connect him only indirectly to evil inasmuch as he describes him as the father of the twin gods Ahra Mainyu (evil spirit) and Spenta Mainyu (holy spirit) (Yasna 30:3f.).[51] The original monotheism was thus bound together with a strict dualism. Ahra Mainyu, however, is not equal to Ahura Mazda, for he is only a spirit of Ahura Mazda and has Spenta Mainyu as his direct adversary. The apparent strict dualism is thus weakened inasmuch as the high god himself stands behind Spenta Mainyu and is one with him (Yasna 47:1). Yet it is the twin spirits who create the world in which Spenta Mainyu is responsible for life and Ahra Mainyu for the absence of life. Each of them has his own followers, through whom Ahra Mainyu is identified with deceit, betrayal, death, sin, and evil. When we now ask where evil comes from, the conclusion must be drawn that Ahura Mazda is also the father of the evil spirit. Hence Ahura Mazda contains within himself the tendency for good as well as for evil.[52]

---

49. Kluger, *Satan,* 135.

50. See in regard to this paragraph the excellent publication by Geo Widengren, *Die Religionen Irans* (Stuttgart: Kohlhammer, 1965), 74–78, where he provides a short summary of the teaching of Zarathustra. For a brief description of Zoroastrianism see Schwarz, *The Search for God,* chap. 5: "The Mystery of Man's Religions II," 124–27.

51. In *The Songs of Zarathustra: The Gatas,* translated from the *Avesta* by D. F. A. Bode and P. Nanavutty (London, 1952), 49, Yasna 30:3f., we read: "(3) Now in the beginning, these two Mainyu, the twins, revealed themselves in thought, word, and deed as the Better and the Bad; and, from these two, the wise chose aright, but not so the unwise. (4) And thus, when these two Mainyu first came together, they generated life and the absence of life, and so shall human existence continue till the end of time; the worst life for the Followers of the Lie, but the supreme beatific vision for the Followers of Truth."

52. So Geo Widengren in his informative article "The Principle of Evil in the Eastern Religions," in *Evil: Essays by Karl Kerenyi and Others,* ed. the Kuratorium of the C. G. Jung Institute, Zürich (Evanston Ill.: Northwestern Univ. Press, 1967), 35f.

The similarity between certain teachings of Zoroaster and the gradual perception of the figure of Satan in Israel is not to be denied. In both cases the cause of evil is excluded from the conception of God and attributed to a power external to God. Some of the characteristics of Ahra Mainyu are again encountered in the New Testament conception of Satan. When we consider that in the Old Testament God is emphasized as creator of history and of the world and that the attempt is consistently made to portray Satan in such a way that he belongs ultimately within the sphere of God's rule, then we recognize the fundamental difference between the monotheism of the Old Testament and the cosmo-ethical dualism of Zarathustra.[53] In contrast to Zoroaster the Old Testament authors never once ventured to express the thought that Yahweh was the father of Satan. For the Israelites it was so important that God is the Lord of history that they were not interested in establishing a causal connection between God and Satan. That does not, however, diminish the strong possibility of a catalytic influence of Zoroastrianism upon the Judeo-Christian tradition that served to reinforce and clarify the conception of Satan.

In the Judaism of the pre-Christian era, which in many respects provides the direct background for the message of the New Testament, Satan was normally understood as the one who sought to destroy the relationship between God and humanity, and especially that between God and his people.[54] Moreover, the Old Testament conception of Satan was continued and enlarged during this period. In Enoch, for example, we read that a multitude of satans are lead by Satan (1 Enoch 53:3).[55] They have regular access to heaven and can appear before the Lord of spirits (1 Enoch 40:7). Their function is threefold: (1) they accuse human beings before God (69:6); (2) they attempt to incite humans to evil (69:6); and (3) they act as angels of judgment (53:3; 56:1). The satans are responsible for the fall of the sons of God and their marriages to the "daughters of the people" (1 Enoch 69:4f.). In 1 Enoch 6 it is said

---

53. Kluger's comment (*Satan*, 157) that "for the Persian religion, dualism is the *point of departure*" is perhaps somewhat exaggerated because the starting point is the one god, Ahura Mazda.

54. So Werner Foerster, "Diabolos (The Later Jewish View of Satan)," in *TDNT* 2:76.

55. For this and the following references to the pseudepigraphal literature of the Old Testament, including quotations, see James H. Charlesworth, ed., *The Old Testament Pseudepigrapha*, 2 vols. (Garden City, N.Y.: Doubleday, 1983, 1985).

that two hundred angels led by Azazel (8:1) took human wives. In the book of Jubilees we read that these evil spirits "practice all error and sin and all transgression" and that they "destroy, cause to perish and pour out blood upon the earth" (Jub. 11:5). Thus Noah asks God to capture the evil spirits and incarcerate them on the site of the destruction (10:5). Sin is here attributed to the fall of the angels and their progeny.[56]

In another passage we read that humans are responsible for their own sins and that sin can be traced back to the fall of Adam (Apocalypse of Abraham 23 and 26).[57] The fall of the angels or of Adam is not, however, the cause of sin, but merely its historical inception. This is expressed clearly in 2 Bar. 54:15, 19: "For, although Adam sinned first and has brought death upon all who were not in his own time, yet each of them who has been born from him and has prepared for himself the coming torment... Adam is, therefore, not the cause, except only for himself, but each of us has become our own Adam." It is here asserted that through Adam's fall physical death came into the world, a thought that is taken up by Paul in the New Testament. The fall, however, is not viewed as the cause of spiritual death. (This latter idea is only occasionally to be found in the Jewish literature of the pre-Christian period, e.g., 2 Bar. 48:42f.; 4 Ezra 3:21.) Occasionally Adam is seen as the cause of the corruptness of humanity. But at no point is a clear connection drawn between Adam's sin and the sin of his descendants.[58] We read for instance in 4 Ezra: "For the first Adam, burdened with an evil heart, transgressed and was overcome, as were also all who were descended from him. Thus the disease became permanent; the law was in the people's heart along with the evil root, but what was good departed, and

---

56. So David S. Russell, _The Method and Message of Jewish Apocalyptic_ (Philadelphia: Westminster, 1964), 252, in his informative work on the understanding of Satan in the Judaism of the pre-Christian era.

57. Naturally, we must take into consideration the relatively late date of this book, which was perhaps written even later than some New Testament writings. See R. Rubinkiewicz's introduction to the Apocalypse of Abraham, in Charlesworth, ed., _Old Testament Pseudepigrapha_, 1:683.

58. It is interesting that in 2 Enoch 31:6 and in the Revelation of Moses the fall of Satan is described. Especially in the later book is the important observation made that Satan, after his expulsion from heaven on account of his disregard for the directives of God, speaks through the mouth of the serpent and ensnares Eve and leads her to sin (Apoc. Mos. 17:4). This identification of Satan with the serpent is then taken up in the New Testament Revelation of St. John (see Rev. 12:9).

the evil remained" (4 Ezra 3:21f.). This means that the free will of humanity was substantially weakened after the fall.[59]

The uninterrupted tenor in the Judaism of the pre-Christian era exhibits itself in the following admonition: "So understand, my children, that two spirits await an opportunity with humanity: the spirit of truth and the spirit of error" (T. Jud. 20:1). Humanity must choose between light and darkness, between the law of the Lord and the works of Beliar (T. Levi 19:1). In the Qumran texts this demand for personal decision takes on cosmic dimensions. The history of the world is understood as a battle between light and darkness.[60] There exists no neutral ground between the sons of light and the sons of darkness who fight in this world for the final victory. Humanity, however, is not a helpless ball being played with in the contest between the two spirits, for humanity receives its destiny from the hands of God. In the Judaism of the pre-Christian era, Satan, Beliar, Mastem, or Azazel, as evil was called, was understood as a power that battles against God and brings his honor in dispute.[61] Because the authors of the later Jewish period lived in a time of colossal political and spiritual crises, their perspective is appropriate to the circumstances. Still, they did not simply see the world suspended in a back and forth, undecided battle. The view continued to prevail that God was the ruler of the world. Through the catalytic influence of Zoroastrian Parsism they could understand a hostile world and its history without compromising their Israelite belief in God's ultimate power. They arrived at a dynamic, ethical dualism, the cornerstone of which was already laid in the Old Testament. This "modified dualism," as William F. Albright terms it, deeply influenced the Christian faith.[62]

---

59. Russell, *Method,* 253 n. 4, repeats a comment from G. H. Box in his translation of 4 Ezra in *The Apocrypha and Pseudepigrapha of the Old Testament in English,* ed. R. H. Charles (Oxford: Clarendon Press, 1963), 2:563, when he says: the claim that the law that is implanted in human nature is not capable of achieving dominion over evil inclinations "contradicts the teaching of rabbinic theology."

60. For the following see Werner Foerster, "Satanas," in *TDNT* 7:156.

61. See H. H. Rowley, *The Relevance of Apocalyptic: A Study of Jewish and Christian Apocalypse from Daniel to the Revelation* (New York: Association Press, 1963), 172.

62. William F. Albright, *From the Stone Age to Christianity: Monotheism and the Historical Process* (1940) (Baltimore: Johns Hopkins Univ. Press, 1957), 362.

Chapter 4

Evil and the Evil One
from the Perspective
of the New Testament

From beginning to end the New Testament message is characterized by the conflict between good and evil, God and the world,
Jesus and Satan. A dualistic worldview, however, with God and
antigod as its two poles, cannot be found in the New Testament.
The New Testament points rather to a dynamic, aggressive conflict
that begins with the work of Jesus and finds its continuation in the
lives of Christians. Beginning with Jesus we could discuss evil as
the adversary of God, or with the apostle Paul we could speak of
sin. First, however, we will look at Jesus' struggle with evil.

Jesus' Struggle against Evil

The story of Jesus, as it is presented in the New Testament, is characterized by the absolute and irreconcilable contrast between God
and Satan and the presence of the kingdom of God in Jesus Christ,
which Satan seeks to destroy.[1] The entire mission of Jesus can be
understood as a continuous confrontation with Satan.[2] This does

---

1. So Werner Foerster in his brief but comprehensive article "Diabolos (The
NT View of Satan)," in *TDNT* 2:79.

2. See for the following the informative analysis by Joachim Jeremias, *New
Testament Theology,* vol. 1: *The Proclamation of Jesus,* trans. John Bowden (New
York: Charles Scribner's, 1971), 93–96. Herbert Haag, *Teufelsglaube* (Tübingen:
Katzmann, 1974), 317f., who sees in Luke 10:18 the only authentic saying of
Jesus concerning Satan, is too critical with regard to the biblical tradition. By
interpreting this saying as meaning that Jesus announced the fall of Satan as
the accuser, Haag recognizes, on the one hand, that Jesus had achieved victory
over the powers aligned against God, while he denies, on the other hand, the

not, however, mean that Satan is constantly referred to in the New Testament. Nevertheless, he appears at the decisive events in the life and ministry of Jesus: at the beginning of Jesus' ministry, as the story of the temptation of Jesus reports (Mark 1:12f.), and at the conclusion of his work, as the betrayal by Judas Iscariot shows (Luke 22:3). The story of Beelzebul (Mark 3:22-27) explains that the entire demonic sphere is under the control and supremacy of Satan. "Baal-Zebul" was originally the name of a Syrian god that was mispronounced as Beelzebub, meaning "lord of the flies" (see 2 Kings 1:2).[3] At the time of Jesus, Beelzebul was, within Judaism, in many respects equated with Satan. In Jesus' casting out of demons the greater act of casting out Satan is made manifest.[4]

But Satan does not make the activity of Jesus easy. The Synoptic Gospels continually indicate that Satan has made it his goal to further subjugate humanity and especially to hinder Jesus of Nazareth in his effort to bring salvation to humanity.[5] Satan is the originator of every possible life-degrading disease (Luke 13:16). Thus the work of Jesus, in contrast to the activity of Satan, was directed toward "doing good and healing all who were oppressed by the devil" (Acts 10:38). Satan, the enemy of everything good, sowed his seeds among the "children of the kingdom" (Matt. 13:38) and also attempted, through Peter, to destroy the work of Jesus (Matt. 16:23). While the destructive power of Satan cannot be overestimated, the New Testament authors reject the popularly held view of the time that every personal misfortune is the result of a person's preceding sins (see Luke 13:1-3). They are, to be sure, convinced

idea that Satan still possessed a threatening function. Yet such an understanding of salvation as fully realized is unfounded. While without doubt Jesus proclaimed the reign of God and actualized this reign, there is still an enduring eschatological component to this reign. The victory is achieved only in a proleptic sense. As the apocalyptic passages in the Synoptics indicate, the reality of Satan cannot be disregarded. Jesus has broken the power of the evil one, but he has not yet fully destroyed him or made him ineffectual. For a contrary view to that of Haag, see Foerster, "Satanas (Satan in the New Testament)," in *TDNT* 7:160. Inasmuch as Haag distinguishes Jesus' understanding of Satan and demons from that of his contemporaries and even from the evangelists, he appears to support an accommodation theory.

3. See Ernst Jenni, "Baal-Sebub," in *BHH* 1:175f.; and Eduard Schweizer, *Das Evangelium Markus, NTD,* 42, on this passage.

4. See in this regard the excellent investigation by Trevor Ling, *The Significance of Satan: New Testament Demonology and Its Contemporary Relevance* (London: SPCK, 1961), 18. This indicates that an exorcism, taken by itself, is not advantageous. What is decisive is by what authority it is carried out.

5. So Foerster, "Satanas," 160.

that Satan causes the evil in the world, but they are not interested in establishing, in the sense of an action-consequence connection, a causal linkage between one's sinfulness and the resulting "punishment" through disease or other evils, even if this belief was widespread among the people of that time. The New Testament writers wish much more to show that these evil events can serve the salvific purposes of God.[6]

The New Testament shows not only the destructive powers of Satan but also knows that he is defeated through Jesus Christ. Through the story of the expulsion of Beelzebul by Jesus (Mark 3:26f.) it is made clear that Satan has found his conqueror. This fact is confirmed through each of the subsequent actions of Jesus up to and including his sacrificial death (1 Cor. 15:57). Satan continues to accuse humans before God, yet Jesus counters these accusations with his intercessions so that their "faith may not fail" (Luke 22:32). Jesus occupies here a position that, in Judaism, was attributed to the angels, especially the archangel Michael. But an important difference existed in this regard between the older Judaism and that of the time of Jesus in that Satan had now lost his position of importance and his access to heaven. Jesus saw the creation as it was liberated from Satan and again placed under the reign of God, and he experienced its reality in his works and those of his disciples. Thus he could claim: "I watched Satan fall from heaven like a flash of lightning" (Luke 10:18).[7] This corresponds with the observation made in the book of Revelation: "For the accuser of our comrades has been thrown down, who accuses them day and night before our God" (Rev. 12:10). Because Satan is defeated it is not surprising that Jesus gives his disciples the authority "to tread on snakes and scorpions, and over all the power of the enemy." They have power over the seductive, antigodly forces of evil (Luke 10:19).

As we see from the New Testament epistles, Satan is once again active, as Jesus is no longer bodily present upon the earth, and seeks to destroy the growing Christian community. Thus Jesus taught his disciples in the Lord's Prayer to pray that they do not be-

---

6. See Rudolf Bultmann, *The Gospel of John: A Commentary*, trans. G. R. Beasley-Murray (Philadelphia: Westminster, 1971), 331, in his exegesis of John 9:3. See also Siegfried Schulz, *Das Evangelium nach Johannes, NTD*, 41, with reference to this passage.

7. See Foerster, "Satanas," 156f., who emphasizes the expulsion of the accuser.

come subject to the power of evil.[8] But Satan nonetheless sought to bring to naught the work of the apostles (1 Thess. 3:5). He persecutes the Christians (1 Pet. 5:8f.) and disguises himself as an angel of light in order to lead people astray with false doctrine (2 Cor. 11:14). Paul can even say that some of the obstacles encountered in his missionary travels are to be attributed to the influence of Satan (1 Thess. 2:18). The God-opposing activity of Satan culminates in the arrival of the Antichrist, who will proclaim himself to be God (2 Thess. 2:3-9). Then the desire of Satan will be fulfilled, as it is expressed in the apocalyptic writing the Life of Adam and Eve, "that he will set his throne above the stars of heaven and will be like the Most High" (15:3). Although Christians dare not underestimate Satan, they need not be afraid of him. They are promised: "The God of peace will shortly crush Satan under your feet" (Rom. 16:20). Through "the shield of faith" they can "quench all the flaming arrows of the evil one" (Eph. 6:16), or they can simply avoid tempting situations (1 Cor. 7:5). Christians are not uninformed as are the heathen, who do not even realize that they are under the reign of Satan (Acts 26:18).

A dramatically dualistic tendency in which the world is divided into two spheres of influence—one in which Christ rules and the other that stands under the influence of Satan—is especially pronounced in the Johannine writings.[9] In the Gospel of John we read, for example, that the devil was "a murderer from the beginning and does not stand in the truth, because there is no truth in him. When he lies, he speaks according to his own nature, for he is a liar and the father of lies" (John 8:44).[10] In contrast to the divine Logos he is not "in the beginning" but is "from the beginning" and is therefore secondary to the Logos. He is, however, a murderer and the father of lies, "the ruler of this world" (John 12:31), and the human inhabitants of the world are his children. The one

---

8. See Joachim Jeremias, *The Lord's Prayer,* trans. John Reumann (Philadelphia: Fortress Press, 1969), 29; and Ernst Lohmeyer, *"Our Father": An Introduction to the Lord's Prayer,* trans. John Bowden (New York: Harper, 1965), 217-29.

9. See in this regard the excellent description by Rudolf Bultmann, *Theology of the New Testament,* trans. Kendrich Grobel (New York: Charles Scribner's, 1951), 2:15-32.

10. See Foerster, "Satanas," 163, in his exegesis of this passage. Foerster rightly observes that this verse emphasizes "that the devil is determined by the fact that he is the devil.... [T]hat forbids us to ask what the devil was before he became the devil." This means that every speculation about the origin of the devil is here rejected, even if such speculation was popular in late Judaism.

who commits sin is from the devil, the one who is born of God, however, commits no sin (1 John 3:8f.). Satan is understood to be the direct cause of evil.

Yet one does not encounter a cosmic dualism in the Johannine writings, that is, two battling principles in the world, for through the coming of Jesus justice is enforced and the ruler of this world is expelled (John 12:31). In contrast to Gnosticism the world is not divided between an evil cosmos that is the domain of Satan and a heaven that is a safe haven for all believers in which the heavenly Father reigns. According to John, the world remains the creation of God that is created through the Logos.[11] Likewise, humanity is not divided into those who can be saved and those who are already irretrievably lost. Repentance and being born again are still possible (John 3:3), for "God did not send the Son into the world to condemn the world, but in order that the world might be saved through him" (John 3:17). Even if Christians through faith in Christ have "conquered the evil one" (1 John 2:13), they are not transported immediately into another sphere. They continue to live in this world, and a caution hence is necessary: "Do not love the world or the things in the world" (1 John 2:15). Rudolf Bultmann was thus correct when he wrote: "Each man is, or once was, confronted with the deciding for or against God; and he is confronted anew with this decision by the revelation of God in Jesus. The cosmological dualism of Gnosticism has become in John a *dualism of decision*."[12] This dualism, however, will not last forever. "The world and its desire are passing away, but those who do the will of God live forever" (1 John 2:17). This is the hope that the New Testament faith highlights and allows to become a living hope.

If we wish to summarize the biblical insights concerning the correlation between Satan and the cause of evil, we must first emphasize that within the biblical writings is to be found the

---

11. Bultmann, *Theology of the New Testament,* 2:17.

12. Bultmann, *Theology of the New Testament,* 2:21. Raymond E. Brown, *The Gospel according to John (I–XII)* (Garden City, N.Y.: Doubleday, 1966), lvi makes an interesting suggestion. While he concedes that Bultmann's claim that John is dependent upon an earlier oriental Gnosticism cannot be refuted, he believes that in many regards such a hypothesis is not necessary. Brown, on the contrary, believes that "OT speculation about personified Wisdom and the vocabulary and thought patterns of sectarian Judaism, like the Qumran community, go a long way toward filling in the background of Johannian theological vocabulary and expression." Such Jewish influence would indicate that the Johannine conception of the function and position of Satan is largely a consistent development of Old Testament and late Jewish thought.

ncreasingly clear view that the cause of evil cannot simply be at-ributed to God. Especially in the political unrest of the postexilic eriod, trust in God as the provider of all good things could no onger be reconciled with belief in God as the source of good and vil. In this regard another significant factor, alongside of the cat-lytic influence of Zoroastrianism, certainly played a role. This actor is simply that God's control of the historical process upon vhich the salvation of humanity depends, in light of the experience f the exile and the postexilic disappointments, could no longer e trusted as long as God also contained within himself the po-ential for evil. Yet the Yahwistic narrative of the fall shows that lready much earlier the power of evil was understood as some-hing so colossal that one could not imagine that it originated from umanity itself, whether from a single individual or from human-y as a whole. Attributing the cause of evil, however, to a power xternal to humanity does not lessen the individual and collective esponsibility of humans for their actions. However, because it is ertain that God is creator of the entire world, the cause of evil nust originate out of God's good creation.

Just how it came to be that something out of God's good cre-tion came to deny its creator might be interesting for speculative ninds, but not for the biblical authors. A clear definition of what recisely is meant by evil also lies beyond the interests of the Bible. lthough evil is often described as something that restricts the fe-supporting process, it is for the most part understood at the ame time as something that hinders the advance of the kingdom f God. Even biological impairments such as diseases, or natural vents such as earthquakes, can fall under the category of evil. he reason why no distinction is made between so-called natu-ally and spiritually caused evil events appears to be based upon he biblical conviction that the world cannot be dualistically di-ided between two original principles in which God is the cause of verything good and Satan the cause of everything evil. The bibli-al witnesses are convinced that the cause of evil must ultimately, nd occasionally even proleptically, glorify God (John 9:3).

We must also inquire here whether the distinction made be-ween God and the source of evil contradicts what we know about he structure of human existence. Pierre Teilhard de Chardin, for xample, believed that within an evolutionary understanding of he universe evil is an unfortunate but necessary by-product of he process of creation. According to this view, it would be difficult to maintain that God and the cause of evil are equally active forces underlying all processes. Sigmund Freud, on the other hand, stressed the instinctual impulses that are active in humanity and society. Yet he was not able to simply locate these impulses within humanity or society. Konrad Lorenz likewise accepted the existence of an aggression drive, which could, however, produce highly unfortunate results within humans. Yet not even this drive could be equated either entirely or in part with the constitutional nature of a single species. A living species is not simply to be identified with the place that it occupies within its contemporary space–time continuum. While a species stands in relationship to its environment, it also reaches beyond even its own being. This applies also to humanity. Therefore one cannot view good and evil as either the causes or results of human activity in such a way that they become ultimately purely human phenomena.

The biblical tradition does not measure good and evil by human standards, but rather compares them to the will of God. Because God desires the triumph of his kingdom and the establishment of a new creation, good and evil are essentially and intentionally oriented toward the future. The principles of good and evil seek to influence the actualization of God's will and play either a constructive or a destructive role in the process of creation. It would, we assume, be a contradiction within the divine reality itself if within God there were to be found a "yes" and a "no" contained in his will. Because our universe is the victim of evil as well as something that provides evil with a space in which to work, evil can be located neither in the universe as a whole nor in any specific part thereof. Perhaps we could illustrate the phenomenon of evil by comparing it with certain structural characteristics of antimatter, though of course in doing so, no identification of antimatter with the cause of evil is intended. Antimatter as a part of a greater field annihilates the matter that it encounters and radiates the product of this annihilation into the surrounding area. By way of theological analogy one could suggest the following conceptualization of evil: the cause of evil does not occupy the same status as God, but inasmuch as it stands in opposition to God's creation, it destroys those parts of the creation with which it comes into contact, producing a radiation, the effects of which are felt in other parts of the creation.

Evil and the Human Person

In the New Testament evil is primarily described by two adjectival or substantival terms, *kakos* and *poneros*.[13] Of these, *kakos* occurs less frequently. Evil (*kakos*) is limited to the human realm, "for God cannot be tempted by evil and he himself tempts no one. But one is tempted by one's own desire, being lured and enticed by it" (James 1:13f.). Jesus also confirmed that evil comes from humans themselves when he said: "For it is from within, from the human heart, that evil intentions come.... [A]ll these evil things come from within, and they defile a person" (Mark 7:21, 23). This evil that arises out of humans themselves is not inconsistent with the simultaneous conviction that an evil that is the ultimate ground of the negative stands behind humanity. Testimony to this ultimate ground of evil is to be found in the negative things that we receive fatefully in our own lives (Luke 16:25). Finally, the human individual is also confronted with the evil actions of others (Rom. 13:3f.). Yet according to Paul, all persons know that they themselves do not accomplish the good that they want to do, but rather the evil that they do not want to do (see Rom. 7:19). From this perspective evil is understood not only as moral evil but also as a complete lifestyle. Evil is the godlessness in which human beings continually find themselves.

Humans, to be sure, want to do good and honor and obey God. They have not yet entirely forgotten their inner purpose and their origin in God the creator. But they are not able to get any further than the most modest approaches to a just way of life. They sink repeatedly into sin so that they are no longer their own masters when they do these things, "but sin that dwells within" them (Rom. 7:20). Sin is thus the activity of humans in alienation from God that expresses itself in evil deeds. Nevertheless, Paul appeals: "Do not be overcome by evil, but overcome evil with good" (Rom. 12:21). This takes place, on the one hand, through the putting to death of evil desires (Col. 3:5), and, on the other hand, through the love that does no evil (Rom. 13:10)—a possibility facilitated through the love that comes from Christ.

When we now consider the second term that is used to indicate evil (*poneros*), it confronts us first of all in the sense of the Old Testament *raah,* as that which is not useful or unsuitable, that is,

---

13. For the following see Walter Grundmann, "Kakos," in *TDNT* 3:479f.

as that which is as such negative. Thus we read that an evil or bad tree produces bad fruit (Matt. 7:18) and that one can be an evil or wicked servant (Matt. 18:32). *Poneros* can also, however, mean "bad," "dangerous," or "disastrous," so that we read of the "evil day" as a critical day that brings with it great distress (Eph. 6:13), or metaphorically of a "foul [evil] and painful sore" (Rev. 16:2) that afflicts humanity. Much more frequently, however, we read of evil people (Matt. 7:11) who stand in contrast to God, who alone is good. Thus Jesus can speak of an "evil and adulterous generation" (Matt. 12:39) that, because it contains evil, can bring forth only evil things (Matt. 12:35). Those who are evil appear to have decided against Jesus and are therefore threatened with eschatological judgment.

When people are evil in their basic orientation, they will be fatefully drawn ever further into the web of evil. Thus Paul speaks of those who are "wicked people and impostors," for they slide ever further into the evil for which they themselves are the agents (2 Tim. 3:13). From the heart come "evil intentions," in which context "evil" can be the translation of *poneros* as well as of *kakos* (Matt. 15:19; Mark 7:21). In addition to individual stirrings of the senses the entire person can be called evil (Heb. 3:12). The wickedness spoken of here consists in "apostasy from faith, in self-will and turning from God."[14] If the human conscience is separated from God it can be called "an evil conscience" (Heb. 10:22). The deeds committed by believers in their pre-Christian lives are also characterized as evil (Col. 1:21) because they occurred under the sign of enmity with God. Paul can thus speak of "every evil attack" from which the Lord will rescue him, whereby he perhaps makes concrete reference to an evil plot against him or to imprisonment or persecution (2 Tim. 4:18). Also interesting is a passage in Matthew, which recurs in a similar form in Luke, in which an "unclean spirit" is spoken of that brings still other spirits "more evil than itself" (Matt. 12:45; Luke 11:26). It appears that reference to a hierarchy of evil spirits is made here, a view that one also finds in late Judaism.

Finally, John speaks of evil actions that are carried out by people in the darkness rather than in the light (John 3:19). The actions of the world, which occur in antithesis to the light and to the revelation of God, are fundamentally evil (John 7:7), for they

---

14. So Günther Harder, "Poneros," in *TDNT* 6:556.

do not originate from God. Whatever is contrary to the gospel is evil, for it is the word of God that decides what is good and evil. Here we encounter once more a dramatic dualism that John introduces through his use of contrasts such as good and evil, or light and darkness.

Alongside of the adjectival use of *poneros,* through which certain forms of behavior or things are more precisely labeled, we encounter frequently in the New Testament the substantival use of *poneros,* through which evil is spoken of in the singular or plural. Thus we hear in a parable of Jesus that at the end of the world those who are evil will be separated from the righteous (Matt. 13:49), or in the Sermon on the Mount that God makes the sun "rise on the evil and the good" (Matt. 5:45). Both passages show that Jesus rejects a strict application of the action-consequence connection. The just and the unjust live together upon the earth, and only at the end of time are they divided, and the evil ones receive the punishment that they have earned. At the same time Jesus also indicates that through God's generosity, evil and good persons live together. This does not mean that God is indifferent toward humanity, but rather that God's generosity rises above our understanding of justice and that he genuinely intends what is good for both evil and good persons, the just and the unjust.[15]

Not only a person or persons can be indicated by *poneros,* but in the singular form this substantive can also represent that which stands in absolute contrast to God, the devil.[16] This is the meaning of the word, for instance, in the parable of the sower in Matthew: "When anyone hears the word of the kingdom and does not understand it, the evil one comes and snatches away what is sown in the heart" (Matt. 13:19). In the parallel passage in Mark, however, we read: "Satan immediately comes and takes away the word that is sown in them" (Mark 4:15). In the version of this parable found in Luke's Gospel, we read that "the devil comes and takes away the word from their hearts" (Luke 8:12), in which "devil" is a translation of the Greek word *diabolos.* Thus we see that Satan or the devil can also be denoted as "*the evil* one." We find this also outside of the Gospels, as for instance in Eph. 6:16, where "the flaming arrows of the evil one" are spoken of. The term *poneros* is

---

15. In regard to this passage see Eduard Schweizer, *The Good News according to Matthew,* trans. David E. Green (Atlanta: John Knox, 1975), 134.

16. So the interpretation from Harder, "Poneros," 560f.

employed on several occasions to indicate Satan in 1 John, where we read of the evil one who is defeated by Christians (1 John 2:13f.). The human individual is the battlefield in the conflict between Christ and Satan. Those who are in Christ, however, have already been victorious and have fought on the side of Christ.

Often "evil" appears to be used in a neuter sense. We see this, for instance, in the explanation of the parable of the tares in which Jesus speaks of the children of the kingdom (of God) and the children of the evil one (Matt. 13:38). A similar usage of _poneros_ in neuter form is to be found in Jesus' high priestly prayer in which Jesus, making reference to his disciples, prays that God will "protect them from evil" (John 17:15). And finally, in the Lord's Prayer, Jesus asks that God deliver us "from evil" (Matt. 6:13). When in regard to this last passage reference is made to the distress of the last days, that is, to eschatological evil—a conception with parallels in the Pauline tradition, as for instance in the promise to the Christians in Thessalonica that God would guard them "from evil" (2 Thess. 3:3)—one may not simply remain with this neuter usage of the phenomenon of "evil." Evil is no simple neuter. Especially in its eschatological orientation it cannot be attributed to sinful human efforts with any less difficulty than it can be derived from God. The term "evil," therefore, must remain open to include the concept of an "evil one." This metaphysical connection gives evil the weight and the threatening force that are repeatedly demonstrated in the New Testament. In the final analysis, this means that humans do not simply have the power to do or not to do evil, but rather they stand under the power of sin; that is to say, they are overshadowed by the power of evil.

Humanity under the Power of Sin

To speak here of sin is already justified by the fact that _hamartia_ (sin) can represent the Hebrew terms _chattat, avon,_ and _pesha._ When we look at the New Testament, we notice that "sin," in both its substantival and verbal forms, appears much less frequently in the four Gospels than in the other New Testament writings. At first glance, one wonders about this phenomenon. Yet we must remember that Jesus did not appear as a prophet of God's judgment to proclaim God's punishment to a sinful world, but rather as the Lord of the world. As Jesus shows, for instance, in the Sermon on the Mount, he was aware of the reality of sin. Yet he understood himself in his speech and activity as the conqueror of sin. Therefore he could say: "I have come to call not the righteous but sinners" (Matt. 9:13), and "there will be more joy in heaven over one sinner who repents than over ninety-nine righteous persons who need no repentance" (Luke 15:7). He reveals himself to those to whom he is sent who live in alienation from God and desires to lead them down the path that brings them back to God. The extent of God's rejoicing over the repentance of humans is illustrated, for example, in the parable of the prodigal son (Luke 15:11-32). In this parable it is also clear that sin signifies the forsaking of the parental home for godlessness and alienation from God.

Jesus desires to lead individuals back to God and shows them that God will once more accept them and rejoice over their return. Sin, however, is no trifling matter, but rather something that requires remorse and repentance (Luke 15:21), as well as the recognition that one has wronged God through the alienation from him. As the one who proclaims the reign of God, Jesus eats with sinners, removes the barrier between the sinner and God, and establishes a new community with God. He does not erect barriers between himself and those who live in alienation from God. This is demonstrated in the symbolic act of the sinful woman (Luke 7:37ff.), in the instance of the tax collector Zacchaeus (Luke 19:1ff.), and in the parable of the prodigal son (Luke 15:11ff.), as well as by many additional words and deeds of Jesus.

Jesus' relationship to sin is expressed most clearly in his sacrificial death. This is to be seen in the explanatory words of the Lord's Supper. Thus Jesus, at the institution of the eucharistic meal, says, as he gives the disciples the chalice with wine: "This is my blood of the covenant, which is poured out for many for the forgiveness of sins" (Matt. 26:28). Jesus describes his death as an eschatological Passover offering. His substitutionary death (for many) puts into effect the final redemption, "the new covenant of God."[17] Jesus understands himself as the eschatological Passover lamb through whose death the realization of salvation is made possible. As promised in Jer. 31:31-34 and explained by Jesus at the institution of the Lord's Supper, a new covenant is being established that through the death of Jesus will be set in force.[18] Analogous to the blood of

---

17. See in this regard Joachim Jeremias, *The Eucharistic Words of Jesus,* trans. Norman Perrin (New York: Charles Scribner's, 1966), 226.
18. So Walter Grundmann, "Hamartia," in *TDNT* 1:304.

the Passover lamb, the blood of Jesus is the blood of the covenant. Thus the words of Deutero-Isaiah concerning the servant of the Lord are fulfilled: "He bore the sin of many, and made intercession for the transgressors" (Isa. 53:12). Jesus is the servant of the Lord who through his suffering and death bears the sins of humanity and overcomes the gulf between God and sinful humanity.

The words and works of Jesus indicate that God seeks communion with sinners and that God's new world is dawning. Through his death and resurrection it is now a reality: sin is defeated and the foundation for God's new world is laid. For this reason, in the Gospel of John, Jesus is described by John the Baptist as the lamb of God "who takes away the sin of the world" (John 1:29). Jesus is the one who builds a bridge over the chasm of sin separating God and the world and who sacrifices himself for the many. Through Jesus, however, a division in the world is also brought about. The judgment announced in the kingdom parables of Matthew 13 becomes a present reality. Those who do not believe that Jesus is the self-disclosure of God will die in their sins (John 8:24). If Jesus, therefore, had not come and confronted humanity with the self-disclosure of God, they would have still been without sin, that is, without the knowledge of their sins (John 15:22). But now they have no excuse for their sins, for they could have recognized who Jesus was and what he required of them. It is precisely for this reason that they see but do not perceive and that they are burdened with sin (John 9:41). Christ has come into the world and has brought with him the decision between life and death. Whoever accepts him receives the word of forgiveness, whoever rejects him remains in his or her own sins. The "helper" or "comforter" that Jesus will send furthers the work of Christ, for he will convict the world "of sin and righteousness and judgment" (John 16:8).

One can also, however, sin out of ignorance in regard to the Son of Man. Such sin carries with it no eternal consequences.[19] It is forgivable. When one rebels, however, in the face of Jesus' message and curses it, even though one recognizes it through the Holy Spirit, then in full awareness of the actual situation one has pronounced judgment upon one's own self. Such sin against the Holy Spirit is unforgivable.[20] Those who in full awareness set themselves

---

19. See Schweizer, *Good News,* 287f., with reference to Matt. 12:31f.

20. So Grundmann, "Hamartia," 307. Otto Procksch, "Hagios," in *TDNT* 1:104, claims that this saying has a "Pentecostal content." Important, however,

against God and his revelation are separated from God, and this separation cannot be removed.

Jesus has given us the possibility to once more draw close to God from our state of sinful alienation from him. This occurrence is reflected in the Gospels. Paul goes one step further and reflects on the consequences of Christ's death and resurrection. First, however, he demonstrates that humans have always fallen short of their own being, for their aspirations are from the very beginning perverted and evil.[21] In the opening chapters of his Letter to the Romans he points out that humans have no excuse for their evil inclinations. They know the will of God, yet do exactly the opposite in their actions (Rom. 1:32). The reason for this is clear, for through Adam sin and death have entered the world as ruling powers (Rom. 5:12). This cannot, however, serve as an excuse for human misbehavior, for humans do willingly the opposite of that which they have recognized to be good. Those who have fallen into sin no longer possess their own will that could lead them to do good. Thus Paul can say: "For I do not do the good I want, but the evil I do not want is what I do. Now if I do what I do not want, it is no longer I that do it, but sin that dwells within me" (Rom. 7:19f.). Humans still have, therefore, the ability to want to do good, but they lack the strength to carry it out.[22] Humans are not the subject of their sinful actions that they do against their own wills, but rather the sin that possesses them. Sin, therefore, can take on directly personal characteristics.

The law plays an important role in the Pauline understanding of sin. Thus Paul speaks next of the law that evil is present in humans even though they want to do good. Law, therefore, is here understood in the sense of a compulsive necessity. Thereupon Paul confesses that he rejoices within over the law of God, whereby he means the law of Moses. Finally, he speaks of another law that exists within his members that is in conflict with the law of his reason and holds him captive to the law of sin from which his members,

---

is the intention of the sin, that it takes place with full knowledge and awareness and thereby excludes itself from the possibility of forgiveness. Whether one can conclude, however, that the sin against the Son of Man is forgivable because God's presence in him is still hidden is questionable because the decision against him has eternal consequences.

21. For the following see Bultmann, *Theology of the New Testament,* 1:227f.

22. So Peter Stuhlmacher, *Der Brief an die Römer, NTD,* 103, on this passage. Stuhlmacher does not, however, touch upon the subject of human responsibility.

that is, his carnal impulses, are ruled. Thus we stand with this testimony before the contrast between the good commandment or law of God and that law that prevails through sin, that is, that which through longings awakened by sin desires that which the law forbids. A means of death and sin, therefore, has developed out of God's good gift of the law. This is to be seen in the example of Adam, who would have never known sin had not the law prescribed that he should not desire, and thus awakened desire within him. Paul will not, however, simply set aside the law, for he knows that the law is good. But the law was and is too weak to fend off sin. Thus it brings sin to our awareness, but does not help us to become free of it. Rather, it is precisely through the holy law (Rom. 7:12) that we are entangled ever more in sin because we are overpowered by desire, violate the law, and bring about our death and our own eschatological judgment.

This fall into sin and death, which Paul emphasizes very strongly, leads necessarily to the question of whether humans still bear responsibility for their actions, on the basis of which they could be held accountable. Two things are here to be noted. Of their own nature, as Paul emphatically states, humans have no chance to escape from sinfulness. Rather, their own efforts lead them only deeper into sin. This is precisely what sinful persons notice when they recognize that they do what they do not want to do. Therefore they do not sin blindly, but rather knowingly and, one could say, also willingly. Regarding the question of individual responsibility, however, a second point, which Paul addresses in the following manner, is even more important: "For the law of the Spirit of life in Christ Jesus has set you free from the law of sin and of death" (Rom. 8:2). Hence humans have a way out and can live freely and responsibly. This way is only open, however, through the will of Christ and not through any human will. The one who rejects this possibility that Christ opens has willingly rejected the freedom from the compulsion of sinning and is fully responsible for his or her own actions.

Paul, therefore, says nothing about the genetic or psychological constitution of humanity. He views humanity, rather, from one of two possible viewpoints, either from the perspective of not having the possibility that Christ has made available or from the perspective of this new possibility. What Paul says about sin, therefore, is "oriented to the revelation of God in Christ. Hence it is not an empirical doctrine of sin based on pessimism. It is the judgment of

God on man without God as it is ascertained from the revelation of Christ and revealed in full seriousness in the cross of Christ."[23] In contrast to Jesus, Paul lived already in a Christian age. From this vantage point he could look back upon what had been made possible through Christ. Paul himself had sought to use the law as a means of salvation and had, for this reason, persecuted the early Christian community. Sin, therefore, not only is an offense to the divine majesty but also constitutes an active enmity against God and a striving against God's will.

In agreement with Judaism, Paul answered the question of the origin of sin by affirming that sin came into the world through Adam. This first human set himself against God, and thus sin was born. With sin, death also came into the world, for it is, so to speak, the consequence of sin, because in alienation from God there is no life. Through the reign of death the universality of sin is to be seen, for all people are marked by death. Death, however, is not a fatalistic power, as it was thought to be in Hellenism and Greek culture, but rather the human individual's own power that pursues sin and through which death gains its mastery. Sin is thus the author of everything evil.

For Paul sin is not only a single deed but a universal context within which all persons find themselves. Human individuals are from the very beginning of their lives placed within a condition of collective sinfulness so that they no longer have the freedom to choose whether to do good or evil. An inseparable connection therefore exists between Adam's action and our own condition. It must, however, be emphasized that Paul did not develop a doctrine of original sin in which sin is passed from one person to the next. Rather, he has seen the entirety of humanity in its alienation from God, which made it impossible for humanity, of its own accord, to return to God. That there is an escape from this context of sin is made apparent to Paul in the Christ event, for Christ has given us the triumph so that death is swallowed up in victory (1 Cor. 15:54ff.).

The death and resurrection of Jesus, as the overcoming of our own entanglement in sin, are bound closely by Paul with baptism. "For if we have been united with him in a death like his, we will certainly be united with him in a resurrection like his. We know that our old self was crucified with him so that the body

---

23. So Grundmann, "Hamartia," 308.

of sin might be destroyed, and we might no longer be enslaved to sin" (Rom. 6:5f.). Through baptism we receive by transferal what Christ has done for us through his death and resurrection, namely, substitutionary atonement for our sins and the overcoming of the barrier of death. In baptism our old humanity dies, and we are born again as new persons. Paul qualifies this, however, by pointing out that as Christians we continue to live upon this earth and thus are not yet released from our sinful context, even if we must no longer sin unavoidably. Paul can therefore admonish Christians to live a Christ-conforming life. Sin shall no longer reign over Christians, for we are no longer under the law but are under grace (Rom. 6:14).

While humans under the law are in the grip of the demonic power of sin that rules them and "rewards" their actions with death, sin has been overcome through the Christ event. The one who knew no sin was made sin for us so that in him we might experience the righteousness of God (2 Cor. 5:21). Through Christ and his overcoming of sin we have become new creatures. The cross is the symbol of victory over sin and the demonic reign of death. The preaching of the cross is thus the power and wisdom of God through which human pursuits of salvation are declared insufficient and irrelevant. Through baptism we are dead to sin and liberated to new life. This great change must continually be brought to the awareness of humans so that they can fend off the lordship claims of sin and not submit once again to a new servitude. Christians stand, therefore, in a suspenseful dilemma: on the one hand, they are liberated from sin, but, on the other hand, they are so menaced by sin and its power that they must continually be called to consecration. Only through the return of Christ will sin and its final effect, death, be fully destroyed and the reign of life that began in Christ be carried out universally and visibly. Thus the Christian, active and witnessing, awaits the future glory that shall be made manifest (Rom. 8:18).

When we summarize how evil is depicted according to the perspective of the New Testament, we notice, in analogy to the Old Testament, that humanity in its being-in-the-world is characterized by its entanglement in evil, a destiny to which humanity willingly acquiesces. The hope shines through, however, as in the Old Testament, that this state of affairs that is characterized by the reign of evil and sin will be settled by the universal reign of God. Moreover, an improvement is recognized, for in the Christ event the foundation for a new world order has already been laid that becomes an experience of present reality for the individual through baptism and participation in the Lord's Supper. Humans, therefore, no longer simply fall into evil. They no longer stand under the disastrous compulsion of alienation from God and rebellion against God. On the contrary, they can already participate in the new communion with God. Humanity has been given a new covenant. This cosmic turning point is made possible through the Christ event, for in Jesus of Nazareth evil has met its vanquisher. Through his self-sacrifice on the cross he has essentially disarmed evil and given us the possibility of new life.

Chapter 5

Monistic or Dualistic Worldview?

We have seen that evil was increasingly excluded from the Judeo-Christian conception of God. The decisive question, however, is whether this gradually arrived at understanding of a force independent of and opposed to God arose out of the Judeo-Christian conception of God or whether external influences came into play. Does not this independence of evil lead to an ultimate dualism that is at odds with the Christian understanding of salvation? When we consider the contextual framework of the question of evil, therefore, we must not overlook the problem of dualism within the Christian faith. In our contextual considerations we will look first of all at the Iranian religion of Zarathustra, because "anyone who has even a superficial knowledge of the Iranian religion cannot but be struck by the parallels that may be drawn between it on the one hand and Judaism and Christianity on the other. The ideas of God, angels and archangels, of Devil, demons and archfiends, as found in both, present so great a similarity that comparisons between the angelology and demonology of the two types of religion become inevitable."[1]

The Dramatic Dualism of Zoroaster

According to our knowledge, the Iranian religion goes back to the priest and prophet Zarathustra (Zoroaster according to the Greek transcription), who probably lived in north-central Asia between 1400 and 1000 B.C., that is, at the transition between the Stone and the Bronze Ages.[2] It is, however, also possible that he lived

---

1. A. V. Williams Jackson, *Zoroastrian Studies: The Iranian Religion and Various Monographs* (1928) (New York: AMS, 1965), 205.

2. For this dating see Hans-Peter Hasenfratz, "Iran und der Dualismus," *Numen* 30 (1983): 35; and Wolfgang Röllig, "Zoroastres," in *Der kleine Pauly*,

from the seventh to the sixth century B.C., as local tradition maintains. Much about him is unknown, yet we are aware of his call experience and his fanatical opposition to his fellow priests. At the center of Zoroaster's teaching stands Ahura Mazda, with Ahura meaning "lord" and Mazda "wisdom," thus, "the wise lord." This highest being is uncreated and incomparable. Apart from him and without him nothing exists.[3] He is the greatest, and no one is like him. He is without any human imperfection and has no anthropomorphic characteristics. Nothing is hidden from him. He dwells in a heavenly realm and distributes good and evil to humanity. As finite beings humans can only describe him using finite analogies. Ahura Mazda is the creator of the heavens and the earth. He created water and trees, formed the human body, and gave it life and conscience. Zarathustra sought communion with Ahura Mazda and found it as he turned to him for refuge in the midst of his persecution and troubles. Although earthly friends and relatives abandoned him, the prophet was not alone, for his heavenly father was with him and heard his prayers.

The highest title of Ahura Mazda, which was itself personified almost to the status of an independent being, is Spenta Mainyu, the holy spirit. Sometimes a distinction was made between Ahura Mazda and Spenta Mainyu as if one was dealing with two distinct beings, but the holy spirit was usually understood as the supreme being. Thus Ahura Mazda was beseeched to provide strength and goodness as well as power and happiness through his holy spirit. Through the holy spirit Ahura Mazda promised the righteous everything good and brought suffering to those who were evil. In Zoroaster's doctrine of the two original spirits, Ahura Mazda is replaced by the appellative Spenta Mainyu, who is seen by Zoroaster as being in direct opposition to Angra Mainyu, the evil spirit. These two spirits can be compared to twins and represent the good and the evil aspects of existence. The evil spirit strives against the good spirit in every regard, for the holy spirit lives in heaven and chooses the righteous way while the evil spirit represents that which is unrighteous.

---

ed. Konrat Ziegler and Walther Sontheimer (Munich: dtv, 1975), 5:1561f., which suggests a different dating.

3. For the following see Maneckji Nusservanji Dhalla, *Zoroastrian Theology: From the Earliest Times to the Present Day* (1914) (New York: AMS, 1972), 19–25.

For Zarathustra evil is an independent entity.[4] It is neither a deficiency of the good nor an illusion, but rather a reality that is continually active within human beings and in the entire world. Angra Mainyu, the evil spirit, is not dependent upon Ahura Mazda for his existence, but is rather independent. His coexistence with Spenta Mainyu, however, does not lead to his being equally eternal with God.

The devas, or demons, have bound themselves to the evil spirit and have chosen him as their leader. In this hierarchical structure an analogy is to be seen with the higher heavenly beings who serve Ahura Mazda. The evil spirit seeks to bring human beings under his spell and to lead them down the path of evil. Humans, therefore, should seek to avoid him. The demons help to lead humans astray through evil thoughts, words, and deeds. Evil persons are, therefore, loved by demons, for they have renounced the good spirit and remain on the path of evil. In the *Gathas,* the heavenly literature of Zoroaster, there is no symmetrical balance between the two powers of good and evil to be found. There is indeed an archdemon and a kingdom of evil, but on the side of evil there is no such marked differentiation within the spirit kingdom as is to be found on the side of the good.

Of significance is that two different camps exist in the world: the one on the side of Ahura Mazda, which follows the law of righteousness, and the other on the side of Drug, that is, wickedness, which follows the law of deceit and evil. Thus the righteous make up the world of righteousness while the unrighteous represent the world of evil and deception. The two opposing, originally divine forces establish a boundary between their respective realms of influence. The one who holds to the truth chooses life, while the one who holds to deceit and dishonesty is given not-life. In this way not only the present but also the final destiny is determined, for Angra Mainyu and his followers are finally defeated in battle against Ahura Mazda and his followers and succumb to the state of not-living, that is, to the death and irrevocable annihilation that they have chosen. Those, however, who through upright actions have remained on the side of Ahura Mazda receive everlasting life. Evil, therefore, will ultimately be annihilated.

We are here confronted with an ethical dualism, or more accurately, an antagonism; but not in the sense that the physical-

---

4. For this and the following see Dhalla, *Zoroastrian Theology,* 46–53.

material is evil and the intellectual-spiritual is good. Rather, the respective behavior is qualified as being either good or evil.[5] This is to be seen already in the two original beings who are not good or evil from the very beginning, that is, from their very nature or through their creation, but rather each of whom makes a conscious decision for either good or evil in accordance with its own nature—a decision that each human being must also make.[6] This freedom of choice transformed the antagonism between the two spirits into a genuine conflict that will only be brought to a resolution by God at the end of the world when he destroys the evil, thereby creating a universe which will be eternally good.

What, then, can we learn about the Judeo-Christian understanding of evil from the Zoroastrian religion, or Parsism? First of all, it is clear that the strict monotheism—or better, the monolatry, that is, the worship of only one god—that is found in Parsism resembles that of the Israelite religion. One can conclude from this that "without the decisive impulses provided by Zarathustra's ethical antagonism the development of the belief in the devil in postexilic Judaism, if not unthinkable, would at least be difficult to imagine."[7] The historical prerequisites for a Zoroastrian influence upon Israelite thought are fulfilled because the concept of a God-opposing adversary developed very late, that is, in postexilic Judaism. At the time of the postexilic period Israel had long been within the field of influence of the greater Persian empire and therefore also within that of Parsism. One can, therefore, at the very least, speak of a catalytic influence of Parsism.[8] Especially clear analogies between the Israelite religion and Zoroaster's teaching are to be found in the relationship between good and evil. In the Qumram sect, for instance, concepts of a son of light and a son of darkness appear that signify, respectively, a realm of truth and a realm of lies. Such concepts point toward a direct dependence upon Parsism. Yet the Qumran writings were not taken up into the Old Testament canon. Even the "conceptual dualism" between light and darkness, as we find, for instance, in the Gospel of John

---

5. So also Hasenfratz, "Iran," 40.

6. So Mary Boyce, *Zoroastrians: Their Religious Beliefs and Practices* (London: Routledge and Kegan Paul, 1979), 20.

7. Hasenfratz, "Iran," 41.

8. See Hans Schwarz, *On the Way to the Future: A Christian View of Eschatology in the Light of Current Trends in Religion, Philosophy, and Science,* rev. ed. (Minneapolis: Augsburg, 1979), 32f.

in the New Testament, resembles only vaguely the ethical antithesis that is so clearly expressed in Parsism.

This ethical antithesis found in Parsism was indeed very important for the development of the understanding of the form of evil in Judaic and Christian thought. Yet alongside of this ethical antithesis was still another dualism in Parsism that left its mark upon Judaism and Christianity, namely, the dualism between spirit and matter or body and soul. This variety of dualism arose within the context of Gnosticism.

The World-Opposing Dualism of Gnosticism

Although a pre-Christian Gnosticism is very difficult to establish, various dualistic conceptions prepared the way for a gnostic worldview.[9] Gnosticism, in many respects a movement rivaling early Christianity, had an expressly negative view of this world. The Gnostics perceived themselves as elect pneumatists who possessed a message that could bring deliverance out of this world. One finds in Gnosticism many points of contact with the Old Testament, especially with the first chapter of Genesis, the Jewish wisdom tradition, and Jewish apocalyptic. But there has "yet to be found any evidence for any sort of developed Jewish gnostic _system_ before the beginning of Christianity."[10] Clear evidence of the establishment of Gnosticism, that is, of a developed system of gnosis, appears to be first contained in the final layers of the New Testament. In 1 Tim. 6:20, for instance, we find the admonition to Timothy: "Avoid the profane chatter and contradictions of what is falsely called knowledge [gnosis]!" In early Christianity there were even Christian Gnostics like Cerinthus, Carpocrates, and Satornilos, of whose writings, however, only fragments have survived. Gnosticism experienced its golden age with the Gnostics Basilides and Valentinus about the middle of the second century, and from this period we possess more extensive written sources.

Due to the complexity and variety of gnostic systems it is impossible to speak of a typical gnostic redemption myth. Yet a fundamental dualism is characteristic of gnostic systems. A subdivision of the human person into two or three component parts is

---

9. See Klaus Berger, "Gnosis/Gnostizismus: I Vor- und außerchristlich," in _TRE_ 13:520, who reports here the findings of E. M. Yamauchi.

10. Robert McLachlan Wilson, "Gnosis/Gnostizismus: II Neues Testament, Judentum, Alte Kirche," in _TRE_ 13:539.

even found in Paul when, for instance, he distinguishes between body and soul or between body, spirit, and soul. Yet he unites these various aspects once more when he emphasizes that humans live their lives in this two- or threefold form either according to the flesh or according to the spirit. In Gnosticism, however, humans are strictly subdivided into different parts, in which their physical, bodily existence is viewed as depraved and evil.[11] Gnostics rejected this world and yearned for another. The world that they rejected was not identified with any particular society or civilization or with any category or group of humans, but rather the whole of existence in the world was characterized as evil and inferior. The spirit, soul, or that which is essentially human is held captive within the body and is limited by it. And woe to the godless who set their hopes upon this bodily captivity that not only itself perishes but also corrupts the soul. According to the gnostic Gospel of Thomas, logion 49, Jesus says: "Blessed are the solitary and elect, for you will find the kingdom. For you are from it and to it you will return."[12] While the doctrine of election is also emphasized in Judeo-Christian tradition, one does not speak there of Jews or Christians returning to where they have come from. In the dualistic worldview of Gnosticism, however, it is precisely this idea that is stressed. Humans must indeed live in the world yet are not from this world but rather come from another world and are momentarily entangled in this one. This position is made clear in logion 87 where Jesus says: "Wretched is the body that is dependent upon a body, and wretched is the soul that is dependent upon these two."

Whereas body and soul are distinguished in the Christian understanding, yet constitute a single unit, in Gnosticism soul and body are ultimately separated from one another. The soul belongs to the sphere of light and is at present trapped in the body. Jesus, therefore, says in logion 50: "If they say to you, 'Where did you come from?,' say to them, 'We came from the light, the place where the light came into being on its own accord and established itself.' "

---

11. For the following see Carl-A. Keller, "Das Problem des Bösen in Apokalyptik und Gnostik," in *Gnosis and Gnosticism: Papers Read at the Seventh International Conference on Patristic Studies* (Oxford, September 8–13, 1975), ed. Martin Krause (Leiden: E. J. Brill, 1977), 85.

12. This and the following citations from the Gospel of Thomas are taken from James M. Robinson, ed., *The Nag Hammadi Library in English* (Leiden: E. J. Brill, 1988), 126–38.

For this reason concepts such as "alien," "the alien," or even "the alien God" are very important in Gnosticism.[13] That which is alien is that which comes from somewhere else and does not belong here. To those who belong here this sounds strange, unfamiliar, and incomprehensible, but for the aliens this world appears equally strange and incomprehensible. The result is suffering in this world and a yearning for the world out of which one has come. This situation has been impressively described in the so-called "Hymn of the Pearl" in the Acts of the Apostle Thomas.

The "Hymn of the Pearl" narrates in verse form the story of a small boy who lives in his father's house and lacks nothing by way of riches, splendor, and a good upbringing. Then, however, his beautiful, radiant garments and his scarlet toga are removed from him. He must go down to Egypt in order to find a pearl guarded in the sea by a snorting dragon. He is then sent away from his home by his parents with provisions for the journey. Upon his return he will once again be allowed to wear the radiant garments and the scarlet toga and, along with his brothers, inherit the wealth of his father.[14] We are told many details of his search. Although the poem is simple and moving, all of the details have a deeper meaning. According to gnostic symbolism, for example, the sea symbolizes the material world and the darkness into which the divine has sunk.[15] The snorting dragon is the original chaos, the ruler or evil principle of the world. One is reminded here of the chaos figure of the Babylonian Tiamat, the chaos dragon. Even Egypt is merely a symbol for the material world, an allusion that occurs frequently in Gnosticism. The biblical story of the Egyptian captivity and the subsequent period of wandering in the desert during which the people thought of the fleshpots of Egypt serves as background to this particular symbol of the material world. Also of importance is the instruction to remove the heavenly clothing so that it would not be sullied in the world. Coming out of a higher world, one must descend into this world. The sought-after pearl is in a supernatural sense the "lost pearl" that must once again be

---

13. So Hans Jonas, *The Gnostic Religion: The Message of the Alien God and the Beginnings of Christianity* (Boston: Beacon, 1970), 49.

14. The text of the "Hymn of the Pearl" can be found in Bentley Layton, ed., *The Gnostic Scriptures: A New Translation* (Garden City, N.Y.: Doubleday, 1987), 371–75.

15. For an interpretation of the "Hymn of the Pearl" see Jonas, *The Gnostic Religion*, 116–29.

found and that is hidden in the depths of this world. One might think here of the soul, or simply of the self, that is entangled in this world and that must be abducted back into the higher world.

In Gnosticism one encounters a conception of redemption very different from that found in the Christian faith. In Gnosticism redemption has nothing to do with the forgiveness of sins but rather with the escape from the world, with the knowledge of where one actually belongs, and with the liberation from this world. Essentially, therefore, one can also characterize the Gnostics as mystics.[16] This world has, for them, no real value; it is to be rejected, for it ensnares us and leads to an oblivion of being.

Reviewing the life and thought of Valentinus (ca. A.D. 100–175) we can easily see why Gnosticism posed a serious threat to Christianity. The great Gnostics like Valentinus and Basilides were mystics. They did not live upon the basis of speculation, but rather appeared to have had an inner experience that, if not actual, was at least convincing and authentic.[17] In the Gospel of Truth, which was perhaps written by Valentinus, or at least someone from his school, we see that the alienation of which Gnostics speak was for him a genuine experience. "He lived in fear and confusion in this world, restless and bewildered; he was possessed by evil dreams and the emptiness of absurdity, his life was a nightmare."[18] The existential experience of alienation stands over against the existential discovery of the subconscious self and one's own identity. Those living in this world hear a voice from above; they learn of the original word of being, come to themselves, and return to their source. These moods and experiences were expressed in mystical systems. The Gnostics were not primarily concerned either with a historical event of the past or with a future occurrence, but rather with the authentic experience of alienation, the reception of gnosis, and a life with one's own identity.

Valentinus was born in Egypt and was educated in Greek thought in Alexandria, where he quite possibly met Basilides. He appears to have been familiar with the work of the Jewish phi-

---

16. So Keller, "Das Problem," 90.

17. So Gilles Quispel, "Gnostic Man: The Doctrine of Basilides," in *Gnostic Studies,* vol. 1 (Leiden: Nederlands Instituut voor het Nabije Oosten, 1974), 103.

18. For this and the following see Gilles Quispel, "Das Lied von der Perle," in *Gnostic Studies,* vol. 2 (Leiden: Nederlands Instituut voor het Nabije Oosten, 1975), 123f.

losopher Philo of Alexandria (ca. 30 B.C.–A.D. 45).[19] Sometime between 117 and 138 he was a teacher in Alexandria. Between 136 and 140 he went to Rome where he was active as a leading teacher in the church. There is even a report that he was elected to the office of bishop. Alongside of his public work he met privately with his disciples, probably for the purpose of pursuing a deeper, allegorical interpretation of the Scriptures. He was sharply attacked, which, in light of the many competing theological streams in the city, was not uncommon, and left Rome about 165. His gifted intellect and his mastery of Greek were recognized even by his sharpest critics. The Valentinian movement, which he began, had the character of a philosophical school that flourished to such an extent that many of his followers from the second and third centuries are still known to us by name. Up to the seventh century Valentinians were spoken of, although these were by this time completely separate from the official church.

The Gospel of Truth, so named for its opening words, does not have as its content a gnostic myth, but rather speaks of the crucifixion of Jesus as the core of the Christian faith. By way of content, therefore, it has much in common with the New Testament. The orientation of the message, however, is quite different. Those who are elect and have a knowledge of God are the ones who will be redeemed.[20] Those who do not belong to the elect and who are formed according to forgetfulness will pass away along with that which is forgotten (Gospel of Truth 21). Along with ignorance, the phenomenal realm, that is, the material world, will also pass away (25). The elect should concentrate upon themselves and not upon the others who have already been banished (33). Those who strive after the redemption that comes from above will discover the abundance of fullness (34f.). The light that remains in the darkness is forgiveness, that is, the word of fullness. The earthly condition is marked by ignorance, angst, and terror as well as privation. Perfection is found in the act of returning, that is, in the recognition of the father and the annihilation of error. Inasmuch as Christ has filled or eliminated the deficiency, he has dissolved

---

19. For an account of Valentinus's life see Layton, *Gnostic Scriptures,* 217, 220f., and 267.

20. See Michel R. Desjardins, *Sin in Valentinianism,* Society of Biblical Literature Dissertation Series, vol. 108 (Atlanta: Scholars Press, 1990), esp. 82f. The *Evangelium veritatis* (Gospel of Truth) is translated into English by George W. MacRae in Robinson, *The Nag Hammadi Library in English,* 40–51.

the external appearance and has revealed to the elect the path to their source and to peace. In the Gospel of Truth we encounter ideas similar to those in the "Hymn of the Pearl." At first glance the variety of proposals and speculations is bewildering, yet upon closer reflection they reveal certain fundamental ideas that occur repeatedly in various forms and that belong to the very core of gnostic thought.[21]

The oldest Gnostic known to us is Basilides, who was active in Alexandria from around A.D. 117 to 138.[22] His thought is much more dualistically oriented than that of Valentinus. According to him, the first born, that is, the intellect, also called Christ, is sent into the world to rescue those who believe him from the authority of those beings who created the world. Christ was not crucified, rather Simon from Cyrene suffered mistakenly for him. He was transformed by Jesus so that he was mistaken for him while Jesus stood there in the form of Simon and laughed over those who wanted to crucify him.[23] Then Jesus ascended again to him who had sent him and laughed at the rulers of the 365 heavens. He cannot be detained or restrained upon the earth for he is invisible. Those who possess this knowledge are liberated from the rulers who created this world. Yet redemption is possible only for the soul because the body is by nature corruptible.

We notice in Basilides the conviction that the material cannot hold on to the spiritual, that is, Jesus Christ. Jesus, therefore, cannot die. Body and soul are spoken of in a similarly contrasting manner. Basilides does not seek God, rather God descended in Christ in order to reveal himself to human beings. Revelation comes from above, and Christ reveals the unknown God. Humans, therefore, receive the knowledge (gnosis) of an unknown, transcendent God. Yet the redemption of humans is not a redemption of individuals but rather the redemption of the entire human race.[24] Yet not everyone we call human is indeed human. "Humans" who are without the spirit feel so much at home in the immanent world that they do not yearn for transcendence and are thus not human

---

21. See Kurt Rudolph, *Die Gnosis: Wesen und Geschichte einer spätantiken Religion* (Göttingen: Vandenhoeck and Ruprecht, 1977), 58–74, which gives a good overview of the most important core elements of Gnosticism under the headings "Die Hauptzüge der gnostischen Ideologie und Mythologie" and "Dualismus."

22. So Layton, *Gnostic Scriptures,* 417.

23. Regarding the teaching of Basilides see the fragments recorded in Layton, *Gnostic Scriptures,* 423.

24. For this and the following quotation see Quispel, "Gnostic Man," 119.

at all. Basilides declares categorically: "We are men, all the others are pigs and dogs." Only a spiritual creature is a genuine human being.

Through Jesus the transcendent world was revealed so that humans became aware of their relatedness to God for the first time. This event is decisive for the entire subsequent course of history, for, similar to Jesus, the elect among the human race remember their divine nature and return to God.[25] The spiritual person is freed by Christ from matter and purified so that the spiritual element is set free from the material world and human beings can separate themselves from this world. The spirit is able to find its way back to its true home. This process continues until all have been purified and have returned to the spiritual world. The restoration of the spiritual kingdom is then complete and all persons occupy the places assigned to them by nature. There are no feelings of nostalgia here but rather an absolute peace, for the process of history has reached its conclusion.

Although human beings find themselves in this world, they do not belong to it. This is the essential experience of a Gnostic such as Basilides. He is conscious of the fact that he lives in an alien world and that this world is also alien to him.[26] As Clement of Alexandria stated, quoting Basilides: "The elect are strangers to the world, being supramundane by nature" (*Stromata* 4.26). The experience of alienation and imprisonment reflects, of course, Platonic thought. The world is a prison for souls, and our sensory impressions are mere shadow images of the real world. When Augustine wrote at a later period that his soul remained restless until it found its rest in God, it is quite probably the expression of a similar feeling. Yet Augustine was neither a Gnostic nor a mystic because for him this world was a part of God's creation. Augustine had, however, experienced a period as a Manichaean in which he supported such a dualism.

---

25. For this and the following see Quispel, "Gnostic Man," 120.
26. See Quispel, "Gnostic Man," 126f. When Quispel, however, states that a misinterpreted doctrine of original sin also plays a role here, one must bear in mind that the doctrine of original sin developed at a later date and cannot lead to one's seeking of redemption at present in a sin-free realm.

The Modified Dualism of Manichaeism

Mani, the prophet and founder of Manichaeism, a gnostic religion influenced by Christianity, Judaism, Zoroastrianism, and Buddhism, was born in 216 southeast of Ctesiphon, a city on the east bank of the Tigris River in what is today Iraq.[27] Although he viewed himself as God's messenger to Babylon and as a physician who came out of the land of Babel, he was not Babylonian but was of Iranian descent. In light of the various gnostic sects, esoteric communities, and philosophical and religious schools as well as a highly developed, urbane civilization found in third-century Mesopotamia, that is, the land of the two rivers Tigris and Euphrates, Mani's syncretistic approach is understandable. Already in his youth Mani joined a baptizing sect, and at a young age received his first revelation. At age twenty-four he received the command of an angel to appear in public and proclaim the true teaching. He understood himself as the apostle of light in whom the Paraclete was incarnate. He was the seal of the prophets who wanted to proclaim to all the world in a language accessible to all the message of the great prophets of the past such as Buddha, Zoroaster, and Jesus, who witnessed only to parts of the world and in languages not universally understood. To this end he also reformed the writing system of the Iranian language.

Mani's first apostolic mission was directed toward India where his greatest success was with King Shapur I, the Persian king who granted him many privileges and who he hoped would make his teaching the official state religion. But under the successors of King Shapur I he fell out of grace as a result of the efforts of Zoroastrian priests and died at approximately sixty years of age in prison. Although Mani has been labeled a hostile archheretic by Zoroastrians, Christians, and Muslims alike, Manichaeism experienced a broad dissemination from China in the East to Egypt, North Africa, southern France, and Spain in the West. In Taoist and Buddhist garb Manichaeism survived in China into the fourteenth century. Neo-Manichaean movements of the Middle Ages, however, such as the Bogomiles, who arose in Bulgaria in the tenth century, or the Cathari of the eleventh century in Italy, Germany, and France (where they were called Albigenses), did not descend directly from Manichaeism. These, in all probability, were simply

---

27. For the following see Gherardo Gnoli, "Mani," in *ER* 9:158ff. Reports that Mani was skinned alive are polemic exaggerations.

a revival of the great dualistic religious systems of antiquity.[28] That Manichaeism was an appealing religion can be seen in the example of the young Augustine who participated for nine years as a "hearer" within the life of the Manichaean community and studied this religion carefully, as one learns from his later, and of course negative, comments about Manichaeism.[29]

Ephraem of Antioch also pointed in his *Refutations* to an interesting connection between Mani and Marcion, who was born toward the end of the first century in Sinope, a city on the south coast of the Black Sea, and amassed great wealth as a ship owner.[30] Marcion traveled to Rome where he came under the influence of Cerdo, a Christian teacher from Asia. After he ran into difficulties with the leaders of the church in Rome, he founded his own church in 144, which spread quickly throughout the Roman empire. Although his critics labeled him a Gnostic, several important points distinguished him from Gnosticism. He did not understand redemption as gnosis, that is, as knowledge, nor did he posit the existence of any sparks of light within humans that could lead them back to God. Rather, humans were the work of the creator God or demiurge. Over against this Old Testament creator God, Marcion sees a God of love, the father of Jesus Christ. The two divinities highlight the idea that two principles are at work in the world. The principle of justice or the law is deeply rooted in the universe and can be called the creator of the world.[31] A second principle, which one could call grace or redeeming love, intervenes in the course of the world and provides a corrective to justice. If humans come under the dominion of this second principle they are freed from bondage to the first. Marcion concerned himself, therefore, like the Gnostics, with a life problem, namely, that that which on earth appears to be an equalizing justice is fundamentally unbearable and must be replaced and overcome by the principle

28. See Gherardo Gnoli, "Manichaeism: An Overview," in *ER* 9:168; and John G. Davies, "Manichaeism and Christianity," in *ER* 9:171.

29. Jes P. Asmussen, *Manichaean Literature: Representative Texts Chiefly from Middle Persian and Parthian Writings* (Delmar, N.Y.: Scholars' Facsimiles and Reprints, 1975), 2. See also the text in *Texte zum Manichäismus,* ed. Alfred Adam (Berlin: Walter de Gruyter, 1969), 65–70, from Aurelius Augustinus, *De Haeresibus* (§46).

30. Regarding the comments of Ephraem, see Francis C. Burkitt, *The Religion of the Manichees* (Cambridge: Cambridge Univ. Press, 1925), 80.

31. For this and the following see Edwin C. Blackman, *Marcion and His Influence* (London: SPCK, 1948), 71.

of the good or grace. Like Mani after him, Marcion rejected the Old Testament as inspired scripture because the God of the Old Testament, the God of the Jews, was a wrathful God who continually subjected humans to bondage. Like Mani as well, however, he did not reject the Old Testament completely, for Adam and Eve remained important figures for him.

In the center of Mani's system exist two primal elements: God and matter. Matter is viewed as something evil. Matter is not assigned any divine attributes, but is rather dismissed as demonic and devilish. Once more we encounter here a modified dualism because good and evil are not viewed as siblings. A Manichaean confession of faith clearly warns: "Should we have said that Ohrmazd and Ahriman were younger and older brothers..., then I repent now and beg for forgiveness of sins."[32] With the figures of Ohrmazd and Ahriman we certainly encounter once again the twin gods of Parsism. Yet Ohrmazd is presented unmistakably as the chief and only god, as the supreme being who is equated with light. Light is, so to speak, his divine substance. Ohrmazd is the "father" of the blessed light. In sharp contrast to Ohrmazd exists the realm of darkness, the material world. Ohrmazd brought forth the mother of life, yet Mani avoids use of the word "create" here and speaks instead of "calling forth" so as to avoid inadvertently applying to him the attributes of the creator God.[33] The mother of life then called into existence the first or primal human, who was also named Ohrmazd. He armed himself and went to battle against the prince of darkness and his hosts but was defeated and robbed of his armor.

This primal human descended voluntarily into the world of darkness and matter and thus permitted himself to be robbed of his elements of light. His intention was that the darkness would swallow the elements of light and would thereby incorporate a substance essentially foreign to its own—a condition that it could not endure. In order to accomplish this he sacrificed his soul to the demons of darkness. This brought serious consequences upon him, for he laid now in a dark dungeon without light and completely helpless. As he awoke from the initial paralysis he prayed to God, who called forth the living spirit. The living spirit, accompanied

---

32. Quoted in Geo Widengren, *Mani and Manichaeism* (London: Weidenfeld and Nicolson, 1965), 45. Quote taken from a translation by Ch. Kessler.

33. For this and the following see Widengren, *Mani and Manichaeism*, 44–63; and A. V. Williams Jackson, *Researches in Manichaeism with Special Reference to the Turfan Fragments* (New York: Columbia Univ. Press, 1932), 7–16.

by the mother of life, went to the border of darkness and extended its right hand to the primal human. Thus he was able to liberate him from the depth of the darkness of the world. They returned to paradise as the victorious light coming out of the darkness. The elements of light, however, remained in the clutches of the darkness. The living spirit, who in later tradition was also called the god Mithra, came here to the rescue. He defeated the demons of darkness, who are also called archons, and formed the sun and the moon out of the light particles that remained unsoiled. Out of those light particles that were partially soiled he formed the stars.

The first humans then came into being through two demons, Adam and Eve. At the instigation of matter Adam was born blind, deaf, and without any knowledge of the shimmer of light that was within him. He was finally rescued by the redeemer, the son of God, that is, Ohrmazd or Jesus, who is called the brilliant light. The goal of the primal human being, nonetheless, is to redeem his own soul in Adam. He awoke Adam from the sleep of death, opened his eyes, and liberated him from the demons by showing him the soul of light that is imprisoned and languishes within all matter. He explained to him his twofold origin out of matter, which originates from the power of evil, and out of the soul or the spirit, which comes from the heavenly world of light. He met him, therefore, with redeeming knowledge, or gnosis, and the understanding of that which was, is, and will be.

Redemption concerns the soul alone. As one writing explains: "The soul is in substance different from the body and is in the body so mixed and fashioned and bound with the spirit of the body, that is wrath and concupiscence and lust, . . . [that] the soul (is bound) in the coarseness and corporeality of the body, that is bone and flesh and skin and blood and breath and . . . dirt, by the bond of the spirit (of the body)."[34] But this process of liberation of the sparks of light is very slow and never comes to an end. The world will come to an end before this process is completed when, through a series of apocalyptic events, the so-called great war begins. Following a final judgment, good and evil will be separated, and the physical universe, along with the damned and the demons, will be annihilated.

Alongside of many speculative elements a low regard for the material, which is portrayed as the epitome of evil, as well as

---

34. Cited in Asmussen, *Manichaean Literature,* 8.

a correspondingly high regard for the spiritual are unmistakable in Manichaean doctrine. Underlying this view is the experience, which since Plato and Aristotle has repeatedly come to expression in philosophy, that only that which is immaterial endures while everything else passes away, and that this transitoriness creates all the negative problems that confront us in this life. The church rejected such speculations because it was convinced of the essential unity of the world. The basis for this is to be found in the recognition that there were not two gods, one who was responsible for the creation of the world and another who redeemed the world, but rather that God as creator, redeemer, and sustainer of the world is one and the same God. Also, within the Christian faith evil was not simply understood as something negative that one could escape, or as an evil power that stood over against humanity. Evil was rather understood much more as something active within humans at the deepest level that drove them into a state of estrangement from God. This antignostic and anti-Manichaean corrective is especially to be seen in Augustine's understanding of evil.

The Existence of Evil
in Created Beings • Augustine

Augustine (354–430), later bishop of the North African city Hippo Regius, joined the Manichaeans at age nineteen although he was already a catechumen, that is, a candidate for baptism, in the Christian church.[35] The young Augustine found the Manichaeans' rational understanding of evil especially attractive. The dualistic proposal to understand the world as a battlefield between the principles of good and evil and to ascribe the origin of the immoral to the latter appeared to free him of personal responsibility for evil. Yet after about ten years he no longer found the Manichaean doctrine satisfying, and he came under the influence of Bishop Ambrose of Milan, whose understanding of the Old Testament greatly impressed him. He also engrossed himself in the study of Neoplatonic philosophy, especially the works of Plotinus. In 385 he had broken free of Manichaeism and the next year decided to once again become a catechumen in the Catholic Church. In this year, late in 386, he wrote a dialogue in two books with the title *De*

---

35. For the following see the introduction in *St. Augustine: The Problem of Free Choice* (in ACW 22:3f.).

ordine (On Order), which, on the basis of its content, one might better translate: "Divine Providence and the Problem of Evil."[36]

In this writing Augustine tackles the problem of evil. He is confronted immediately with the dilemma that, if evil is real, then God either is not almighty or himself wills evil. In the face of these alternatives he admits that he would rather portray God as limited in his sphere of activity than label him as the author of evil and thereby also as cruel. Augustine next distinguishes natural evil, as it is manifest, for example, in natural catastrophes, from moral evil, which is seen in the human will.[37] Evil within nature can, according to Augustine, either have a goal or be completely senseless. Because many natural occurrences surpass the limits of human ingenuity, one cannot simply attribute them to chance. They must fulfill some purpose that transcends humanity. Yet Augustine nevertheless admits that many natural occurrences appear to be completely senseless. Augustine suggests, however, that we probably have too anthropocentric a starting point to easily perceive a divine purpose within such events. Rather than occupy ourselves with detailed questions that could be painful for us we should seek to view our own misfortune in light of a universal plan.

The perfection of the universe postulated by Augustine is not easily reconciled with his unmerciful openness to the reality of evil. Another problem is to be found in his assumption that God is always just. In light of the fact that there is always injustice in the world, it is a short step to the conclusion that evil exists eternally alongside of God. Neoplatonism appears to offer a solution to this dilemma that Augustine follows in locating the origin of evil in nonbeing. God did not, therefore, cause evil, because no positive reality exists outside of divine providence. Yet the examples given by Augustine are not convincing. He mentions, for instance, the example of cock-fighting and believes that beauty is to be found even in this brutal sport because it occurs in accordance with the laws of nature. In another place he brings forward the example of the gruesome office of executioner, which is indeed something negative, yet contributes to the order of a well-functioning state. He

---

36. For the dating of this work see the edition in H.-P. Migne, *Patrologiae Cursus Completus, Series Latinae,* 32:977–1022.

37. For a summary of this dialogue see David E. Roberts, "The Earliest Writings," in *A Companion to the Study of St. Augustine,* ed. Roy W. Battenhouse (New York: Oxford Univ. Press, 1969), 100–103.

similarly describes prostitution as evil, yet suggests that its elimination could lead to even greater evils. Everything evil, according to Augustine, contributes to perfection because its nonoccurrence would destroy perfection. At this point one is tempted to ask why evil should be resisted at all when it contributes to good.[38]

Although not completely satisfying, this dialogue is Augustine's first attempt to free himself from a Manichaean type of dualism. Evil is allowed no place of its own, but must rather always contribute to the good. Augustine does not remain, however, with the enigmatic character of evil, probably out of fear that this could once again be interpreted dualistically.

In another dialogue, begun two years later and completed in Africa, Augustine made a further decisive step. As he wrote in his *Retractations* at the end of his life, the work was written in order to refute the Manichaean objection against Christian belief that evil is ultimately attributed to God.[39] This work, *De libero arbitrio* (On Free Will), was highly rated by Augustine as well as by his contemporaries. He commented in a letter to Jerome: "A few years ago I wrote some books on free will—which have gone out into many hands and are possessed by many more.... [I opposed] with all my might those who were trying to prove that nature was endowed with its own principle of evil in conflict with God. These were the Manichaeans."[40] This relatively short writing, in the form of a dialogue between Augustine and Evodius, a youth from his hometown of Tagaste, begins with the fundamental question: "Is not God the cause of evil?"[41]

Augustine distinguishes between committing evil and suffering from evil. Because God is good he can commit no evil. Yet because God punishes evil and this punishment is itself experienced as something evil, God is the cause of suffering from evil in the sense of a divine punishment. The evil that we do is done by us freely, otherwise it could not be justly punished. Augustine goes here a step further and maintains that the evil deeds of humans are not learned because learning and teaching are good. To this Evodius asks from whence evil comes if it is not learned (1.2.4). Augustine replies that this question had driven him into heresy be-

---

38. See Roberts, "Earliest Writings," 106, who asks this same question.

39. Augustine, *Retractations* 1.8.2 (in FC 60:32).

40. Augustine, *Letters* 166.7 (in FC 30:12f.).

41. For this and the following see *St. Augustine: The Problem of Free Choice* 1.1.1 (in ACW 22:35).

cause he wanted to find an answer to it. Finally, he came to the following explanation: "We believe that everything which exists is created by one God, and yet that God is not the cause of sin. The difficulty is: if sin goes back to souls created by God, and souls go back to God, how can we avoid before long tracing sin back to God?" (1.2.4). In order to avoid this conclusion me must, according to Augustine, assume that God is almighty and completely immutable. He is the creator of all good things, although he transcends these, and he is the perfectly just ruler over everything that he has created. He is self-sufficient and unassisted by any other being in the act of creation.

After clarifying his understanding of God, Augustine sought to establish his conception of evil. When something evil takes place, its dominant motive is to be located in the *libido* or the *cupiditas,* that is, in human passion (1.4.9). Evil deeds such as murder, blasphemy, and adultery arise out of human passion. Even when one commits evil deeds out of fear, the motive is still to be found in covetous desires, namely, in the desire for a life without fear. Of course, human law can permit something that we perceive as evil so that passion is excluded from an evil deed. But such a law would be contrary to the eternal law that consists of principles that, in contrast to human laws, never change. That which is correct in temporal laws is derived from the eternal law that alone should be our point of orientation. Augustine speaks next of the distinction between humans and animals and explains that humans possess a spirit that determines and directs all other elements within them so that they are directed according to the divine order (1.8.18). Human wisdom, then, consists in giving such place to the human spirit that passion cannot reign over humans, for apart from God there is nothing better than a sensible and wise spirit. The spirit is therefore rightly punished when it enslaves passion and sins.

At the beginning of the second book Evodius asks why God has given humans a free will, to which Augustine replies that without a free will humans could not live as humans. Evodius then asks why this decision of God was correct if we are able to misuse our free will. Augustine attempts to explain that the free will is good. According to Augustine, we possess three types of good things: virtues, which we cannot misuse, bodily things, which he does not regard as being of particular importance, and the power of the soul as a good of secondary status. This latter can be either rightly or wrongly used. It is used correctly when we place our trust in God, for he is unchanging good, truth, and wisdom, and humans can obtain a happy life through him. Evil consists of turning away from the unchanging good. Because we do this freely, the consequent punishment is just.

In the third book Augustine takes up the subject of God's foreknowledge and declares that no predestination is implied here. Yet what Augustine says concerning natural evil is hardly convincing. He dismisses, for example, the problem of suffering among children by saying that there is no need to suffer any longer once suffering (along with this life) has come to an end. Additionally, one does not know what compensation God has in store for such children who suffer. Also, the question concerning the suffering of animals only shows that we understand nothing of the nature of the excellence of the supreme good, for animals are by nature mortal. We see also by the suffering of animals that the souls of all creatures "strive for unity in governing and animating their bodies." They resist division and corruption and through their struggle against suffering point to the fact that they were created for unity (3.23.69). Finally, Augustine reflects on the possibilities possessed by the first human pair and claims that they had the means by which, if they had used them well, they could have risen to what they did not possess, that is, wisdom (3.24.72). There is a distinction between whether humans are wise or merely blessed with reason. Humans, however, have forsaken the heights of wisdom. For Augustine, Satan also comes into the picture here. He writes: "And that is 'pride, the beginning of all sin; and the beginning of the pride of man is to fall off from God' (Sir. 10:13). The devil added malevolent envy to his pride when he persuaded man to share his pride, through which he knew he was damned. So it was that man suffered a punishment designed to correct him rather than to destroy him" (3.25.76).

Finally, Augustine comes to the subject of *superbia,* that is, pride, the beginning of all sin. This writing, therefore, does not pursue the question of free will, although this topic is repeatedly touched upon, but rather aims to demonstrate, as the opening sentence announced, that God is not the cause of evil. The problem of free will, however, cannot thus be passed over, for it is closely bound with the problem of evil. When at the end of this writing Augustine addresses once again the question of why there is not only good but also evil he cannot, in contrast to his earlier work

De ordine, simply answer that evil belongs to the good. Rather, he must maintain that evil stems from *libido, cupiditas,* and *superbia,* whereby God, however, cannot be made in any way either directly or indirectly responsible for evil because he is immutable and essentially good. Yet Augustine has not yet understood evil dynamically enough as an actual opponent of God. Owing to his own Manichaean past he did not have the courage to do this because he feared that he might lapse into "heresy." He viewed evil as something that contradicted *ratio* and was essentially connected with the will. It is the power that continually opposes, that is separated from God, and that sinks into corruption and base actions.

Only one side of reality is thus addressed, namely, that there is just one primal principle: God. This God is just and good. Everything that is evil has no causal relationship with God but exists on the basis of its own self and the opposition to God. As Augustine correctly admitted in his *Retractations,* there is yet another side: "For it is one thing to inquire into the source of evil and another to inquire how one can return to his original good or reach one that is greater. Hence the new Pelagian heretics who treat free choice of the will in such a way as not to leave a place for the grace of God, for they assert that it is given according to our merits, should not boast as though I have pleaded their cause."[42] Because Augustine said very little here about the necessity of grace for the attainment of salvation, the Pelagians sought, albeit unjustly, to cite him as a supporter of their own position. In this publication Augustine dealt almost exclusively with the question of the origin of evil. This in turn raises the question of how evil can be overcome or avoided.

---

42. Augustine, *Retractations* 1.8.2f. (in FC 60:33).

Chapter 6

Freedom and
Human Responsibility

We have seen that Augustine argued for the unity of God over against the dualistic worldview of Manichaeism. According to Augustine there are not two separate principles, one good and one evil, nor is there a graduated order of reality in which, so to speak, good is stronger than evil so that it will ultimately prevail. Rather, there is only one God and one creation. When evil exists, and Augustine never entertained the slightest doubt as to its reality, then it exists only to the extent that a part of God's good creation has risen up against its creator and entered into conflict with him. Many questions, however, remain unanswered, such as issues concerning the origin and function of that within nature that is objectively bad. Likewise, despite Augustine's assertion that humans themselves are responsible for their sinfulness, this was not thought through so thoroughly as to overcome all contradictions in relation to human freedom and responsibility. Is is no wonder, therefore, that there has been much conflict over the question of the relationship between freedom and accountability in the early church, at the start of the Reformation, and at many other periods in the history of the church.

At the beginning of this conflict Augustine himself brandished the banner of attack. His opponent, Pelagius, even imagined himself a confederate of Augustine until he was taught differently by Augustine and transformed by him into one of the most denounced heretics in the history of the Christian faith.[1] Even Karl Barth threw Pelagianism, fatalism, and heathenism together and wrote

---

1. So Robert F. Evans, *Pelagius: Inquiries and Reappraisals* (London: Adam and Charles Black, 1968), 66.

in his *Church Dogmatics:* "Pelagianism and fatalism are alike heathen atavisms in a Christian doctrine of God. They both ascribe to the creature an autonomy in relation to God's will which it cannot possess."[2] Yet Pelagius laid much stock in being an orthodox theologian of the entire church.[3] In his published writings he clearly separated himself from the Arians, Marcionites, and, of course, the Manichaeans. In a positive sense he wanted to underline the moral responsibility of humans over against God and thus decisively distinguish the Christian position from Manichaean anthropology. Without overlooking divine grace he appealed to human responsibility.

The Appeal to Human Responsibility • Pelagius

We know very little about Pelagius himself. He came from Britain, was ascetically influenced, and between 384 and 409 lived primarily in Rome, where he enjoyed a good reputation from all sides. Afterwards he traveled with Caelestius, a young man of aristocratic birth, first to Sicily, then to North Africa, and later to Asia Minor.[4] While Pelagius was reserved, Caelestius took up his cause with zeal so that, indeed, without him the matter of free will and human responsibility would not have become a controversy so quickly, if at all. Caelestius had a sharp, analytical mind and felt within his element in debate. The question was taken up for the first time at a synod in Carthage in 411. Caelestius was accused there of holding to the following seven positions, which were considered false: "1. That Adam was created mortal and would have died even if he had not sinned. 2. That the sin of Adam injured himself alone and not the human race. 3. That infants at the moment of birth are in the same condition as Adam was before the fall. 4. That infants, even though they are not baptized, have eternal life. 5. That the race of man as a whole does not die by the death or fall of Adam, nor does the race of man as a whole

2. Karl Barth, *Church Dogmatics,* 2/1: *The Doctrine of God* (Edinburgh: T. and T. Clark, 1957), 562f.

3. For this and the following see Evans, *Pelagius,* 92.

4. See John Ferguson, *Pelagius: A Historical and Theological Study* (Cambridge: W. Heffer and Sons, 1956), 39–49. It is uncertain, however, whether Pelagius was a monk, as claimed by Reinhold Seeberg, *Lehrbuch der Dogmengeschichte,* vol. 2 (Darmstadt: Wissenschaftliche Buchgesellschaft, 1965), 488. Caelestius, on the other hand, desired to enter the priesthood and probably later achieved this goal.

rise again by the resurrection of Christ. 6. That the Law has the same effect as the Gospel in introducing men into the kingdom of Heaven. 7. That even before the coming of Christ there were men without sin."[5] Although Caelestius skillfully defended himself through his eloquence at the proceeding, he was nevertheless excommunicated. Caelestius, as a result, turned to Asia Minor while Pelagius went to Jerusalem, where he made the acquaintance of Jerome.

For Pelagius himself the suspicion of heresy was a very serious matter. He wrote in his commentary on Col. 4:6: "Other than the heathen, other than the Jews, other than heretics and anyone else who contradicts the truth: hence Peter says: 'always give a satisfactory answer.'"[6] He sought in his exegesis of the Pauline epistles to avoid every suspicion of heresy. At the center of his explanations one finds moral admonitions. In his exposition of Eph. 4:27, for example, we read: "Sin is the gateway for the devil, but the Holy Spirit the gateway for righteousness" (370). The primary causes of vices are unrighteousness and an evil will as well as impurity and greed (see 317 [Rom. 1:29] and 373 [Eph. 5:3]). It is important that we reject evil desires and have a good conscience, by which Pelagius equates the conscience with the natural law that exists within our spirit (see 60 [Rom. 7:23]). When he comes to the subject of virtues, it is clear for him that the greatest of all virtues is *caritas,* that is, love (337 [Gal. 5:22]). *Caritas* is the law of Christ, as Jesus himself said: I give to you a new law (339 [Gal. 6:2]). *Pax, caritas,* and *fides,* that is to say, peace, love, and faith, make for a perfect Christian, for love without faith is unfruitful just as faith without love and peace bears no fruit. Yet "love is greater than peace" (386 [Eph. 6:23]). From the high estimation of love it follows that faith does not become active through fear but rather through love, as Pelagius emphasizes in reference to the

5. Ferguson, *Pelagius,* 51. See also Carl Joseph Hefele, *A History of the Councils of the Church from the Original Documents,* vol. 2, trans. H. N. Osenham (Edinburgh, 1896), 447. Hefele leaves out the fourth point, as does Marius Mercator. According to Augustine, this point comes not from Caelestius but from Sicilian Pelagians. See Augustine, *On Original Sin* 12.11 (in *NPNF* 5:241); see also 3.3 (237f.) for Augustine's comments on the synod of 411.

6. According to the Latin edition of Alexander Souter, *Pelagius's Exposition of Thirteen Epistles of St. Paul,* vol. 2: *Text and Apparatus Criticus* (Cambridge: Cambridge Univ. Press, 1926), 471; text references in the following pages are to this edition, and the biblical passage discussed by Pelagius is given in brackets.

words from the Gospel of John: "Whoever believes on God will keep his commandments" (333 [Gal. 5:6]).

The concept of a works-righteousness finds no place in the exegesis of Pelagius. Indeed, he frequently stresses in agreement with Paul that one is justified alone through faith and not through the works of the law (12 [Rom. 1:17]). The unjust who repent are justified by God through faith alone and not through the good works they have done (36 [Rom. 4:5]). It is, however, important that faith be accompanied by deeds, "for the faith which proceeds purely through the mouth and is denied through deed is fabricated" (476 [1 Tim. 1:5]). Only heathen conduct themselves so. We must not be Christians in name only, confessing God with the mouth while doing evil deeds. Rather, as far removed as the devil is from God, so clearly should the works of the children of God be distinguished from those of the children of the devil (367 [Eph. 4:17]). God must be glorified through our works according to the example of Christ (390 [Phil. 1:11]).

The exemplary behavior of Christians was an important concern for Pelagius. He therefore wrote at the beginning of his exposition of the Epistles to the Thessalonians: "The Thessalonians had not only achieved personal perfection in every regard, but others had profited as well through their word and example. Therefore the apostle praised them and encouraged them and invited them to do still greater deeds" (417 [in the intro. to 1 and 2 Thess]). The imitation of Christ is also important. Pelagius thus asks rhetorically: "If we are saved through the death of Christ, how much more will we be glorified when we have followed him?" (44f. [Rom. 5:10]).

More problematic, however, are comments such as: "The example of Christ is sufficient for our life," or: Christ has given us an example through his victory on the cross of how we should also be victorious (458 [Col. 2:6] and 461 [Col. 2:15]). Although following Christ is important for believers, the redemption effected through Christ cannot be reduced to an example that we should follow. Though Pelagius never tired of pointing out that we are saved through the free grace of God and not our own efforts, it was very important for him that we make progress in a moral sense and move toward being just. Indeed, Pelagius correctly emphasized that grace was given to us through baptism apart from the works of the law. But he nevertheless maintained that "grace indeed justifies the unrighteous who repent" (32f. [Rom. 3:24] and

246 [2 Cor. 3:6]). In this manner he also emphasized human initiative. There must be something already present upon which the grace of God works.

Also, on the question of baptism a shift of emphasis appears discernible.[7] Pelagius emphasizes the validity and necessity of baptism because it is in baptism that we receive the forgiveness of all our sins. Yet at the same time he qualified himself by stating that the water (of baptism) washes only the body, while teaching cleanses the soul (377 [Eph. 5:26]). Teaching can also serve as admonition, which is not possible in the case of the sacrament.

Finally, Pelagius makes reference to the significance of Adam. It is obvious for him that death came into the world through Adam because he was the first one who died (217 [1 Cor. 15:22]). Through his sin death came into the world. Yet once again Pelagius qualifies himself by saying that through Adam's example offense and sin entered the world (45f. [Rom. 5:12-16]). It is unusual, however, that he quotes the inquiries of those who reject original sin (*tradux peccati*) without lending his approval to these. His intention seems to be to show that the doctrine of original sin is not meaningful because sin is passed along through imitation.

In regard to the question of what sort of theological presuppositions Pelagius brought into this discussion we must not overlook the social context of his time. The Roman empire was internally and externally on the verge of political and moral bankruptcy. Even for the "Christian" emperors their words were often hollow, and a human life had little meaning. The church had become a part of the establishment that, while enjoying many privileges, had largely forgotten its task of reforming society. Within this context Pelagius, who spent nearly twenty-five years in Rome, sought to remind people that each individual was responsible for his or her own life and sins. It would have been a complete reversal of emphasis had he stressed the context of original sin and the necessity out of which we continually commit new sins. Instead, he underlined the accountability of the individual and the possibility of human sinlessness.[8]

Pelagius did not view sin as a "substance" that could be passed

---

7. See also Ferguson, *Pelagius*, 135, in this regard.

8. See Ferguson, *Pelagius*, 159, who presents a similar contextual argument. See also Hans Schwarz, *Our Cosmic Journey: Christian Anthropology in the Light of Current Trends in the Sciences, Philosophy, and Theology* (Minneapolis: Augsburg, 1977), 205f.

on to others or could influence human nature. He saw it rather as a "form" or quality of individual human actions. Thus he addressed the question of the avoidability of sin, for one can always improve a quality and can, therefore, always further repress sin. This is also to be seen in his contention that Adam's sin did not contextually or organically damage humans, but rather is simply spread further through imitation. With this thought Pelagius had broken with the Western tradition. He probably would have felt more at home with theologians of the East such as Clement of Alexandria, who died in 220 and who, in his *Exhortation to the Heathen,* advised: "Wisely cultivate the fruits of self-command, and present thyself to God as an offering of first-fruits, that there may be not the work alone, but also the grace of God; and both are requisite, that the friend of Christ may be rendered worthy of the kingdom, and be counted worthy of the kingdom."[9] The Eastern tradition did not shy away from the idea of human initiative, as can still be seen today in the predominant idea of the divinization of humans (*theosis*) in the Eastern church. Human initiative and grace are not mutually exclusive, rather both contribute to preventing evil from gaining the upper hand as well as toward God's ultimate overcoming of evil. This view, however, did not set well with Augustine.

Captive, Yet Responsible • Augustine

Three phases in Augustine's understanding of evil can be distinguished:[10] first, the controversy over the Pelagian teaching in Carthage and Sicily (411–15); then the direct attack on Pelagius himself, which, together with the continuation of the battle through the dispute with Julian of Eclanum, represents the high point of the controversy (415–24); and, finally, the controversy with the so-called Semi-Pelagians (425–29).

Phase 1: After the capture of Rome in 410 by Alaric, chief of the Goths, Pelagius found himself among the refugees fleeing to North Africa by way of Sicily. In Carthage he met up with Caelestius, who had brought his ideas among the people in pregnant form. At

---

9. Clement of Alexandria, *Exhortation to the Heathen* 11.117.5 (in *ANF* 2:204).

10. See the fourfold division by Ekkehard Mühlenberg, "Dogma und Lehre im Abendland," in *HDT* 1:447. Mühlenberg indicates four phases, the first of which we have already dealt with in the context of Augustine's controversy with the Manichaeans.

a synod in Carthage (411) six theses of Caelestius were rejected. Augustine rose immediately to the challenge of this attack against the Catholic faith and wrote three books in 411–12 with the title *A Treatise on the Consequences and Forgiveness of Sins, and on the Baptism of Infants* as well as an additional writing in 412 titled *The Spirit and the Letter.* We do not wish to give here a detailed analysis of Augustine's doctrine of grace but rather to inquire to what extent, according to Augustine, the human is ensnared in evil.

Caelestius claimed that Adam was mortal and would have died whether he had sinned or not. Augustine, too, admitted that the body of the first human was made from dust and was destined to return to dust. If, however, he had not sinned, his body would have been transformed into a spiritual body with an incorruptible condition as had been promised to the saints and believers so that they would no longer be confronted with the possibility of death.[11] Had Adam not sinned, he would have become immortal and incorruptible. Through his sin, however, he pulled humanity not only into spiritual death but into the death of the body as well (4.4 [16]). Death, therefore, has nothing to do with earthly frailty but with sin. Before the fall the body was capable of dying, but it was not destined to die (5.5 [16]). Sin and death pass via natural descent from one human to all humans and not through emulation. Augustine admits that all humans emulate the example of Adam, who through his disobedience violated the commandment of God (10 [18f.]). But Adam is not only the example for those who sin, but rather the ancestor of all who are born with sin.

Augustine distinguishes between the sins that humans commit themselves and that simply belong to them and the one sin through which all have sinned because all have been this one human (10.11 [19]). Augustine appears to assume a unity of all humans in the first human so that they, so to speak, all have a common genetic genealogy in Adam. This original or inherited sin is sufficient for the damnation of humans so that no additional personal sins are needed (12.15 [20]). This original sin cannot be escaped, for one acquires it "by the generation of the flesh" (15.20 [22]). Of course, therefore, everyone born of the flesh was in need of spiritual renewal, that is, rebirth through baptism (21.30 [26]).

---

11. So Augustine, *A Treatise on the Consequences and Forgiveness of Sins, and on the Baptism of Infants* 2.2 (in *NPNF* 5:16); references in the following pages are to this edition.

Because humans possess no superior merits that would earn God's grace, it is not problematic when seemingly unworthy individuals receive this grace or when those equally unworthy are denied it (23.33 [28]). On the basis of original sin we can, at any rate, only anticipate alienation from God. That which transcends this condition and changes our hopeless situation for the good is just as much unmerited as the retention of this condition would have been merited. Similarly, one also cannot inquire as to why one person may receive baptism and another may not and on this basis be denied the kingdom of God as well as eternal life and salvation. All such transformations are connected not with the behavior of the individual but rather with the unfathomable will of God, while the continuation in our condition comes from the fact that on the basis of original sin we deserve nothing other than death.

When children are not baptized, explained Augustine, they remain in darkness (see John 12:46), that is, in the state of punishment (35 [29]). Only through baptism can they escape from the sphere of influence of sin and the antigodly and gain access to the kingdom of God. Augustine was even of the opinion that the crying and screaming of infants at baptism demonstrated with what reluctance they accepted this sacrament, for they are not aware of how important it is for them (36 [29]). It is not sufficient, however, that one simply be informed about the word of truth. Through the word one recognizes and knows that the law is true, but the spirit must be fed internally through the sacraments. For Augustine the word alone is not sufficient, for the power of God must be added to the word in order that it be understood. This takes place through baptism.

Humans are therefore completely incapable of coming to God on their own. The reason for this is that humans do not stand within the sphere of God's influence but rather under the dominion of the devil, who is "the author of sin" (26.39 [30]). The question as to whether two rival powers of light and darkness are thereby once more introduced must at this point at least be asked. Augustine appears to vindicate himself of this charge in that he views God as the all-encompassing power within whose sphere the devil has created an enclave of his own power. Augustine now opposes two states of being with one another. First, no one dies who is brought forth according to the will of the flesh except through Adam, in whom all have sinned. Second, no one is equipped with life who is born again through the will of the spirit for it is through

Christ in whom all will be justified. Because through one person all have been condemned and also through one person all will be justified, there exists no neutral territory between the two. When individual persons are not with Christ, they are with the devil (28.55 [36]). There is no neutral territory in the world in which one is not either under the influence of evil or under the reign of God. This insight was later further developed by Luther.

Humans have no position of their own. Similar to iron shavings within a magnetic field they are oriented according to the structure of the field. Augustine thereby naturally rejects the Pelagian view that only one's own actual sins are forgiven in baptism because at the very beginning of our lives in this sinful world we already stand within the realm of sin. It is primarily original sin that is forgiven in baptism. Through the grace of God original sin is canceled out. Yet concupiscence, that is, the sinful desire that lives in humans, is not completely destroyed so that it no longer exists because even as baptized persons we live within the sphere of influence of this world (39.70 [43]). Concupiscence is restricted only insofar as it must no longer necessarily lead humans to death because baptized persons no longer live in the realm of death but are able to overcome concupiscence with God's help. A similar transformation is to be seen in the case of adult baptism. Although the bonds of guilt through which the devil had taken the soul captive have been released and the barrier that divided humans from their creator destroyed, concupiscence nevertheless remains so that we continue to give in to sin.

At the end of the first book of this inquiry Augustine asks whether, in light of this situation, there could ever be a person who already had or could ever live without sin. This in turn leads to the question of how free humans are, on the basis of their acceptance through baptism, to determine either for better or for worse their own destiny. The genuine threat posed by evil is, for Augustine, already clear inasmuch as Christians are admonished to pray to God: "Lead us not into temptation!"[12] Of course, Augustine does not contend that humans are condemned to an absolute passivity. In order to overcome our evil desires and misplaced fears we must put forward an effort and indeed sometimes employ the full power of our will. When we perform works of mercy after our baptism, for example, Augustine holds these to be helpful against

12. For this and the following see 2.3.3–2.4.4 (44f.).

guilt and the bonds of sin. The concupiscence and the desires that are at work within humans must be overcome through a battle. When those who are baptized and are blessed with reason go along with concupiscence and allow evil deeds to result, this is to be attributed to their own will. Every appeasement of these desires conceals within it a consent. New guilt is thereby accumulated when it is not removed from us through penance, works of mercy, or Christ's intervention. A second death and complete damnation would then occur. Therefore we pray in the Lord's Prayer: "Forgive us our sins as we forgive those who sin against us, and lead us not into temptation, but deliver us from evil."

The evil that operates in us and remains in us cannot be blamed upon our nature that was given us by God at creation. It is our own will that is at work when we find it easier to sin than not to sin and must be warned not to let sin reign within us. Augustine thus advises us to make certain of God's assistance when we feel that concupiscence is welling up within us so that we are not without God's help but are rather victorious through it and not swept away in temptation. Finally, our hope is that at some point concupiscence will no longer exist in us and our request, expressed in the Lord's Prayer, will become reality. Yet the hope for perfection, for the freedom from the predilection for concupiscence, is an eschatological hope (2.8.10 [48]). For the present we need the help "of divine grace assisting the human will" so that we can do what is right. When we do the opposite and act evilly, however, we act out of our own free will.

Augustine even believed that humans could live without sin in this life, otherwise the biblical admonitions to live a sinless life would be senseless. Yet a life lived according to the will of God is not possible without God's help.[13] Nevertheless, no one can actually live free of sin, for humans repeatedly look in the wrong direction. The necessity of daily renewal for the Christian also speaks against a completely sinless life. Augustine is also able to argue in a different manner and ask why it is that humans, though they are able to live without sin, do not do so. Augustine answers succinctly that humans are not willing to live sinlessly either because they do not want to do what is right because they do not know what is right or because it is not attractive enough. Humans have, therefore, a willful predilection toward evil's sphere of influ-

---

13. For this and the preceding quote see 2.17.26–2.27 (55).

ence. The primary ground for this predilection is to be found in human pride, which lays behind all transgressions.

Through these explanations, which are repeated in various forms and are always supported by Scripture references, Augustine seeks to show that humans are plunged into the realm of evil through original sin and can escape only through the grace of God. The grace is offered to humans in the first place in baptism. Yet even after their baptism humans do not fully escape evil's sphere of influence, for they continue to sin willfully and deprive themselves of God's grace. Although Augustine also speaks of holiness and maintained that humans should strive to do good, there is little trace of this dynamic of human existence, which was so prominent in the thought of Pelagius. Likewise, there is little emphasis upon the imitation of Christ, which ultimately, according to Augustine, could only be imperfectly accomplished.

Although Augustine continually addressed Pelagius's position, he names him by name only in the third part, which is appended to the work as a letter. There he characterizes Pelagius as "a holy man...who has made no small progress in the Christian life" (3.1.1 [69]). The reason that he does not mention Pelagius's name at first and then at the end only in a very positive light is to be found in his statement that he hoped for a peaceful settlement of the issue with him.[14]

In a writing from the same period, *The Spirit and the Letter* (412), Augustine pursues the same question that he touched upon in his work *A Treatise on the Consequences and Forgiveness of Sins, and on the Baptism of Infants*. He expressed the opinion there that it was indeed possible for a human to live without sin but that, with the exception of Jesus, there had not yet been anyone who had accomplished this. Almost the entire writing is given over to addressing the question as to what extent the law leads to a righteous life. Only at the end does he come back to the original question, why he maintains that a person could live a sinless life when this had never been accomplished by anyone. He concluded that one must only apply one's will sufficiently in order to achieve such a great accomplishment.[15] The fact that this never happens is not because it is impossible but is due to God's juridical activity.

---

14. Augustine, *Retractations* 2.33 (in FC 60:188).

15. For this and the following see Augustine, *A Treatise on the Spirit and the Letter* 35.62–36.66 (in NPNF 5:111f.).

Humans could indeed achieve righteousness in this life, desisting from all that is forbidden. It is much more difficult, however, to genuinely love God because he is hidden from us. Correct behavior is facilitated not only by the teaching of the law but also by the infusion of grace through the Spirit. God is able to lead the human will in such a way that it becomes righteous not merely in regard to faith but also so that it lives eternally in the presence of God. Why then, asks Augustine, does this not take place? He can only answer that with God nothing is indeed impossible, but he is also not unjust. There is a hidden depth to the righteousness of God that cannot be plumbed by humanity. Finally, Augustine humbles himself before the sovereignty of God, who has reserved the perfection of humans for the eschaton.

Phase 2: In the second phase of the dispute with Pelagius, beginning in the year 415, Augustine authored an entire series of writings. With *On Nature and Grace* (415) Augustine sought to respond to a book by Pelagius in which human nature is so portrayed that humans are also capable of being justified without the grace of God.[16] Once again the name Pelagius is not mentioned by Augustine, for he continued to hope that Pelagius would return to the right path. Augustine once more emphasizes that humans were created without imperfections and sin. Yet our nature is from Adam. Thus all the gifts of nature we possess, such as life, mind, and understanding, are in need of enlightenment and healing because of Adam's sin.[17] All of humanity has rightly merited punishment because of original sin. It is pure grace that God sent Jesus Christ into the world in order to save sinners whom he has foreknown and predestined, and whom he calls, justifies, and glorifies (5.5 [123]). Augustine raises here the subject of predestination, that is, the doctrine that certain individuals are chosen for salvation. This is not a problem for him because humans have nothing but condemnation awaiting them and therefore any rescuing out of the predicament of sin is unmerited grace. Grace does not belong to the human constitution and its natural functions but is rather directed toward the restoration and justification of human beings (11.12 [125]).

God not only shows his grace to humans but also makes use

---

16. See Augustine, *Retractations* 2.42 (207).

17. Augustine, *On Nature and Grace* 3.3 (in *NPNF* 5:122); references in the following pages are to this edition.

of "bad" things to help us. Augustine thinks here in the first instance upon the death of Christ, which he submitted to in order to
rescue us from death and the power of darkness (24.26f. [130]).
Alongside of this there are also "bad" things or experiences that
we encounter and that can serve to help us overcome our pride.
Even sin can contribute to the conquest of sin just as an operation
may bring about pain in order to alleviate pain. As previously, Augustine comes once more to speak of pride that is the beginning of
all sin. In order to conclude his argumentation, Pelagius, according to Augustine, confuses nature and grace. Pelagius believed that
humans were so created that of their own will they had the power
either to sin or not to sin. Augustine argues in a very similar fashion. Yet according to him, grace must also be added for us to be
able to avoid sin (59.69 [145]). Only falling from grace is possible
for us through our own free will; if we want to turn toward God
we need God's assistance.

Finally, Augustine's writing from this period, *Marriage and
Concupiscence* (418/20), must also be examined. In this writing
Augustine defends himself against the accusation that he rejects
marriage on the grounds that original sin manifests itself in the
sexual union of man and woman.[18] Of course, according to Augustine, all persons born of human parents are under the influence
of the devil unless they have been born again in Christ and through
his grace snatched from the powers of darkness and brought into
the kingdom of God. Yet Augustine does not wish, for this reason,
to condemn marriage because the person born within marriage is
a work of God and not the devil. Because of original sin marriage
is a much greater good than that which comes out of adultery
and sexual promiscuity. "For as sin is the work of the devil, from
whencesoever contracted by infants; so man is the work of God,
from whencesoever born."

In this writing, therefore, Augustine distinguishes between the
evil, fleshly concupiscence, through which humans are set loose
and by which they incur original sin, and the good of marriage.
According to Augustine, there would have been no shame caused
by concupiscence if humans had not sinned. Marriage, however,
would have existed even if humans had not sinned because the

---

18. For this and the following quote see Augustine, *On Marriage and Concupiscence* 1 (in *NPNF* 5:263f.); text references in the following pages are to this
edition.

bringing forth of children is inherent to this life. Yet this would have taken place without the sickness that, in our present bodies, is death, that is, without concupiscence. For Augustine neither marriage nor the bringing forth of children is evil, rather only the fleshly desire that, since the first human sin, is associated with procreation. Augustine views marital purity as a gift of God that, however, is not held in as high esteem by unbelievers as by believers because the former misuse this gift of God. One can speak properly of marital fidelity only when it occurs out of no other motive than as an act of devotion to the true God (4.5f. [265]). That which is naturally good within marriage is the unity of man and woman in procreation. Yet this degenerates to animal passion when it takes place for the satisfaction of lust rather than out of the desire for children.

The fact that Augustine held a diminished view of marriage does not need to be belabored here. In his argument he is primarily concerned with whether marriage is something bad because it is bound to concupiscence. For Augustine the sickness of concupiscence is not the result of marriage but of sin. On account of fleshly desire, which is to be condemned, marriage itself cannot be condemned. The sickness of concupiscence is to be kept in check within marriage so that marital cohabitation is not a decision of the will but rather a necessity for procreation, even if the will cannot be switched off (8.9 [267]). As we have already seen, fleshly concupiscence is forgiven through baptism. It is, however, not simply eradicated but afterward is no longer counted as sin (25.28 [275]). The concupiscence remains a human weakness that, through progressive renewal of the inner person, can be healed to the extent that the outer person becomes imperishable (1 Cor. 15:53).

Concupiscence is neither substance nor body nor spirit, rather, it is much more an expression of an evil quality. Although concupiscence is closely bound with sexuality, Augustine does not equate the two. The connection between them is made clear when Augustine asks rhetorically: "For why is the special work of the parents withdrawn and hidden even from the eyes of their children, except that it is impossible for them to be occupied in laudable procreation without shameful lust? Because of this it was that even they were ashamed who first covered their nakedness [see Gen. 3:7]. These portions of their persons were not suggestive of shame before, but deserved to be commended and praised as the work of God" (2.5.14 [288]). What is negative in regard to concupiscence is lust. Reason has no control over it so that humans react impulsively and even animal-like. If humans do not master their minds, they are delivered over to concupiscence, which can seduce them to do things to which, as beings blessed with reason, they would not normally consent. The reason that Augustine so often brings up the subject of sexual reproduction is probably because he can thereby best illustrate how it is that original sin is passed on when it is not something material but rather something intentional.[19] Because the Pelagians reject the doctrine of original sin, they can describe concupiscence within the act of reproduction as something good while Augustine, who calls the act of reproduction good and the will of God, distinguishes it from concupiscence, which he rejects as sinful. At the beginning of the life of a human, just as in the life of the Christian, we perpetually encounter a mixture of God-willed creatureliness and God-opposing sinfulness.

Phase 3: In the last phase of the dispute with the Pelagian teaching Augustine had to deal with questions that arose from the ranks of the church, as for instance from the monks of a monastery in Hadrumetum, an ancient city on the east coast of present-day Tunisia. In his *Retractations* Augustine reports that the monks there asked how the freedom of the will fit with the grace of God and whether the one excludes the other.[20] By way of an answer to this question he wrote, along with several letters, his book *Grace and Free Will* (426 or 427).

Augustine once more argues that God has given us certain commandments and that these would be completely useless if we had no free will that enables us to follow them.[21] We are thus able to choose freely to live and behave as we should (4.7 [258f.]). Similarly, he also says that eternal life is not only a free gift of grace but also a reward for our service. He seeks to overcome this contradiction by maintaining that justification is a completely gracious act of God, and our good life is, therefore, nothing other than God's grace at work within us. If a reward is given it is grace that is rewarded on account of its own merit and not because anyone has earned it (8.19f. [270ff.]). Even belief does not come from our own free will, for we pray that one who does not believe might believe. God is able, therefore, to transform the will which strives against

---

19. See also the comments of Mühlenberg, "Dogma und Lehre," 460.
20. Augustine, *Retractations* 2.66 (268).
21. See Augustine, *Grace and Free Will* 2.4 (in FC 59:253); and for the dating of the writing, 245ff.; references in the following pages are to this edition.

him and to take away the hardness of the heart (14.29 [282]). He changes evil to good. Yet we also read in Scripture that we should not harden our hearts (Ps. 95:8), which causes one to think here of a free will. Augustine concludes from this, as earlier, that the free will acts of its own accord when it serves evil. When it does that which is good, however, this occurs through the grace of God.[22] Yet how should one separate the divine activity from the human? Augustine gives the following answer: "God, then, works in us, without our cooperation, the power to will, but once we begin to will, and do so in a way that brings us to act, then it is that He cooperates with us. But if He does not work in us the power to will or does not cooperate in our act of willing, we are powerless to perform good works of a salutary nature." Augustine therefore follows the biblical insight that God works both within us: the willing and the effect.

Augustine wants to emphasize God's complete dominance of the will. This is also clear when (in predestinarian manner) he claims that God turns humans when and whither he will, that he shows favor to some and punishes others according to his will, and yet remains just.[23] He makes use of both good and evil, as with Judas, that Christ might be betrayed, or with the Jews, that he might be crucified. "He even makes use of the devil himself, the worst of all, but does so in the best way possible to exercise and put to the test the faith and piety of good men; not for His own sake, since He knows everything before it happens, but for our benefit, since it was necessary that He should deal with us in this fashion." Similar to Luther after him he maintained that God does what he wills in the hearts of evil persons but at the same time lets them continue in their own evil deeds. Despite this apparent contradiction we must hold fast to the fact that there is no unrighteousness with God, even when his own judgments are not always comprehensible. When we read in Scripture, for example, that people are hardened by God in their striving, we should never doubt that they suffer justly when they perpetrate evil deeds (21.43 [303]). When it comes to God's grace, however, everything is turned around. Here we do not receive what we earn but rather that which we have not earned. Nevertheless, Augustine suggests that even in evil persons the evil is not brought about by God but came originally

---

22. For this and the following see 16f.32f. (285ff.), and for the quote, 289.
23. For this and the following quote see 20.41 (297ff.).

from Adam and gained strength through his will. If God does not transform evil persons for the good, then he works within them according to their own desires.

Finally, Augustine addressed a second treatise to the monks of Hadrumetum, *On Rebuke and Grace* (426 or 427), in which he speaks of the gift of perseverance that is necessary for one to remain in faith until the end. No one can fall away who is elected and predestined because the grace of perseverance is always given to the end. Yet it belongs to the hidden councils of God why one person should receive this gift but another not. This was especially problematic in the case of Adam. Because he did not have the gift of perseverance, evil came upon him, as it were, out of necessity. Augustine argues in the following manner: God, who through his power created all things good, "foreknew that evil things would arise out of good." He knew that it was within the power of his almighty goodness to turn the evil into good "rather than not to allow evil to be at all."[24] Adam was given a free will and, because he was not aware of his coming fall, he was content. He thought that it was within his power not to die and not to end in evil. When he had desired of his own free will, without the experience of death and misfortune, to remain in the condition of uprightness and freedom from sin, he would have thereby earned through his perseverance the fullness of the blessing that was also given to the angels. Then it would have become impossible for him to fall. Because he forsook God of his own free will, however, he received God's just condemnation. And with him the whole of humanity was condemned, which is identified with him and sinned in him.

Adam possessed a different grace from that which was given after the fall because he was not yet in a context of evil. He did not need divine assistance as do those who have been justified after the fall. Augustine distinguished, therefore, between the original freedom that was in every respect free and was not yet burdened with evil, and the freedom of fallen humanity that is fundamentally restricted because without divine assistance it continually turns away from God. With Adam, however, a turning away was not something to be taken into consideration, even if God did foresee such a turning away. But predestination and the gift of perseverance are necessary for us fallen humans if we are to escape from evil in the long run. So that no one becomes proud and self-confident,

---

24. Augustine, *Treatise on Rebuke and Grace* 10.27ff. (in *NPNF* 5:482f.).

Augustine points out that no one knows whether or not they will persevere to the end. The grace of perseverance and predestination is a divine mystery (13.40 [488]). We cannot empirically establish who will belong to those who will be accepted by God, or who will belong to those who will be left to their self-deserved fate.

It is extremely difficult to compare Pelagius's position with that of Augustine because both have different starting points and deal with different problems. For Pelagius, sin remains primarily the action of an individual person that can be either carried out or avoided. Augustine, on the other hand, sees the individual as bound to the destiny of the corporate community, the orientation of which has been determined by the first human. The individual's activity is, therefore, preformed and his or her freedom already decisively qualified. In order for the individual to achieve and retain the ability of free choice, which is Pelagius's starting point, a prevenient grace is necessary. Because the individual can never completely escape the human context, a special act of grace, as occurs for instance in justification, is indispensable but is nevertheless insufficient. If humans are to act freely, they need the continual support of God's grace. For Augustine, however, this poses a problem because it is apparent that not everyone has this support. Therefore some are, so to speak, predestined to salvation while others are not. Although Augustine insists on the accountability of the individual, it seems that ultimately God distributes good and evil, and we do not know why some receive the one and others the other.

Augustine consistently thought through this double predestination, yet the danger nevertheless exists that one might question the goodness of God. This danger was also recognized by the Second Synod of Orange (529), which dealt expressly with the Augustinian heritage and the Semi-Pelagians, who were especially active in France.[25] At the urging of Pope Felix IV this synod, which met on the occasion of the dedication of a new church in Orange in southern France, produced a series of basic articles that were largely extracted from Augustine. The prevenient grace of God was strongly emphasized by the synod so that, for example, all good thoughts and deeds are a gift of God (article 9) and that even the saints stand in need of divine assistance (article 10). It was

---

25. For information on this synod and the articles formulated by it see Hefele, *A History of the Councils,* 4:152–67.

also pointed out that when humans commit evil deeds, they fulfill their own will; when they do good, however, then they freely fulfill the will of God (article 23). Yet we hear nothing of a double predestination. With these articles the problem of the relationship between God and evil was not explained, but only pushed aside. Although Augustine taught, based upon a questionable exegesis of Rom. 5:12, that all persons have sinned in Adam because they were all somehow present in him, he draws the right conclusions about the human situation.[26] Humans do not live in a vacuum but are always influenced by the context in which they live.

The question about free will as well as the question about the extent to which we are given over to evil have always occupied theology whether we think here of Anselm of Canterbury, St. Bonaventure, or Thomas Aquinas. Especially in late scholastic theology a position arose concerning human free will that, in its essentials, was very similar to that rejected by the Synod of Orange.[27] Martin Luther was one of the few theologians of the late Middle Ages who tenaciously defended the old Catholic doctrine of Augustine and of the Synod of Orange.[28] The representatives of humanism, along with late medieval theologians like John Eck, were especially opposed to him on this issue. Finally, after much hesitation and under pressure from Pope Hadrian VI, King Henry VIII of England, and other Catholic leaders, Erasmus of Rotterdam decided to take up the dispute against Luther and Luther's writing *Assertio omnium articulorum M. Lutheri per bullam Leonis X. novissimam damnatorum* (Defense of All Articles of Martin Luther Which Have Been Condemned through the Latest Bull of Leo X).

This defense of Luther's was published in 1520 at the behest of his prince, Frederick the Wise, and deals in detail with the accusa-

---

26. See Julius Gross, "Das Wesen der Erbsünde nach Augustin," in *Augustinus Magister: Congrès International Augustinien* (Paris, 21–24 September 1954), *Communications* 2 (1954): 774.

27. See the detailed study by Harry J. McSorley, *Luther: Right or Wrong? An Ecumenical Theological Study of Luther's Major Work, "The Bondage of the Will"* (Minneapolis: Augsburg, 1969), 129–215, who provides here a helpful historical-theological overview.

28. See McSorley, *Luther,* 293. Thus Ernst-Wilhelm Kohls, *Luther oder Erasmus,* vol. 1 (Basel: Reinhardt, 1972), 29, can rightly say that the conflict between Erasmus and Luther "was a renewal of the great conflict between Augustine and Pelagius." Unfortunately the second volume of this work, which was to treat the dispute over *The Bondage of the Will* and was "promised" to appear soon, has not yet appeared.

tions that were brought against Luther in the papal bull *Exsurge Domine*. Most of the forty-one theses treat the question of the extent of human freedom. Especially instructive is thesis 36, which is identical with thesis 13 of the *Heidelberg Disputation* (1518). It reads: "Since the fall of Adam, or after actual sin, free will exists only in name, and when it does what it can it commits sin."[29] As sinners humans do not have a free will but contribute only to their condemnation by their actions. With this position Luther stands in alignment with the Synod of Orange and Augustine. It is with this position that Erasmus takes issue. As we will see, however, he does not refute Luther's position but rather speaks past him.[30] We have here a situation similar to the conflict between Augustine and Pelagius in which the two disputants begin from very different starting points and are ultimately speaking of two entirely different matters.

Overcoming Evil through Human Willpower • Erasmus

In his book *On the Freedom of the Will* (1524) Erasmus takes up the question of free choice. He begins with the assumption that, with the exceptions of Mani and John Wycliffe, no one had yet totally denied humans the power of choice.[31] Erasmus first discusses the biblical texts that support free choice, such as Sir. 15:14-17, where we read: "Before each person are life and death, and whichever one chooses will be given [to them]." Although this quote applies especially to the first humans, it is also important for us because we have the freedom to choose between good and evil. This freedom has admittedly been damaged by sin, but it has not been destroyed by it (51ff.). Before we receive the grace of God, we incline more toward evil than good, yet free choice is not completely absent. In the first place, according to Erasmus, there is freedom of choice in external things that we can make decisions about, as for instance whether we will sit or stand, speak or re-

---

29. Martin Luther, "Defense and Explanation of All the Articles," trans. C. M. Jacobs (in *LW* 32:92).

30. So McSorley, *Luther,* 284.

31. See Erasmus of Rotterdam, *On the Freedom of the Will,* trans. E. Gordon Rupp, in *Luther and Erasmus: Free Will and Salvation,* ed. E. Gordon Rupp and Philip S. Watson (Philadelphia: Westminster, 1969), 43; references in the following pages are to this edition.

main silent, and so on. This freedom cannot help us acquire eternal life, and it has not been destroyed through sin. The ability to make such decisions is the first gift of grace.

Erasmus distinguishes this from the second or operative grace, through which we have the freedom to surrender ourselves to the will of God, for example through prayer, study of the Scriptures, or hearing the preached word. Erasmus seeks to support his contention that the human will is free through further quotations from the Bible like Matt. 23:27 or John 14:15—texts that appear to presuppose a freedom of choice.

Erasmus next takes up those texts that seem to deny the freedom of choice. The most important example is the hardening of Pharaoh (Exod. 9:12), which is taken up by Paul in Rom. 9:17. Erasmus explains that Pharaoh was given a will that was able to turn toward either good or evil (66). Of his own will Pharaoh chose the evil and followed with his heart evil rather than God's commandments. God nevertheless took the depravity of Pharaoh and used it for his own glory and for the redemption of his people in order to make it clear that human attempts to strive against the will of God are vain. Similarly, according to Erasmus, a smart king or lord makes use of the cruelty that he hates in order to punish evil. Hardening is therefore a pedagogical measure of God, but is not to be viewed as predetermined. Even the foreknowledge of God is not determining, for he does not foreknow something so that it will occur but because it occurs. Yet with God what he wills and what he foreknows coincide. But not every necessity involved in human events excludes the freedom of our will (68). God foreknew, for example, that Judas would betray the Lord. If one considers, however, the infallible foreknowledge of God and his unchangeable will, then one must conclude that Judas necessarily betrayed his Lord. Yet Judas could have changed his will. Thereby the foreknowledge of God would not have been compromised, for God would have foreknown even this and changed his own will accordingly.

But how is it with the story of Jacob and Esau where it is said that God had loved Jacob but hated Esau?[32] Here also Erasmus claimed that God contains within himself no contradictions but loves and hates upon just grounds and that this does not preclude human free will. When, for example, he hates one who is not yet

---

32. For this and the following see 69ff.

born, this is because he knows that this person will commit acts that will merit hate, and when he loves one who is not yet born, then this occurs upon the same grounds, albeit based upon deeds of an opposing nature. When he points to the Old Testament picture of humans as clay in the potter's hand so that God can do with us what he will (see Jer. 18:6), this is an expression of the fact that we should entrust ourselves to God just as a vessel is entrusted to the hands of the potter. "Yet in truth this is not to take away free choice wholly, nor does it exclude our will from cooperating with the divine will in order to attain eternal salvation." When Paul takes up this passage in Rom. 9:21ff., this is likewise done in order to silence the evil grumblings of the Jews against God, but not with the intention of completely excluding the freedom of choice.

If humans cannot do anything positive, then, according to Erasmus, there is no place for merits, and where there is no place for merits, there is also no place for punishment or reward (73). On the other hand, if humans do everything, then there remains no place for grace. When one views the effort of the human will together with the support of divine grace, then those scriptures that appear to oppose one another quickly lose their contradictory character.

When Erasmus comes to Luther's publication, he criticizes that not enough place is given to the human will. From statements such as "No one can receive anything except what has been given from heaven" (John 3:27), one cannot conclude, according to Erasmus, that there is no strength or use in our freedom of choice. The fact that fire warms comes from heaven just as much as the fact that we seek that which is advantageous for us and avoid that which is harmful to us. The fact that after the fall our will is spurred on to seek better things is likewise from heaven. It is also from heaven that we find favor with God through tears, alms, and prayers, which make us acceptable before God. God, therefore, always goes before us as creator and sustainer so that we are able to make use of our free will.

Without the assistance of grace, according to Erasmus, we of course are unable to achieve even part of that which we seek (79). The situation here is similar to that of a ship's captain who, after a severe storm, does not say that he has saved the ship but rather that God has, although his own skill and effort were not completely useless. With reference to Phil. 2:13: "For it is God who is at work in you, enabling you both to will and to work for his good pleasure"; and calling upon the authority of Ambrose's interpretation of this passage, Erasmus concludes that "a good will cooperates with the action of grace" (81). The entire Scriptures speak so often of help and assistance that one must here bring humans and God together. Over against those who claim that humans can do nothing without the grace of God and conclude therefore that no human work is good, Erasmus maintains that which seems to him much more probable: "There is nothing that man cannot do with the help of the grace of God, and . . . therefore all the works of man can be good" (85).

In his epilogue Erasmus speaks out again against the idea that human merit remains completely worthless and that the works even of godly persons are sinful (87). He also rejects the claim that an absolute necessity be ascribed to everything we do or desire. He assures his readers once again that he readily admits that all human efforts are traced back to God, without meaning that we can do nothing. Our share of free will is very small, and it is a part of divine grace that we can turn our souls toward that which leads to salvation and can cooperate with grace. Erasmus seeks in this way to establish that we are able to cooperate with God's grace and to contribute something toward our salvation. He also suggests the following: "After his battle with Pelagius, Augustine became less just toward free choice than he had been before. Luther, on the other hand, who had previously allowed something to free choice, is now carried so far in the heat of his defense as to destroy it entirely" (90).

In order once more to clarify his position for Luther, Erasmus distinguishes three stages in the efforts of humans toward salvation: beginning, progress, and end. Divine grace is ascribed to the first and last of these stages while the freedom of choice has its place in the stage of progress. Yet even here the grace of God is the primary factor while human freedom of choice remains a secondary cause. Although Erasmus attempted to explain his position to Luther through repeated entreaty, no new impetus was produced. Decisive for him is that humans themselves can contribute something to their salvation. Erasmus's goal was a virtuous life. Gustav Adolf Benrath characterized Erasmus's position accurately as follows:

> External enemies such as the world, the devil and death play no
> role in this battle as individual powers. The battle takes place

within humans themselves. Reason must continually defeat the rebellious "outer person."...Being a Christian consists largely of
the heart's desire to become a Christian. Everyone will be victorious; only those who do not want to be victorious will not
achieve victory. The one who makes an effort will be brought
along further by the Spirit, for everything depends upon moral
progress and advancement. Christ is thereby not only the teacher
and leader into battle but also the goal toward which we must
orient ourselves....In this way the Christian way of salvation becomes for Erasmus a way of sanctification. Indeed, it would be a
way of self-sanctification were it not for the Christian sign of baptism at the beginning, the progress with the help of the Spirit, and
the heavenly reward at the end.[33]

The Person
as Torn between Two Powers • Luther

Martin Luther waited more than a year before he responded to
Erasmus with his publication of _The Bondage of the Will_ (1525),
which numbers among the most impressive writings ever produced
by Luther. Luther's "response" was approximately four times the
length of Erasmus's publication. Erasmus answered back with a re-
joinder titled _Hyperaspistes_ (The Defender), which was longer than
his original writing and Luther's response put together. Although
at the beginning Luther wrote very respectfully and congratulated
Erasmus on having understood the essence of his teaching, thus
making a response worthwhile, Erasmus was hurt by the intensity
of Luther's response. Even a letter from Luther in which he sought

---

33. Gustav Adolf Benrath, "Die Lehre des Humanismus und des Antitrinitaris-
mus," in _HDT_ 3:29. Of course one can portray Erasmus in a more conservative
light and make of him a representative of orthodox theology. Ernst-Wilhelm
Kohls, _Die Theologie des Erasmus,_ vol. 1: _Textband_ (Basel: Reinhardt, 1966),
152–58, writes, for example: "The Erasmian concept of sin rises above every le-
galistic or sociological-moral standardization. Such a standardization is likewise
avoided through the fact that Erasmus ultimately views the battle of the Christian
against actual sins as an extension of the battle between God and Satan. In this
sense sin appears to him as nothing short of 'the power of the devil.' Nothing
of this godly/antigodly dynamic, however, is to be detected in this writing against
Luther. The accent is not upon an antigodly action nor upon the aggravating
severity of evil, but rather clearly upon the _cooperatio,_ the cooperation of humans in the salvation process." Also in this regard see the comment of E. Gordon
Rupp in his introduction to the translation of _De libero arbitrio,_ "The Erasmian
Enigma," in _Luther and Erasmus,_ 8, where he says of Kohl's evaluation: "One is
bound to have reservations about a demonstration taken almost exclusively from
the early writings [of Erasmus]."

to justify the passionate nature of his argumentation could not reconcile Erasmus (*LW* 33:11).[34] This was not surprising, for Luther did not simply put forward his own position over against that of Erasmus, but rather took Erasmus's publication apart almost sentence for sentence in order to refute it. At the very beginning Luther made clear that the main point of conflict between himself and Erasmus was the question of whether the human will is able to contribute something to the eternal salvation of humans.[35] This in turn raised the question of whether God foreknows something and we all act out of necessity or whether a free will exists within us. Luther's conviction is clear, for he says, similar to Augustine before him, that it is fundamentally necessary for the salvation of the Christian to know that God does not foreknow contingently, but that he foresees, aims, and carries out all things through his immutable, eternal, and infallible will (37).

Luther begins with the presupposition that nothing takes place accidentally, but that God's eternal plan and providence stand behind all things. The divine power is sovereign, and it cannot be restricted. Salvation lies beyond our power and depends wholly upon God. Luther concludes from this that when God is not present and at work in everything that we do, the result will be evil, and we will necessarily do that which is of no avail for salvation (64). Luther does not mean, thereby, that without the Spirit of God humans do evil against their will as if they were physically forced to do this, but rather that they do evil out of their own obliging will. One is quite naturally reminded here of Luther's hymn "A Mighty Fortress Is Our God" (LBW 228), where he writes: "No strength of ours can match his might! We would be lost, rejected."

Luther speaks of a necessity of unchangeableness, that is, that the will not only is unable to change itself and go in a different direction but is at the same time also inclined to continue in its original evil direction. When God works graciously within us, the will is changed and acts likewise out of its own inclination and its own willing and not out of coercion so that it cannot be changed toward another direction through an opposing will. Just as the will previously willed and found satisfaction in evil, it now wills and

---

34. For further literature on the dispute between Luther and Erasmus see Bernhard Lohse, "Dogma und Bekenntnis in der Reformation: Von Luther bis zum Konkordienbuch," in *HDT* 2:33.

35. Martin Luther, *The Bondage of the Will* (1525) (in *LW* 33:35); in what follows, text references to this work are to this edition.

rejoices in that which is good. Luther thus comes to the point that
is most discussed and that he explains as follows:

> If we are under the god of this world, away from the work and
> Spirit of the true God, we are held captive to his will, as Paul says
> to Timothy [2 Tim. 2:26], so that we cannot will anything but what
> he wills. For he is that strong man armed, who guards his own
> palace in such a way that those whom he possesses are in peace
> [Luke 11:21], so as to prevent them from stirring up any thought or
> feeling against him; otherwise, the kingdom of Satan being divided
> against itself would not stand. And this we do readily and willingly,
> according to the nature of the will, which would not be a will if it
> were compelled; for compulsion is rather (so to say) "unwill." But
> if a Stronger One comes who overcomes him and takes us as His
> spoil, then through his Spirit we are again slaves and captives—
> though this is royal freedom—so that we readily will and do what
> he wills. Thus the human will is placed between the two like a
> beast of burden. If God rides it, it wills and goes where God wills,
> as the Psalm says: "I am become as a beast [before thee] and I am
> always with thee" [Ps. 73:22f.]. If Satan rides it, it wills and goes
> where Satan wills; nor can it choose to run to either of the two
> riders or to seek him out, but the riders themselves contend for the
> possession and control of it. (65f.)[36]

The first impression of Luther's argument is that a dualism is
here being introduced that divides the world into two spheres of
influence. The two powers, God and Satan, however, are not the
focus here, but rather humanity. Humans, according to Luther,
never live in a neutral vacuum but always in a particular context that decisively influences them and from which and in which
they live. If this context is formed by God, then they desire and
do that which is of God. If, however, it is determined by the antigodly powers, then humans desire and do what the interests of
these powers demand. Even when one takes both powers into consideration, Luther leaves no doubt that God as the stronger of the
two wins. Satan is not equal in power to God but is a creature,

---

36. For a discussion of the image of the beast of burden and the two riders
as well as of the relevant literature see McSorley, _Luther,_ 335–40. McSorley's
argument, that Luther does not discuss where Satan comes from, is not valid.
Luther's intention is not to explain evil, but rather to show that humans do not
have a free will when it comes to their own salvation. Therefore it is also not
correct to say, with McSorley, that, according to Luther, God himself appears to
be the author of evil (343). At this point McSorley has missed the actual intention
of Luther, which focuses in a different direction.

even if he has antigodly rank, and is ultimately dependent upon God for his being. Humans have freedom only within a context that is determined either by God or by the antigodly powers. As creatures humans do not have the freedom to choose their context, but rather live within a context that they can leave only if they are transferred into the other context. The questions of freedom of the will and freedom of choice are not thereby touched upon but rather the question of whether humans can choose of their own power the sinful context, a possibility that Augustine always emphasized. Luther, however, appears to reject this possibility.

Luther next distinguishes between the preached and offered grace of God, on the one hand, and the hidden and frightening will of God, on the other. In the latter, God determines through his own counsel which persons shall be the recipients of his preached and offered grace.[37] One can only worship the divine will in reverence but cannot penetrate it. This awesome aspect of the divine majesty is reserved for God alone. "God must therefore be left to himself in his own majesty, for in this regard we have nothing to do with him, nor has he willed that we should have anything to do with him. But we have something to do with him insofar as he is clothed and set forth in his Word, through which he offers himself to us and which is the beauty and glory with which the psalmist celebrates him as being clothed. In this regard we say, the good God does not deplore the death of his people which he works in them, but he deplores the death which he finds in his people and desires to remove from them." We must distinguish "between God preached and God hidden, that is, between the Word of God and God himself." Because God is all-working and there is no other power equal to him, Luther must necessarily distinguish between two wills in God, the revealed will, out of which good comes to us, and the hidden will, which we ultimately cannot ground and which contains, so to speak, that which is cruel and evil. The latter also predestines certain persons to evil. It is through God's will, as it were, that it is decided whether certain persons come to stand under the sphere of influence of God the redeemer or whether they spend their lives under the reign of evil in alienation from God. Why someone would be excluded from salvation is not answered

---

37. For this and the following quotes see Martin Luther, *The Bondage of the Will*, 138ff.

by Luther, who instead points to the hidden will of God that we can ultimately only worship and honor but not fathom.[38]

Luther sought to shed light upon the evil that God works in still another way and gives the hardening of Pharaoh as an example. The starting point here is the assumption that God does not cause sin.[39] Luther begins with the efficacy of God and reminds Erasmus that he himself admitted that God works all in all (1 Cor. 12:6):

> Now, Satan and man, having fallen from God and been deserted by God, cannot will good, that is, things which please God or which God wills; but instead they are continually turned in the direction of their own desires, so that they are unable not to seek the things of self. This will and nature of theirs, therefore, which is thus averse from God, is not something nonexistent. For Satan and ungodly man are not nonexistent or possessed of no nature or will, although their nature is corrupt and averse from God.... Since, then, God moves and actuates all in all, he necessarily moves and acts also in Satan and ungodly man. But he acts in them as they are and as he finds them.... When God works in and through evil men, evil things are done, and yet God cannot act evilly although he does evil through evil men, because one who is himself good cannot act evilly; yet he uses evil instruments that cannot escape the sway and motion of his omnipotence. (175f.)

Because of the omnipotence with which God moves all things, Satan is able to hold on to his followers. Yet God does not work in such a way that he himself brings about evil, a fact that Luther continually stressed, but he rather moves further along and hardens that evil that he finds already before him. Evil does not occur through a mistake of God's but rather through our false behavior because we are by nature evil through our fallen nature. In accordance with the nature of God's omnipotence, evil persons are driven further along in their own evil activity although God, in accordance with his wisdom and for his glory and our salvation, can also use this evil for good.

Two points are here worthy of special consideration: first, Luther's statement that the evil will cannot do anything other than evil (*aliter facere non possit*); and second, the statement that

---

38. Philip S. Watson, "The Lutheran Riposte," in *Luther and Erasmus,* 23, rightly observes: "His doctrine of predestination, like Calvin's after him, is from one point of view a confession of ignorance and a very proper piece of Christian agnosticism."

39. Luther, *The Bondage of the Will,* 174; text references in the following pages are to this work.

Satan became evil in that God forsook him and Satan sinned (*deserente Deo et peccante Satana malam factam*) (178). The fact that God made Pharaoh's will unrepentant can be derived from God's omnipotence. That he could not have changed Pharaoh's will, however, appears at the very least unusual and would seem to contradict God's omnipotence. Also, the fact that Satan became evil because God forsook him and he sinned seems to trace evil back to God, a consequence that Luther does not want. He wishes rather to show that it is an aspect of God's omnipotence to move everything further along, whether good or evil, according to its own character. In this way he answers the question of why God does not transform evil into good but instead actually strengthens evil in its wickedness. He also advises that this belongs to the mystery of God's majesty, which we can only worship but cannot explain. When we ask, therefore, why God allowed Adam to fall and why he created all of us infected with the same sin because he could have protected Adam or created us with a different constitution, then we must not forget, according to Luther, that God is God. For God's will there is no cause or rule of reason that we could use as a measure because nothing is equal or superior to his will, but his will is itself the ruler of all things (180f.). Hence God himself is the final rule and measure of his action and his judgment.

At the conclusion of his document Luther summarizes his argument once more in three points (293): (1) God foreknows and predetermines all things. He can make no mistakes in his foreknowledge nor be hindered in his predetermining. Nothing happens that he does not will to happen. (2) Satan is the ruler of this world who constantly battles against the kingdom of Christ with all his might. He would allow no one to escape the sphere of his power if he were not forced to do this through the divine power of the Spirit. (3) Original sin has so damaged us that it causes many problems in the fight against evil even in those who are led by the Spirit of God. Without the help of the Spirit of God, therefore, there is nothing in humans that is able to turn toward the good but rather only toward evil.

Luther understands humans as having a tendency toward evil placed upon them by original sin and as turning themselves away from God and seeking to please themselves. If it were possible for humans to contribute something to their own salvation, then a certain amount of uncertainty would enter into and interfere with our human assurance of salvation. Erasmus, on the other hand, interprets this perspective of Luther's as determinism. He desires, therefore, despite the recognition that humans are sinful, to hold fast to the idea that humans can contribute at least something to their salvation. Luther, however, does not embrace determinism. This is clear when he concedes that there is a kingdom of the left in which humans can do through their own choice and counsel what they will, while in the other kingdom (of the right) things are directed by the choice and counsel of God (119). Erasmus makes no distinction between a kingdom of the left and a kingdom of the right. Worldly respectability leads simultaneously to heavenly acceptance for Erasmus. It is not surprising, then, that the key thoughts of *The Bondage of the Will,* even if they appear to be extreme, are necessary for Luther's dispute "with a theology that is largely Semi-Pelagian or has even become Pelagian."[40]

The basic statements of Luther on this subject were of such importance that they found their way into the Formula of Concord of the Lutheran Church. There, with reference to Luther's writing, we read that "there is ... no cooperation on the part of our will in man's conversion," but that "God himself must draw man and give him new birth."[41] Yet no mechanistic understanding of the Christian's transfer out of one sphere of influence into the other is thereby intended, for the confessors also explain that "conversion is that kind of change through the Holy Spirit's activity in the intellect, will, and heart of man whereby man through such working of the Holy Spirit is able to accept the offered grace." Humans, therefore, are not wholly passive. If they wish to escape evil's sphere of influence, however, they are dependent upon the grace of God. We continue to encounter here two spheres of influence, that of good and that of evil. It is therefore profitable at this point to take a closer look at the structure of evil's sphere of influence.

---

40. So Lohse, "Dogma und Bekenntnis," 39.

41. For this and the following quote see "The Formula of Concord," in *The Book of Concord,* trans. and ed. Theodore Tappert (Philadelphia: Fortress Press, 1959), 529 and 537.

Chapter 7

The Kingdom of Evil

When we speak of the "kingdom of evil" we are not thinking of a dualistically structured principle of evil that stands in opposition to the good, but have in mind, rather, that individual manifestations of evil are derived from a communal existence. The concept of a kingdom of evil addresses a genuine New Testament state of affairs. We read, for instance, in the Gospel of John of the "prince of this world" and of the "battle of darkness against the light." Also in the Synoptics the destiny of Jesus from the first moment until the last stands in opposition to the antigodly powers. Even Paul writes of the "powers and authorities of this world." In Christianity the concept of a kingdom of evil was first systematically developed in Augustine's *City of God* (or more accurately stated, "On the City of God against the Heathen")—a book that he wrote between the years 413 and 426. The immediate occasion for the writing of the manuscript was the capture of Rome in 410 by Alaric and his Goths. Concerning this event Augustine wrote in his *Retractations:* "Meanwhile, Rome was destroyed as a result of an invasion of the Goths under the leadership of King Alaric, and of the violence of this great disaster. The worshipers of many false gods, whom we call by the customary name pagans, attempting to attribute its destruction to the Christian religion, began to blaspheme the true God more sharply and bitterly than usual. And so, 'burning with zeal for the house of God' [Ps. 68:10; John 2:17], I decided to write the books *On the City of God* in opposition to their blasphemies and errors."[1]

---

1. Augustine, *Retractations* 2.43.2 (in FC 60:209).

137

Jerusalem and Babylon
in Conflict • Augustine

Augustine made use here of an image that was already familiar among African Christians and that he was probably first introduced to through Tyconius, a North African representative of the Donatists.[2] According to this view, humanity has been divided into two great cities or communities, that is, into two great camps of allegiance, since the fall of Adam. The one city serves God and his faithful angels while the other serves the rebellious angels, the devil, and his demons. These cities appear to be inextricably mixed together within the church as well as in the world, but they will be separated from one another at the last judgment. When Christ passes judgment, the two cities, Babylon and Jerusalem, will clearly emerge, one to the left and the other to the right.

Already before Augustine wrote *The City of God* he had spoken of these two communities. We read therefore in his writing *The First Catechetical Instruction* (ca. 400):

> There are two cities, one of the wicked, the other of the just, which endure from the beginning of the human race even to the end of time, which are now intermingled in body, but separated in will, and which, moreover, are to be separated in body also on the day of judgment. For all men who love pride and temporal dominion together with empty vanity and display of presumption, and all spirits who set their affections on such things and seek their own glory by the subjection of man, are bound together in one fellowship; and even though they frequently fight one with another for these ends, still they are flung headlong by an equal weight of desire into the same abyss, and are united to one another by the likeness of their ways and deserts. And again, all men and all spirits who humbly seek God's glory, not their own, and who follow Him in godliness, belong to one fellowship. And yet God is most merciful and long-suffering toward ungodly men, and offers them room for repentance and amendment.[3]

The two communities encompass not only humans but also spiritual beings. Their separation has existed since the beginning of humanity, that is, since the fall of Adam, and will last so long as the earth exists. Externally one cannot determine to which of

---

2. For this and the following see Peter Brown, *Augustine of Hippo: A Biography* (London: Faber and Faber, 1967), 314.

3. Augustine, *The First Catechetical Instruction* 19.31 (in ACW 2:61).

the two communities a person belongs because only their wills are structured oppositely to one another. It is also difficult to distinguish the two groups because they are mixed together and there exists no visible dividing line separating the one community from the other.

In *The City of God* Augustine sought to divide history into seven epochs following the pattern of a seven-day schema:[4] the first epoch extends from Adam until the flood, the second from the flood until Abraham. The third epoch covers the period between Abraham and David, the fourth that between David and the exile, and the fifth extends from the exile until the coming of Christ. Currently we find ourselves in the sixth epoch. Augustine rejects immediately the possibility of an exact prediction of the course of history because one cannot measure the length of these epochs according to a certain number of generations. "The seventh [age] shall be our Sabbath, which shall be brought to a close, not by an evening, but by the Lord's day, as an eighth and eternal day, consecrated by the resurrection of Christ, and prefiguring the eternal repose not only of the spirit, but also of the body." Augustine describes, then, a linear progression of history from the beginning to the end of this world.

Augustine explains that God originally chose to derive all humanity from one individual in order to unite humans into a community and to bind them together in a harmonious unity and a bond of peace.[5] According to this plan humanity would not have been subject to death. Yet the first humans brought death upon themselves through their disobedience. This sin was so serious that human nature was altered and resulted in enslavement to sin and unavoidable death for all their descendants. This reign of death left such a mark on humanity that they ran directly into a second death, which was their well-deserved punishment, although no small number of persons were saved through the unmerited grace of God. We now have the result before us: a great number of different peoples who are spread over the entire world and who are distinguished through their various religious and moral practices and their different languages.

---

4. See Augustine, *The City of God* 22.30, trans. Marcus Dods (New York: Random House, 1950), 864ff., quote, 867; references in the following pages are to this edition.

5. For this and the following see 14.1 (441).

Nevertheless, there are really only two main groups within human society, which one might call two cities. The one city prefers to live according to the principles of the flesh, the other according to those of the spirit. The citizens of these two different cities all want to pursue their own peace, and they achieve this goal. According to Augustine, the world does not disintegrate into two societies in which one is characterized by the power of Satan and the other by the power of God, but rather, both exist through the unmerited grace of God. Both, however, organize their lives in contrasting fashion, for they pursue either the goals of the spirit or those of the flesh, whereby Augustine takes up a Pauline distinction.

When Augustine distinguishes between spirit and flesh or spirit and body, he in no way intends to place the blame for sin upon the latter. As he expressly states, the flesh is not the cause of every kind of moral failure, but rather, the ground for evil behavior is to be found in the soul or spirit of humans. "For it is not by having flesh, which the devil has not, not by living according to himself— that is, according to man—that man became like the devil. For the devil too, wished to live according to himself" (14.3 [443ff.]). If humans live according to their own criteria and not according to God's, then, according to Augustine, they become like the devil. But if they live according to the criterion of truth, then they do not live according to their own standards but according to those of God. "In enunciating this proposition of ours, then, that because some live according to the flesh and others according to the spirit there have arisen two diverse and conflicting cities, we might equally well have said, 'because some live according to man, others according to God'" (14.4 [445]).

In this way love of self is contrasted to the love of God. The love of self is at the same time the love of the flesh, that is, of one's own flesh. Those who love themselves are not concerned for the truth, for this is not a human possession. Augustine characterized the two cities as follows:

> Two cities have been formed by two loves: the earthly by the love of self, even to the contempt of God; the heavenly by the love of God, even to the contempt of self. The former, in a word, glories in itself, the latter in the Lord. For the one seeks glory from men; but the greatest glory of the other is God, the witness of conscience. The one lifts up its head in glory; the other says to God, "Thou art my glory, and the lifter up of mine head" [Ps. 3:3]. In the one, the

princes and the nations it subdues are ruled by the love of ruling; in the other, the princes and the subjects serve one another in love, the latter obeying, while the former take thought for all. (14.28 [447])

We encounter here two entirely different and opposing types of conduct that characterize these two communities.

The earthly city is able to live in peace only when its life is not grounded upon belief. A harmonious agreement among its citizens is achieved through the establishment and following of ordinances so that a certain compromise is reached between people concerning those things that are necessary for mortal life. Because the heavenly city has a pilgrim existence upon the earth and must dwell here, it makes use of this earthly peace. So it is that the heavenly city "lives like a captive and a stranger in the earthly city" (19.17 [696]). The heavenly city, however, does not hesitate to obey the laws of the earthly city, for through these are regulated those things that serve toward the maintenance of this mortal life.

Christians live in the earthly city and are active within it so that their lives, to the extent necessary, can be provided with earthly goods. Although Augustine is no friend of the earthly city and criticizes it correspondingly, he views it nevertheless as necessary and lends it his support. The heavenly city, during its earthly pilgrimage, calls citizens out of every nation together to form a community of foreigners. This does not, however, mean that the laws and ordinances of the earthly city are abolished. Rather, the heavenly city makes use of and defends these laws and seeks a compromise with the human will for those things that are important for the mortal nature of humans without compromising true religion or piety in the process. Even if the earthly city is called a city of the devil, it cannot be rejected. It is necessary for the material aspect of our humanness and requires our support. This is made easier by the fact that as a Christian one lives within this city and has a dual citizenship in both cities.

Augustine never portrays the evil world as being equivalent to the secular state. But because the city of God may be conceived of as the empirical, physical church, the reader might very naturally think of the city of the world as being equivalent to the (Roman) state.[6] Augustine's thought demands this equating of the two inas-

---

6. So Reinhold Seeberg, *Text-Book of the History of Doctrines,* trans. Charles E. Hay (Grand Rapids: Baker, 1954), 1:327.

much as he recognizes and affirms the necessity of earthly laws, although everything that is truly and lastingly good is to be found only in the city of God. It must be asked, however, whether one may really bind the earthly city to the devil, as Augustine does, while at the same time attributing to it an important function for the earthly living together of humans. But the other side of this identification is also problematic. Augustine is able to mention together in one breath the city of God and the church, indeed even in connection with the kingdom of God. Yet the visible church is not, for Augustine, an ideal community.[7] Within the visible church dwell the good and the lost, and both are gathered in by the dragnet of the gospel. Within this net both swim together unseparated until the shore is reached. There the evil will be separated from the good.

Augustine knew that in his time many entered the church only because they hoped to gain personal advantage by doing so. It was therefore difficult to precisely identify the city of God and the world in regard to their members. Augustine's proposal is based simply upon the assumption that humanity is able to live upon this earth only because of God's grace. Two possibilities then present themselves: to live one's life either according to the will of God or according to one's own will. The latter is understood as sinful. Yet sin, as Augustine demonstrated in his dispute with Pelagius, is not an individual phenomenon. It has, as do all things in the world that are evil, a social dimension. Therefore it is used for the self-glorification of humanity and is, at least potentially, self-destructive. Augustine is, however, aware that God can use even evil for good. In this way human self-interest also serves human self-maintenance, a fact from which even Christians benefit. We must not forget, however, that *The City of God* was written in the context of the destruction of Rome by Alaric and his followers. Augustine therefore points clearly to the fact that human history, as a history of the earthly city, is a history of evil, behind which lies the judgment God.

---

7. For this and the following see Augustine, *The City of God* 15.26 (516f.), 18.49 (660), and 20.9 (725ff.). See also Gordon L. Keys, *Christian Faith and the Interpretation of History: A Study of St. Augustine's Philosophy of History* (Lincoln: Univ. of Nebraska Press, 1966), 172.

The Kingdom of the Devil • Luther

It is not surprising that Martin Luther, who learned a great deal from Augustine, also adopts his distinction between the kingdom of God and the kingdom of the devil.[8] Luther writes:

> There are two kingdoms. The first is a kingdom of the devil. In the Gospel the Lord calls the devil a prince or king of this world [John 16:11], that is, of a kingdom of sin and disobedience. To the godly, however, that kingdom is nothing but misery and a vast prison.... Thus he who submissively serves the devil in sin must suffer much, especially in his conscience, and yet, in the end, he will thereby earn nothing but everlasting death. Now all of us dwell in the devil's kingdom until the coming of the kingdom of God. However, there is a difference. To be sure, the godly are also in the devil's kingdom, but they daily and steadfastly contend against sins and resist the lusts of the flesh, the allurements of the world, the whisperings of the devil. After all, no matter how godly we may be, the evil lust always wants to share the reign in us and would like to rule us completely and overcome us. In that way God's kingdom unceasingly engages in combat with the devil's kingdom.... The others dwell in this kingdom, enjoy it, and freely do the bidding of the flesh, the world, and the devil. If they could, they would always stay there.... The other kingdom is that of God, namely, a kingdom of truth and righteousness.... It is the state when we are free from sin, when all our members, talents, and powers are subject to God and are employed in his service.... That comes to pass when we are ruled not by sin, but only by Christ and his grace.[9]

The kingdom of the devil, therefore, is the world in which everyone lives, whether Christian or non-Christian. Luther takes up here, along with Augustine, the testimony of John 16:11, which tells us that Satan is the prince of this world.

In his familiar, realistic manner Luther does not glorify the world as the already in-breaking kingdom of God, but rather characterizes it as a place plagued by many problems and evils. In this kingdom of the devil we must persevere and defend ourselves, for we are constantly in conflict with the devil. Luther indicates much the same thing in his Small Catechism when he says that the old

---

8. On the distinction between the two kingdoms see Cargill Thompson, *Studies in the Reformation: Luther to Hooker*, ed. C. W. Dugmore and Philip Broadhead (London: Athlone Press, 1980), 45, who also traces the distinction of the two kingdoms back to Augustine.

9. Martin Luther, *An Exposition of the Lord's Prayer for Simple Laymen* (1519) (in *LW* 42:38ff.).

Adam within us must daily be drowned by sorrow and repentance and that a new person must daily rise up. The kingdom of God struggles with the kingdom of the devil although the former is, in a strict sense, an eschatological phenomenon that fully breaks into the world only when the latter passes away. Luther also points out that the kingdom of God does not come with outward signs but is already present inside of humans and that we should pray that it will be established and increase within us and grow strong. God's grace and his kingdom together with all virtues shall come to us just as "Christ came to us from heaven to earth; [for] we did not ascend from earth into heaven to him" (*LW* 42:41). While the kingdom of the devil manifests itself outwardly, the kingdom of Christ is an inner power active in Christians.

Christians and non-Christians differ from one another in that the latter follow the will of the devil. They seek to advance his kingdom and to destroy the kingdom of God. Therefore they do not come out of the kingdom of the devil into the kingdom of Christ but, according to their own desire, remain eternally in the kingdom of the devil. Humanity is then divided into two kinds of persons: the one belongs to the kingdom of God but must live in the kingdom of the devil while the other not only lives within the kingdom of the devil but belongs to it as well.

One cannot simultaneously belong to both kingdoms. Luther expressed this clearly in *The Bondage of the Will* when he wrote:

> For Christians know there are two kingdoms in the world, which are bitterly opposed to each other. In one of them Satan reigns, who is therefore called by Christ "the ruler of this world" [John 12:31] and by Paul "the god of this world" [2 Cor. 4:4]. He holds captive to his will all who are not snatched away from him by the Spirit of Christ, as the same Paul testifies, nor does he allow them to be snatched away by any powers other than the Spirit of God, as Christ testifies in the parable of the strong man guarding his palace in peace [Luke 11:21]. In the other kingdom, Christ reigns, and his Kingdom ceaselessly resists and makes war on the kingdom of Satan. Into this Kingdom we are transferred, not by our own power but by the grace of God, by which we are set free from the present evil age and delivered from the dominion of darkness....We are bound to serve in the kingdom of Satan unless we are delivered by the power of God.[10]

---

10. Martin Luther, *The Bondage of the Will* (in *LW* 33:287f.).

If the kingdom of God or the kingdom of Christ did not exist, all humans would be delivered over to the kingdom of Satan. There is no escape from this kingdom unless Christ liberates us so that we are freed from its sphere of influence and transferred into that of the other kingdom. In *The Bondage of the Will* Luther compared the individual to a beast of burden that is ridden either by God or by Satan. The members of the kingdom of God follow Christ and are one with him and he with them, whereas the members of the kingdom of the devil follow him and are one with him. In contrast to Augustine an individual and existential perspective is clearly to be seen in Luther. He does not stress so much the opposing structure of the two kingdoms as he does the opposing manner in which Christians and non-Christians conduct themselves.

If Satan is indeed the prince of this world, as Luther continually emphasizes in agreement with John 12:31, then should one not simply write off this world as evil? Should we not hope to be taken out of this world, and should we not lead a life of withdrawal and detachment from the world? In regard to Luther one can confidently answer these and similar questions in the negative, for he was no proponent of either Manichaeism or Platonic philosophy. For Luther this world was God's creation and therefore the place in which we were placed by God. It would be a distortion of Luther's position if the world were simply given over to the devil. It is rather the other way around, for the devil's power in this world is limited. He is a created being, for he was originally a part of God's good creation. As such he cannot be equal to God. Although Luther sometimes dramatizes the devil dualistically, for him, the devil does not stand primarily beside God and over humanity but rather between God and humanity.[11] The devil, so to speak, obstructs the view of God so that humans mistake the devil for God and in presumed obedience to God serve the devil.

In Luther's view angels are the soldiers, keepers, guides, and governors of God's creation.[12] It is their task to watch over and lead us and the creatures of this creation whereby they do battle not only for the pious but for all people. Of course Satan, in

---

11. See in this regard the comments of Hans-Martin Barth, *Der Teufel und Jesus Christus in der Theologie Martin Luthers* (Göttingen: Vandenhoeck and Ruprecht, 1967), 208, on the place of the devil in Luther's theology.

12. For this and the following see Martin Luther, *Lectures on Genesis* (1535–45) (in *LW* 6:87f.); text references in the following pages are to this work.

Luther's view, because he is the god of this world, has under him many other devils, that is to say, evil angels. These evil angels govern everywhere from the pope and the emperor to the princes and even in private homes. Through them the works of the devil are produced that we see and experience but that the world does not recognize for what they are.

As experience shows, the good angels contend with the evil angels. Yet we should not let ourselves be too intimidated. Even if Christ calls Satan the prince of this world, it is God who is the creator and ruler of all. Satan cannot even harm a hair on our head "except by God's will and permission" (*LW* 6:90). Luther even says consolingly:

> The power of the devil is not as great as it appears to be outwardly; for if he had full power to rage as he pleased, you would not live for one hour or retain safe and intact a single sheep, a crop in the field, corn in the barn, and, in short, any of those things which pertain to this life.... You will find more good than bad things and you will also see that a very small part is subjected to the power of the devil. For he is compelled to leave the fish in the rivers, the birds in the air, the men and animals in the villages and cities, which he would not do if it were not for the protection of the angels. At times, however, he causes great disturbances, brings kingdoms and monarchies into conflict with each other, and throws provinces, states, and households into confusion. To be sure, he causes disturbance, and yet he is not able to carry out what he most desires, to overthrow all things and to mingle heaven with earth. So strong are the walls, fortifications, and hedges of the angels round about us and all things. (*LW* 6:90f.)

If, when considering evil, we disallow that which occurs through God when he leads us, for example, into temptation or punishes or chastises us because we have fallen away from him, then, according to Luther, considerably more good than evil occurs. The kingdom of evil upon this earth is sharply curtailed through God's all-encompassing activity. It is not able to destroy the foundational orders of God that belong to his creation and its preservation. These orders can be impaired and even brought into question, but the kingdom of evil and the devil are not able to transform this world into chaos.

But why does God, if he is ultimately the creator and preserver of all things, tolerate at all the kingdom of evil that seeks to transform the good creation into a sea of blood and tears and injustice?

Luther's answer is that there should be no discussion about the wisdom of the counsels of God (*LW* 6:91). He speaks of the goodness of God that is not limited as is ours but that remains unlimited and unfathomable. One should let God govern as he does and praise him for his great mercy that even with evil persons more good than evil occurs. If God and his angels would cease only for a single day to rule the world, the devil would bring everything to an end in a terrible chaos. Luther therefore avoids theodicy, that is, the question of God's righteousness, and points instead to God's unfathomableness and to the fact that, seen as a whole, God is merciful and good. Luther realistically recognizes that there is evil in the world. He does not explain this evil individualistically inasmuch as he would trace it back to humans. Yet he also does not view evil as simply an outgrowth of human society. For Luther there is a metaphysical power that stands in the background and battles against God's creation, seeking to destroy it.

For the preservation of temporal order God has established the worldly regiment or kingdom. According to Luther's categorization humans belong either to the kingdom of God or to the kingdom of the world. "Those who belong to the kingdom of God are all the true believers who are in Christ and under Christ, for Christ is the King and Lord in the kingdom of God."[13] These persons do not, in principle, need the temporal law or sword, that is to say, the worldly force that is exercised against persons who do not observe the law. Because the Holy Spirit works in their hearts and teaches them that they should do no one injustice and love all people, they do of their own accord what one would require of them. But there are also those persons in this world who belong to the kingdom of the world. "The unrighteous do nothing that the law demands; therefore, they need the law to instruct, constrain, and compel them to do good" (*LW* 45:89). For non-Christians, who actually belong to the kingdom of the world and do not just live within it as do Christians, temporal law is necessary for the preservation of law and order. Luther, exhibiting his typical realism, said that if it were not for temporal authority,

> men would devour one another, seeing that the whole world is evil and that among thousands there is scarcely a single true Christian. No one could support wife and child, feed himself, and serve

---

13. Martin Luther, *Temporal Authority: To What Extent It Should Be Obeyed* (1523) (in *LW* 45:88); text references that follow are to this work.

> God. The whole world would be reduced to chaos. For this reason God has ordained two governments: the spiritual, by which the Holy Spirit produces Christians and righteous people under Christ; and the temporal, which restrains the un-Christian and wicked so that—no thanks to them—they are obliged to keep still and to maintain an outward peace. (*LW* 45:91)

The temporal regiment of God, through which he keeps the world from self-destruction, is a divine order of preservation that is implemented, as it were, through the law, that is, through temporal law and corresponding punishment. All persons are subject to this regiment of God whether Christian or non-Christian, the Christian willingly, however, while the non-Christian often unwillingly. From this regiment is to be distinguished God's government through the gospel, that is, through grace and consolation, through which humans find entry into the kingdom of God. Law and force have no place here, for faith cannot be forced upon anyone but is rather God's own work. Hence there is a necessary connection between Luther's two-kingdoms doctrine, that is, Luther's conviction that there is a kingdom of God and a kingdom of the devil, and the two-regiments doctrine, his view that God governs differently in the temporal sphere than he does in his very own kingdom of the gospel.[14]

Luther thus goes a decisive step beyond Augustine. With Augustine it was difficult to understand how the ordinances of the city of the world could be affirmed because its purpose and its citizens were earthly and estranged from God. Luther, however, through his distinction between the temporal kingdom of the devil and God's kingdom of the left, has made it unmistakably clear that although the kingdom of evil exists and reigns in the world, it is not identical with the good ordinances of God that also exist in the world. On the contrary, the kingdom of evil always has the goal of destroying God's regiment and holding all persons bound within the kingdom of the devil. The result is that Luther not only sees a dynamic power struggle between the sphere of influence of God and that of the antigodly powers but is also able to affirm

---

14. Thompson, *Studies in the Reformation,* 47f., has convincingly demonstrated a necessary connection between the two kingdoms and the two regiments. He writes: "Luther's concept of the two divine orders or regiments is profoundly influenced by his doctrine of the eschatological conflict between the kingdom of God and the kingdom of the Devil." Yet he concedes that Luther does not always strictly distinguish between "kingdom" and "regiment."

God's creation as an unqualified good that cannot be usurped even by the greatest efforts of the antigodly powers. Additionally, the kingdom of God, in contrast to the city of God, is not a *corpus permixtum,* a mixture of good and evil, but is rather a community of those sanctified by Christ. The kingdom of God, therefore, cannot be confused with the church.

The Kingdom of Sin • Kant, Ritschl

In the person of Albrecht Ritschl (1822–89) we encounter a representative of modernity who greatly influenced German Protestant theology during the second half of the nineteenth century. We are not taking Ritschl into consideration here because of his stature, however. His significance for us is to be found in the fact that, on the one hand, he saw himself as building upon the tradition of Luther, while, on the other hand, he was influenced by the ethics of Immanuel Kant (1724–1804), which led him especially to the idea that a kingdom of sin stood in opposition to the kingdom of God.[15]

In his book *Religion within the Limits of Reason Alone* (1793) Kant treats in detail the problem of human sinfulness and the kingdom of evil. Kant begins his treatment of evil by asking how it expresses itself in humans and from whence it comes. According to Kant, persons are not called evil because they carry out activities that are contrary to the law and are accordingly seen as evil. Rather, these activities appear to be of such a nature that we can conclude that evil maxims or precepts exist in humans.[16] That means that one can sometimes see how it is that activities will end in opposition to the law and one is fully aware that they are illegal. Nevertheless, the maxims themselves are not always observable. According to Kant, humans are by nature neither morally good nor evil, but they are only in certain respects good, and in others evil (BA 8,9 [17f.]).

The human capacity to do evil can be shown in three ways. First, it is part of the weakness of the human heart to not consistently observe accepted precepts. A frailty of human nature

---

15. This is especially pointed out by David L. Mueller, *An Introduction to the Theology of Albrecht Ritschl* (Philadelphia: Westminster, 1969), 69.

16. Immanuel Kant, *Religion within the Limits of Reason Alone* (BA 5,6), translated with introduction and notes by Theodore M. Greene and Hoyt H. Hudson (New York: Harper, 1960), 16; references that follow are to this edition.

manifests itself here.[17] Second, there is a tendency in humans to mix morally and nonmorally motivated causes, hence a so-called impurity of motivation. Finally, Kant comes to speak of a tendency of humans to take up evil whereby they demonstrate a wickedness of human nature or of the human heart. This latter is present in all persons, even the best, so that one can say that a general tendency toward evil exists in humans. Humans are understood to be evil to the extent that they are aware of moral laws but nevertheless incorporate occasional deviations from these laws into their maxims (B27f., A25 [27]). Kant speaks of a radical, inborn evil in human nature that originates, however, through our own selves.

According to Kant, the cause of evil can be seen in the nature of human thinking and in the natural inclinations that arise out of it. But this would restrict evil too much because humans would thereby be degraded to the level of animals. If one would locate this depravity in the moral, lawgiving reason, so as to imply that reason could destroy the authority of the law out of which it comes, this would be to attribute too much to evil. We would then have to do with a reason that is wicked, and humans would be turned directly into demons. If there is an inclination to evil in human nature, then it must be sought in human free will that is capable of becoming morally evil. Evil is then radical, for it perverts the fundament of all maxims through the human will (B36,37, A33 [32]). Hence Kant guards human free will and neither degrades humans into subhumans nor elevates them into superhumans. Nevertheless, it is difficult for him to adhere to a traditional doctrine of original sin, a deficiency that he seeks to compensate with his doctrine of the kingdom of evil.

Kant relates the biblical story of the fall including the appearance of two opposing principles with the prince of this world as the leader of the kingdom of evil.[18] The evil principle is not overcome through Christ, for his kingdom remains standing. Before it can be defeated, a new epoch must begin. Yet the power of the kingdom of evil is broken so that it can no longer hold people against their will as it had previously done. Another kingdom, one that is moral, is offered as asylum to humans as a place where they can find support for their morality if they desire to leave the sphere of influence to which they previously belonged. Humans must stand under one

---

17. For this and the following see B21, A19 (24f.).
18. For this and the following see B106–15, A99–106 (73–78).

lordship or another. According to Kant, there is no salvation for humans when they do not thoroughly adopt genuine moral principles in their character. Yet Kant entertained doubt as to whether humans could conduct themselves correctly, not because of their sensual nature, but because of a certain self-afflicted perversity, or however one wishes to describe this wickedness that humans have brought upon themselves, and through which evil came into the world.

Kant summarizes:

> Now man is in this perilous state through his own fault.... When he looks around for the causes and circumstances which expose him to this danger and keep him in it, he can easily convince himself that he is subject to these not because of his own gross nature, so far as he is here a separate individual, but because of mankind to whom he is related.... Envy, the lust for power, greed, and the malignant inclinations bound up with these, besiege his nature, connected within itself, *as soon as he is among men.* And it is not even necessary to assume that these are men sunk in evil and examples to lead him astray; it suffices that they are at hand, that they surround him, and that they are men, for them mutually to corrupt each other's predisposition and make one another evil. (B128f., A120f. [85])

In order to counter this situation one must build an alliance against evil and promote the good in the human. Of course, humans are continually at risk of falling back under the sway of evil.

In order to unite individual humans, who by themselves are unable to resist evil, in the pursuit of this common goal, the concept of a higher moral being is necessary. Through this concept the insufficient powers of individuals are united. In this way one can resist the evil that is to be found within one's self and within all others (B137–42, A129–34 [90ff.]). Kant sets the kingdom of sin, therefore, against the kingdom of God, which is exemplified in the church. Sin is not an individual offense but rather manifests itself in the community through which it is continually strengthened and set anew into motion. As an individual one cannot resist this sin but needs the community and the goal toward which this community is directed. Kant understands evil neither atomistically nor as a mystery that plagues human nature. He rejects every natural understanding of sin and maintains a deliberate, intentional deviation of the human will. In what manner, then, does Ritschl, who was strongly influenced by Kant's ethics, take up these ideas?

Ritschl, like Kant, assumes that the kingdom of sin, as he calls it, "is a substitute for the hypothesis of original sin" that expresses that which the idea of original sin was meant to describe.[19] He thus distances himself from Augustine and Luther inasmuch as he accuses them both of having succumbed to a false exegesis. Luther saw the doctrine of original sin revealed in Scripture while Augustine, in his well-known exegesis of Rom. 5:12, was of the opinion that all humans had sinned in the person of Adam. Paul, however, was not speaking here of the relationship between cause and effect, as was the case with the law and the chain of natural descent. Rather, Paul recognized the divine decision as the interceding factor, even if he had spoken of sin coming into humanity through Adam's single transgression (344f.). If we view the concept of original sin as the background against which sin stands out, one cannot, according to Ritschl, adequately understand sin in the life of the individual or in humanity as a natural species. "The subject of sin, rather, is _humanity as the sum of all individuals,_ in so far as the selfish action of each person, involving him as it does in illimitable interaction with all others, is directed in any degree whatsoever towards the opposite of the good, and leads to the association of individuals in common evil" (335). Ritschl felt himself here to be in formal agreement with Friedrich Schleiermacher in opposition to Pelagius and Augustine.

According to Ritschl, Pelagius made the will of the individual exclusively responsible for sin, which meant for him that sin was passed along through example and imitation. Imitation, however, in Ritschl's view, becomes more infrequent in the later years of one's life, something that is not true, however, of sin. If one were to start with the example nature of sin, sin would not go beyond the limits of the individual will. The cooperation of humans in sinful deeds, therefore, is testimony against the example theory. Augustine views humanity as a natural race as the subject of sin so that all persons, as descendants of the first human pair, are burdened with the highest level of sin. Humans are therefore equal in regard to sin. With this deduction, however, Augustine, according to Ritschl, overlooks the interaction of actual sins. Additionally, justice is not done to the phenomenon of the will in

---

19. Albrecht Ritschl, _The Christian Doctrine of Justification and Reconciliation: The Positive Development of the Doctrine,_ trans. H. R. Mackintosh and A. B. Macaulay (New York: Charles Scribner's, 1900), 344f. (§41); text references that follow are to this edition.

the case of the actions of humans, which one could trace back to a common source, for the will disappears from the picture in the natural interpretation of sin.

Ritschl, on the other hand, claimed: "If we discover in the individual action the proof-mark of the independence of the will, can we ascribe to ourselves, not merely individual actions, but likewise evil habit or evil inclination?...Even if we find radical evil working within us to the extent affirmed by Kant, responsibility for it can only be vindicated if it is assumed to be the result of the empirical determination of the will, for it can be derived neither from the natural origin of every man, nor from the pretended intelligible act of freedom" (337). Important for Ritschl, as well as for Kant, is evil's determination of the will. With Ritschl this is also grounded upon the fact that he wishes to overcome evil through education. This is possible, however, only when persistent bad behavior or evil inclinations are understood as the results of acts of the will. If one assumes a doctrine of original sin, however, which is passed on from one generation to the next, then education would be of little help. Ritschl further maintained that one must distinguish among sinful transgressions according to their severity. With the concept of original sin, however, this is hardly possible because original sin is seen as a universal constant (337f.).

In order to take into consideration the various degrees of habitual sin and to view them as facets of sinful activity, Ritschl introduces the idea of the kingdom of sin. Guilt can only be shared when one not only owns up to one's own sinful deeds but also recognizes how these cause other sins, although one cannot always precisely say how far this effect extends. This sinful federation with others does not exclude anyone, so that we are all burdened with sin. Ritschl thus reaches the conclusion that, from the perspective of a discerning conception of guilt, original or hereditary sin can no longer be understood as the primary form of the concept of sin (341f.). Nevertheless, Ritschl did not feel that he was betraying his Lutheran heritage but sought to show that his understanding of sin, in rudimentary form, was already to be found in the Lutheran confessional writings and especially in Melanchthon. Finally, he even sought to find support in Paul when he wrote: "And finally, since Paul neither asserts nor suggests the transmission of sin by generation, he offers no other reason for the universality of sin or for the kingdom of sin than the sinning of all individual men" (348).

When we compare Ritschl's concept of the kingdom of sin with Luther's kingdom of the devil we notice that Ritschl's conception produces an unusually static effect. This is somewhat moderated in that sin is not viewed as an end in itself but as the opposite of universal good. Sin always strives, desires, and acts against God; the kingdom of sin finds its counterpart in the kingdom of God. "This whole web of sinful action and reaction, which presupposes and yet again increases the selfish bias in every man, is entitled 'the world,' which in this aspect of it is not of God, but opposed to Him" (350). We are, so to speak, caught up in a dragnet of evil, which is created and strengthened through us. Yet Ritschl claims that it is not inevitable that each individual be caught in this sinful web and make his or her own contribution to wickedness and untruthfulness. Moreover, one can act egotistically when one appears to be fighting for the kingdom of God and, for example, for certain goods like family pride, class feeling, patriotism, or loyalty to the confession of the church. Ritschl made it clear, therefore, that the church, as it manifests itself upon this earth, must not be equated with the kingdom of God. The church belongs to the world and must be distinguished from the kingdom of God.

If we wish to do justice to Ritschl, we must take into consideration the context from which he argues. Optimism reigned supreme in the nineteenth century. It is therefore of no surprise that Ritschl should claim that "there exists in the child a general, though still indeterminate, impulse towards the good" (337). There is no place here for a doctrine of original sin with which humans are burdened from birth on. Humans are capable of improving. At the same time, however, Ritschl emphasizes that humans are not isolated individuals but always live within a context that necessarily influences them. This is made especially clear in his *Instruction in the Christian Religion* (1875) where he writes:

> The unified action of many individuals in these forms of sin leads to a reinforcement of the same in common customs and principles, in standing immoralities, and even in evil institutions. So there comes to be an almost irresistible power of temptation for those who with characters yet undeveloped are so much the more exposed to evil example because they do not see through the network of enticements to evil. Accordingly, the kingdom of sin, or the (immoral human) world, is reinforced in every new generation. United sin, this opposite of the kingdom of God, rests upon all as a power which at least limits the freedom of the individual to good. This

limitation of the freedom of the individual by his own sin and by connection with the common condition of the world is, taken strictly, a lack of freedom to good. This, however, outside of the kingdom of God, is the common condition of all men.[20]

The recognition and emphasis of the superindividual form of sin and evil, clearly expressed in the preceding quotation (Ritschl used sin in the theological sense, whereas evil represented the morally bad), were needed correctives in the nineteenth century. At least in the case of theologians this did not go unheard, as is shown by Walter Rauschenbusch and later Reinhold Niebuhr in the United States as well as by the religious socialists Leonhard Ragaz and Hermann Kutter in Switzerland at the beginning of this century. They took up Ritschl's terminology and spoke of a kingdom of evil that perverts humans and institutions.[21] One could, thereby, no longer push sin and evil off onto the individual and seek to convert the individual in order to make possible better living conditions upon the earth. One must, therefore, concern oneself with the structures of injustice and evil and seek to reform these.

Evil as Societal Power • Rauschenbusch, Reinhold Niebuhr

Walter Rauschenbusch (1861–1918), one of the most prominent representatives of the Social Gospel in America and a person influenced by his experience working with the innumerable immigrants who flooded New York at the end of the nineteenth century, recognized better than many the reality of sin in its far-reaching, societal context. In his 1912 book, *Christianizing the Social Order,* he wrote: "Sin is a social force. It runs from man to man along the lines of social contact. Its impact on the individual becomes most overwhelming when sin is most completely socialized. Salvation, too, is a social force. It is exerted by groups that are charged with divine will and love. It becomes durable and complete in the measure in which the individual is built into a social organism that is ruled by justice, cleanness, and love. A full salvation demands a Christian social order which will serve as the spiritual environment

---

20. Albrecht Ritschl, *Instruction in the Christian Religion,* trans. Alice Mead Swing, in Albert Temple Swing, *The Theology of Albrecht Ritschl, together with "Instruction in the Christian Religion"* (London: Longmans, Green, and Co., 1901), 206f. (§30).

21. So also Mueller, *An Introduction,* 73.

of the individual."[22] Sin is a societal power that stands in opposition to redemption, which is likewise described as a social force. In this and other publications Rauschenbusch mentions sin only infrequently while his primary attention is directed toward societal structures and their problems. It is first in his *A Theology for the Social Gospel* (1917) that more space is given to a discussion of sin. This book also contains a chapter entitled "The Kingdom of Evil."[23] Although Rauschenbusch was never entirely content with Ritschl, because he supposedly gave too little attention to social analysis, this publication is nevertheless clearly influenced by Ritschl.[24]

In *A Theology for the Social Gospel* Rauschenbusch distinguishes between three forms of sin; sensuousness, selfishness, and godlessness, in which we sin against our higher self, against the good in humans, and against the universal good.[25] With remarkable unanimity theology has essentially categorized sin as selfishness and thereby provided an ethical and social definition that manifests itself in the irrepressible social spirit of Christianity. When theology, however, characterizes sin as an assault against God, this is foreign to reality, for we seldom sin against God alone. This can be seen already in the Ten Commandments. If we describe sin, however, more as selfishness, then this definition fits better with the Social Gospel than with an individualistic type of religion. A sinful spirit is unsocial and antisocial.

In contrast to many of his contemporaries Rauschenbusch defended the doctrine of original sin, for he claimed that this was one of the few attempts of an individualistic theology to achieve a collective view of its field of study.[26] The doctrine of original sin views humanity as a unity that descended from a single individual and has been held together through the centuries through the unity of its origin and its bond of blood. Natural science, according to Rauschenbusch, confirms this view, for evil flows through the

---

22. Walter Rauschenbusch, *Christianizing the Social Order* (1912) (New York: Macmillan, 1915), 116.

23. For a brief summary see the detailed biography, *Walter Rauschenbusch,* by Dores Robinson Sharpe (New York: Macmillan, 1942), 328–34.

24. Paul M. Minus, *Walter Rauschenbusch: American Reformer* (New York: Macmillan, 1988), 145 and 221 (n. 11). See also Walter Rauschenbusch, *A Theology for the Social Gospel* (1917) (Nashville: Abingdon, 1978), 138f. (n. 1); references that follow are to this edition.

25. For this and the following see 47–50.

26. For this and the following see 57–61.

generations in the channels of biological connections. Yet conventional theology goes too far when it makes original sin responsible for such an all-encompassing corruption of humans. The evil that arose out of the sin of the individual was trivial and irrelevant in contrast. Rauschenbusch also doubted whether one could achieve a responsible freedom when original sin is so strongly emphasized. Theology forgot that sin is transmitted along the line of community tradition, a channel that is, however, much more accessible to religious influence and religious control than is nature.

The persistent depravity and transgressions of adults are not transmitted through genetics, but they are instead socialized. Sin resides in social practices and institutions and is taken up by the individual as well as by the individual's social group. According to the theology of the Social Gospel, original sin is for this reason partly conditioned by society and partly biologically inherited. This has something to do not only with the instinct for imitation, as Pelagius thought, but also with the spiritual authority of the community over its members. The emphasis upon the biological transmission of evil, as is almost exclusively stressed in the doctrine of original sin, distracts attention from the power of societal transmission, from the authority of the social group that justifies, stresses, and idealizes that which is bad, and from the decisive influence of economic profit, all of which can defend and spread evil (67). Yet these aspects are just as important as creationism or traducianism—doctrines that are often coupled with original sin. When one speaks of sin, one cannot speak only of the community but must also speak of spiritual power and of the value of the combined, superpersonal powers in the community such as governments or society's many groups and organizations. These "organizations are rarely formed for avowedly evil ends. They drift into evil through sinister leadership, or under the pressure of need or temptation" (72).

If one considers the various aspects of sin, it is a short step to speak about the kingdom of evil. "The life of humanity is infinitely interwoven, always renewing itself, yet always perpetuating what has been. The evils of one generation are caused by the wrongs of the generations that preceded, and will in turn condition the sufferings and temptations of those who come after" (79). While destructive insects are unable to change natural constellations in order to increase damage, this is possible for destructive humans. They can gain control of legislation, police, military, and religion and alter the constitutions of nations in order to increase the damage that they are capable of inflicting. Our theological conception of sin remains fragmentary if we do not recognize that all persons in their natural groups are bound together in a solidarity of all times and places and bear the yoke of evil and suffering (81). The understanding of the kingdom of evil, according to Rauschenbusch, is not new. "But while our modern conception is naturally historical and social, the ancient and mediaeval Church believed in a Kingdom of evil spirits, with Satan at their head, which is the governing power in the present world and the source of all temptation" (82).

According to Rauschenbusch, the belief in a satanic kingdom exists today only where religious and theological traditions keep this belief alive. Yet in Rauschenbusch's view we cannot deny that Satan and his angels are increasingly disappearing today and that an actual belief in demonic powers is in conflict with modern life. We can no longer view the kingdom of evil as a demonic kingdom. Rauschenbusch saw the Social Gospel as the only influence that could "renew the idea of the Kingdom of Evil in modern minds, because it alone has an adequate sense of solidarity and a sufficient grasp of the historical and social realities of sin" (87). This modern form would then offer religious values that were similar to the old ideas because both, according to Rauschenbusch, were of a kind. The belief in a satanic kingdom, to the extent that this was not pure theology but rather living religious belief, has always been related to societal realities. One sees this in Judaism as well as in the early church and in the Middle Ages.

When the collective consciousness of sin and evil, which Rauschenbusch holds to be important for the religious spirit, continues to disappear, our understanding of sin as well as our understanding of the necessity of redemption will become increasingly shallow. The societal conception of the kingdom of evil is meant to battle this loss of reality. If we accept this understanding, then we can no longer restrict redemption to the soul and its personal interests but must conceptualize redemption societally. Walter Rauschenbusch impressively demonstrated that evil cannot be understood individually but must rather be understood transpersonally and thereby also societally. He saw the kingdom of evil in opposition to the kingdom of God and stressed that one cannot appropriately describe the kingdom of evil when one does not understand the kingdom of God because the latter is hindered in its coming-to-be through the kingdom of evil. We would agree with Rauschenbusch that evil has a societal dimension. Today one would expand this perspective in order to include the natural realm as well because it, too, is a creation of God that has not escaped the corruption-causing activity of humans. Yet one must still ask whether one can merge the kingdom of evil with the unjust structures of society, as does Rauschenbusch, or whether perhaps these structures point beyond themselves to a first cause of evil that is not simply the first manifestation of evil.

Reinhold Niebuhr (1892–1971) taught together for many years with Paul Tillich at Union Theological Seminary in New York City. Although he did not make use of the designations "kingdom of evil" or "kingdom of sin," it is clear from publications such as his *Children of Light and Children of Darkness* that he recognized that evil was rooted societally in the world.[27] He proceeds from the biblical viewpoint that "the 'mystery' of 'original sin'...has the merit of being true to the facts of human existence."[28] Original sin is not an inertia of natural impulses that stands in opposition to the purer impulses of the spirit; rather, it is a perversion that exercises a universal reign over all persons even though humans do not sin by nature but in freedom. This "mystery" of original sin, which makes it impossible to expect redemption through the development of human power or freedom, will always be an intellectual insult for rationalists.

"The Christian doctrine of sin in its classical form offends both rationalists and moralists by maintaining the seemingly absurd position that man sins inevitably and by a fateful necessity but that he is nevertheless to be held responsible for actions which are prompted by an ineluctable fate."[29] Niebuhr does not reject this doctrine but rather, after a detailed critique of the Pelagian and Augustinian interpretations, comes to the conclusion that "we cannot...escape the ultimate paradox that the final exercise of freedom in the transcendent human spirit is its recognition of the false use of that freedom in action" (260). The majority of

---

27. Reinhold Niebuhr, *Children of Light and Children of Darkness* (New York: Charles Scribner's, 1945).

28. Reinhold Niebuhr, *Faith and History: A Comparison of Christian and Modern Views of History* (New York: Charles Scribner's, 1949), 122.

29. Reinhold Niebuhr, *The Nature and Destiny of Man: A Christian Interpretation,* vol. 1: *Human Nature* (New York: Charles Scribner's, 1953), 241; references that follow are to this volume.

Pelagians and many Augustinians did not take these paradoxes sufficiently into consideration, the former having emphasized too much the integrity of human freedom. For this reason they were unable to recognize that the discovery of human freedom brought along with it the discovery of human guilt. The representatives of the Augustinian tradition, on the other hand, were overly concerned to hold fast to the insight that human freedom was perverted by sin. They therefore almost entirely overlooked the fact that the discovery of this sinful characteristic must be attributed to human freedom. Niebuhr, in contrast, maintained that humans can recognize that they are not free only because they are free. Therefore one must emphasize along with classical theology human freedom and responsibility.

In viewing human sinfulness, however, one must not overlook that evil that is not to be traced back to the individual but to the collective behavior of humanity. Niebuhr wrote, therefore, of "collective egotism" in his treatment of the doctrine of sin. For Niebuhr it was important to distinguish between the egotism of the individual and the pride of the group because the claims of a collective or societal self far transcend those of the individual "I." "The group is more arrogant, hypocritical, self-centered and more ruthless in the pursuit of its ends than the individual. An inevitable moral tension between individual and group morality is therefore created" (208f.). Strains similar to Rauschenbusch are here detectable. According to Niebuhr, it is clear that the egotism of racial, national, and societal economic groups is the most constant in the national state because this exhibits a collective identity in the minds of individuals. Even here he is able once again to point to biblical example when he says that the prophetic religion of Israel stood from the very beginning in conflict with national self-deification.[30] Israel wanted to identify God and Israel with one another so that God would be the exclusive property of Israel. But only the prophetic faith, which rejected such nationalism, has a future. This faith allowed Augustine to withstand the collapse of the Roman empire without despair and to confront the charge that Christianity was responsible for its destruction with the assertion that its downfall was, to the contrary, the result of sinful pride. Niebuhr offers, therefore, an interpretation of history and society

---

30. For this and the following see 214f.

upon a biblical basis that especially stressed the societal dimension of evil.

One might expect that the thoughts of Rauschenbusch and Niebuhr would be echoed by those European theologians who were especially concerned with social questions, as for instance the Swiss Religious Socialists. Yet such a parallel or a mutual dependence of thought forms is difficult to demonstrate. Leonhard Ragaz (1868–1945) had indeed developed sympathies for American ideas, but not for the emphasis upon a societal dimension of evil but rather for the concepts of progress and brotherhood. He wrote, for example, of the League of Nations proposed by President Woodrow Wilson: "We remain with the choice between the destruction of the world and the League of Nations, yet the bow of peace of the League of Nations has appeared to us in the clouds as a promise that it is not the destruction of the world but its renewal which is coming."[31]

Ragaz's involvement in socialism was not prompted by the knowledge that the world is threatened by evil but stemmed rather from an intensive hope and certainty concerning the kingdom of God.[32] Ragaz saw in the appearance of socialism, social democracy, and, to a certain extent, also in communism, "a knocking of the living God in judgment and promise upon the gates of the world and especially of Christianity."[33] Important for him is not so much the dimension of evil, but rather that through its onslaught the "forgotten truth of the kingdom of God is being brought once again to remembrance." This salvation-optimism did not demand an extensive analysis of evil. Where such an analysis was carried out, as by Hermann Kutter, the result was a clearly optimistic perspective.

The interpretation of Kant by Hermann Kutter (1869–1931), *Am Anfang war die Tat* (In the Beginning Was the Deed), contained a chapter on "radical evil." Kutter's direction is immediately clear when we read: "But we of course know that all human suffering stems from denial. The sickness of humanity is relative,

31. Leonhard Ragaz, *Die Bedeutung Woodrow Wilsons für die Schweiz und für die Welt,* Schriften der Schweizerischen Vereinigung für den Völkerbund, no. 2 (Weinfelden, 1924), 18.

32. So also Arnold Pfeiffer, ed., *Religiöse Sozialisten* (Olten: Walter-Verlag, 1976), 152.

33. For this and the following quotation see Leonhard Ragaz, *Die Erneuerung der Schweiz* (Zürich, 1933), 191.

human life is absolute."[34] The absolute, God, or the good, is set over against the relative, the evil. Because evil is understood as being only relative, there is no life-threatening power that can actually harm us. This is made clear when Kutter explains further: "How then should we understand evil differently when not as a break with the absolute? What is the good within the good? The absolute. What is evil within evil? The opposite of the absolute. A powerless counterpart, an evil will which seeks, within the absolute—in which we always remain enclosed—to make its own self absolute." Seen from the perspective of the good, evil is simply powerless. It can oppose the good only in deluded self-overestimation. In another place Kutter even describes evil as nothing, "as the power, the nothing, which we must think, feel and desire, which has empowered our existence. We know that it is *nothing,* but we also know that it is nothing. We recognize it as our guilt, that we have loved something that is nothing, and as our weakness, that we have sought something within nothing. This nothing is the imprisoned reality of averted will, which we could also call unwill."[35]

With this statement one encounters not only a terminological but also a clearly substantial connection to Karl Barth, who also characterized evil as nothing, or nothingness. On the basis of this interpretation of evil, therefore, it is justified to describe Kutter as a father of dialectical theology.[36] In this connection, however, we are not so much interested in the genetic dependence between the Religious Socialists and dialectical theology as we are in the fact that the Religious Socialists placed the certainty of the victory of the kingdom of God so much in the center of their reflections that they no longer had a proper grasp of evil in its profound depth and in its societal context. When the analysis of the context is neglected, the danger arises that the proposed therapy will also overlook reality and will provide little remedy for solving the problem of evil. This is precisely the situation in which contemporary theology finds itself today.

---

34. Hermann Kutter, *Im Anfang war die Tat: Versuch einer Orientierung in der Philosophie Kants und den von ihr angeregten höchsten Fragen. Für die denkende Jugend* (Basel: Kober, 1924), 237; for the following quote see 238f.

35. Hermann Kutter, *Das Unmittelbare: Eine Menschheitsfrage* (Basel: Spittler, 1921), 82.

36. See in this regard Pfeiffer, *Religiöse Sozialisten,* 89.

Chapter 8

Evil in Contemporary Theological Discussion

The phenomenon of evil was first illumined in this book with the aid of the social sciences. After an examination of biblical foundations, important aspects of evil were then traced through the history of theology and dogma. At this point we intend to take up the contemporary theological discussion of evil. Once again, this examination must of necessity be selective because there are so many positions and aspects of the problem to consider that we can highlight only the most significant points of discussion.

The Enigmatic Shape of Nothingness • Barth

The most interesting, as well as perhaps the most confusing, proposal as to how to do justice to the phenomenon of evil came from Karl Barth (1886–1968) in his *Church Dogmatics*. He spoke there of nothingness as contradiction and opposition, as a "disruptive element," which comes into being as a foreign body under the providence of God. It is, however, of such a unique character that it "can never be considered or mentioned together in the same context as other objects of God's providence."[1] In the first part

---

1. Karl Barth, *Church Dogmatics* (hereafter CD), 3/3, trans. G. Bromiley and R. Ehrlich (Edinburgh: T. and T. Clark, 1960), 289. Additionally, Karl Barth also treats sin in a detailed fashion within the structure of the doctrine of reconciliation in CD 4/1 (1956). He also emphasizes that sin can be recognized only christologically in the mirror of Jesus Christ (p. 240). He understands sin as arrogance against God, as resistance against following the path that God has indicated and planned, and as a lie, in that humans seek to know better than God what the real truth is in the salvation process (pp. 142ff.). The lie is, according to Barth, self-destruction, for humans lie before God and deceive themselves and thus destroy themselves, bringing about death and misery. With these assertions

of his doctrine of creation Barth had already spoken of a shadow side of existence. The self-revelation of the creator, however, is not bound to this shadow side of existence as a sort of negative foil needed to hold himself up as positive.[2] It is God's yes to creation that first empowers the no that characterizes the realm of creation. There appears to have been something preexistent within the creation that neither belongs to its essence nor stands over against it as something entirely distinct from it, but rather finds its continued existence through God's yes to the creation. This nothingness (*das Nichtige*), or shadow side, is bound by Barth very closely to God's activity.

Similar to nothingness is the situation with human sin, through which the person "has covered his own creaturely being with shame."[3] The human being as sinner remains a creature of God. God's word, that is, the testimony of the Holy Scriptures, reveals the human being, however, to be "a betrayer of himself and a sinner against his creaturely existence." According to Barth, one cannot recognize the human being as human, or even as sinner, when one does not view humanity from the perspective of God's self-revelation. The recognition that the human person is a sinner depends directly upon "the recognition that he shares in divine grace" (*CD* 3/2:32). To the grace of God belongs the justice of God that is revealed and carried out in the word of God. One recognizes thereby that one is other than what one should be.

It is extremely difficult to reconcile nothingness with the grace of God. Indeed, the creation in its shadow side, in its negative aspect, stands very close to nothingness (*CD* 3/3:296f.). Yet nothingness is not part of creation, even when it can force itself into creation. Barth calls sin "the concrete form of nothingness because in sin it becomes man's own act, achievement and guilt" (*CD* 3/3:310). Barth follows thereby the biblical model, for despite the accountability of humans for their behavior, sin as an action is continually described in the Bible as a succumbing to a foreign power. Sin is, on the one hand, human action, but, on the other hand, it is a result of nothingness. Yet, according to Barth, noth-

---

Barth reveals his commitment to traditional teachings. Through their sinfulness humans not only alienate themselves from God and other people but also create evil for themselves and for others in a destructive sense.

2. Karl Barth, *CD* 3/1 (1958), 372f.

3. For this and the following quotation see Barth, *CD* 3/2 (1960), 27, 26.

ingness does not exhaust itself in sin, for then it would simply be a part of creation.

What is then this nothingness? According to Barth, one cannot say of nothingness that it "is," like one might say, for example, that God or a created being "is."[4] Yet it would be playing down the significance of this nothingness if one thus concluded that nothingness is simply nothing. Rather, God takes account of it, is occupied with it, struggles against it, bears it, and overcomes it. It is not simply identical with that which does not exist, and it is also not the counterpart to God, nor is it a created being, but it is rather the *other* "from which God separates himself and in the face of which He asserts Himself and exerts His positive will." Nothingness, according to Barth, has no existence or recognizability except as the object of God's activity. This means that God's affirmation implies a no toward that to which he does not say yes, that is, to nothingness. God is Lord both on the right hand and on the left. Precisely because he is also Lord of the left, "he is the basis and Lord of nothingness too." Nothingness is not merely an accident, an oversight of God, but rather under his no it is the object of his wrath and judgment. "Nothingness 'is,' therefore, in its connexion with the activity of God. It 'is' because and as and so long as God is against it" (*CD* 3/3:353). A lively debate has been spawned over this statement about the being of nothingness, for it is incomprehensible to our "common logic," and it appears to such common logic that Barth comes very close to declaring God to be the cause of nothingness.[5]

Karl Barth, as we have seen, declined to ascribe to nothingness a self-sufficient existence independent from God. He also denied, however, that one could derive nothingness from the activity of God alone, in which God has the role of one who foreknows and permits. Finally, nothingness does not simply represent a deficiency of good or perfection because it is not thereby ascribed a ground of being and is thus not an active power. But how can one then still rule out that nothingness comes from God himself? If nothingness corresponds with the divine nonwilling, then the divine nonwilling is, as it were, the archetype for nothingness.

---

4. For this and the following see *CD* 3/3:349ff., quotations, 351.

5. Regarding this assessment and for references to further literature see Wilfried Härle, *Sein und Gnade: Die Ontologie in Karl Barths Kirchlicher Dogmatik* (Berlin: Walter de Gruyter, 1974), especially his chapter entitled "Das Nichtige," 227–69.

Nothingness would then have its final parallel in God, namely, in God's negative will.[6] Despite all the attempts at interpretation one must agree with Barth that we have to do here with the "ontic peculiarity" of nothingness.[7]

The gracious will of God is so strongly emphasized by Barth that that which strives and works against him cannot approach a genuine existence. Ultimately, everything will be received into the salvific scope of God. Barth argues always from the grace of God, from God's covenant with humanity. Evil is the opposite of that which God wills. Nevertheless, it becomes the object of his *opus alienum,* that is, the work that is not proper to him, that of anger and judgment. The negation of the grace of God is "chaos, the world which He did not choose or will, which He could not and did not create, but which, as He created the actual world, He passed over and set aside, marking and excluding it as the eternal past, the eternal yesterday. And this is evil in the Christian sense, namely, what is alien and adverse to grace, and therefore without it." Nothingness opposes the grace of God inasmuch as it offends God and threatens his creation and breaks into the creation as sin, evil, and death and produces chaos.

Barth emphasizes that one cannot deal with nothingness in a frivolous manner. It is such a threatening power that the conflict with it, its conquest, removal, and settlement, is primarily a matter for God. Nothingness, therefore, is above all God's own problem (*CD* 3/3:355). Humans are affected by nothingness only insofar as they fall willingly victim to it and thus become sinners. In this way suffering, want, and destruction come to humanity. Yet Barth is optimistic in face of the destructive power of nothingness because the "kingdom of nothingness" is already destroyed. "But its dominion, even though it was only a semblance of dominion, is now objectively defeated as such in Jesus Christ. What it still is in the world, it is in virtue of the blindness of our eyes and the cover which is still over us, obscuring the prospect of the kingdom of God already established as the only kingdom undisputed by evil" (*CD* 3/3:367).

When one reads these words, one must quite naturally ask to whom this blindness applies. These lines were published just five years after the close of World War II in which the satanic power,

---

6. See in this regard Härle, *Sein und Gnade,* 241.
7. For this and the following quotation see *CD* 3/3:353.

in its destructive and dehumanizing way, celebrated one victory after another. Barth can, of course, refer to the Gospels in which Jesus comments that Satan has fallen from heaven and has lost his position as our accuser at the right hand of God. Also, Martin Luther wrote in his hymn "A Mighty Fortress Is Our God" that the "old evil foe" can be subdued by "one little word." But, nevertheless, both the Gospel writers and Luther took this nothingness, this propagator of chaos, with utmost seriousness. Even Barth, however, wishes to remain a biblical realist. Thus in connection with nothingness he also spoke of demons.

In his treatment of demons Barth proceeds in a way similar to his classification of nothingness, for one dare not understand demons as the opposite of angels (*CD* 3/3:519f.). Just as heaven and hell have nothing in common, Barth instructs us that we cannot speak in the same breath of God and the devil, or of angels and demons. "The demons are the opponents of the heavenly ambassadors of God, as the latter are the champions of the kingdom of heaven and therefore the kingdom of God on earth. Angels and demons are related as creation and chaos, as the free grace of God and nothingness, as good and evil, as life and death, as the light of revelation and the darkness which will not receive it, as redemption and perdition, as *kerygma* and myth" (*CD* 3/3:520). Barth does not want to introduce a dualism here, but wishes rather to make clear that one must speak of demons in an entirely different way than of angels. The origin and form of the devil and demons are nothingness, whereby Barth once more makes reference to the left hand of God through which they receive their "improper" existence (*CD* 3/3:522f.). They are ungodly and against God, and because God did not create them, they are also not creaturely. They are not other than nothingness, but rather have their origin in nothingness. Because of the death and resurrection of Jesus and his elevation to the right hand of God, nothingness and demons "have nothing to declare." Therefore we are able to celebrate with Christ "our liberation from demons" (*CD* 3/3:530).

Karl Barth demonstrates clearly and in an impressive way the different quality of the antigodly powers of destruction. He does not limit evil to the human realm, but rather sees the metaphysical realm included in the battle against the God-opposing powers. The greatest problem with Barth's position occurs, however, in his many attempts to demonstrate that the God-opposing powers do not originate in God's creation. Though he declares, in agreement with the Gospel of John, that the devil *is* from the beginning and is the father of lies (*CD* 3/3:531), he must pass over the passage in the same Gospel that says that the devil is the ruler of this world (John 14:30). In Barth the God-opposing powers are seen so much within the context of the gracious and redemptive activity of God that they are nearly overwhelmed by this activity. He does not, however, do justice thereby to the phenomena of the negative and perverse within our world. Evil is not an accompanying apparition of the salvific activity of God, but rather a power that, from our human perspective, leaves open the question of who will prevail in the end.

Estrangement and Self-Destruction • Tillich

Paul Tillich (1886–1965) takes up the biblical heritage in his understanding of evil, but does not, however, shy away from contradicting certain aspects of the development of doctrine. He begins by recognizing that "the symbol of 'the Fall' is a decisive part of the Christian tradition,"[8] whereby a symbol is understood as something that participates in the reality of that which it represents (*ST* 1:239). Although this symbol is usually bound to a specific biblical story, its meaning goes beyond Adam's fall and has universal, anthropological significance. We find here a symbol that has to do with the entire human situation, for it expresses the transition from essence to existence. This is a matter of fact and not some derived dialectical step. Tillich thus seeks to separate himself not only from idealism, which points toward an ideal through which human freedom can be achieved, but also from naturalism, which takes existence for granted and denies its negativity (*ST* 2:29f.).

Before the fall—if one can even make use of such a temporal expression—humanity was in a condition of dreamlike innocence. The possibility of a fall is grounded in the fact that humanity alone possessed finite freedom. Humans can deny their essential nature and destroy their own humanity. Nevertheless, the freedom of human beings is not absolute, for it can come to fruition only within the context of universal destiny. Although this "event" con-

---

8. Paul Tillich, *Systematic Theology* (hereafter *ST*), 3 vols. (Chicago: Univ. of Chicago Press, 1951–63), 2:29.

cerns only the fall of a human being, it has cosmic significance.[9] Freedom awoke within humanity and chose not to preserve the dreamlike innocence but to seek self-actualization. The transition from essence to existence bears both a moral and tragic character. It is not itself an event within space and time, but rather has transhistorical significance for all events that take place within space and time.[10] According to Tillich, there is no state before the fall from which one could begin. "The actual state is that existence in which man finds himself along with the whole universe, and there is no time in which this was otherwise." Tillich finds it "absurd" to speak of a moment in time in which humanity and nature were transformed from good to evil. Thus Tillich maintains that nature is included in the fall because one cannot separate human beings from nature, for "man reaches into nature, as nature reaches into man. They participate in each other and cannot be separated from each other" (*ST* 2:43). If the intimate connection between time and fall is problematic for Tillich, it is just as problematic when one, with Tillich, correlates too closely the concepts of creation and fall.

Reinhold Niebuhr charged that Tillich's view of creation and fall as coinciding was an ontological speculation that portrayed the fall as unavoidable. Tillich countered that the unavoidability of the fall is indeed derived "from a realistic observation of man, his heart, and his history."[11] Later he expanded upon his statement to the effect that "creation and the Fall coincide in so far as there is no point in time and space in which created goodness was actualized and had existence" (*ST* 2:44). Actualized creation and estranged existence are essentially identical for Tillich. Also, when he argues that existence cannot be derived from essence, one must at least inquire to what extent God is the author of this estranged existence. At this point Tillich's logic is not clear. He wishes to explain the origin of estranged existence instead of allowing it to remain a mystery as most theologians do. Tillich calls the state of existence one of estrangement. "Man is estranged from the ground of his being, from other beings, and from himself. The transition from essence to existence results in personal guilt and universal tragedy" (*ST* 2:44f.). Tillich thus appears to prefer the word "es-

---

9. See Carl J. Armbruster, *The Vision of Paul Tillich* (New York: Sheed and Ward, 1967), 171.

10. See *ST* 2:40f. for this and the following quotation.

11. Paul Tillich, "Reply to Interpretation and Criticism," in *The Theology of Paul Tillich,* ed. Charles W. Kegley, rev. ed. (New York: Pilgrim Press, 1982), 388.

trangement" to the concept of "sin" because estrangement shows to what humanity actually belongs—to God, to the own self, and to the world. Sin is therefore viewed from the vantage point of estrangement.

Tillich next characterizes estrangement as unbelief—a definition of sin that is also to be found in article 2 of the Lutheran Augsburg Confession. Interesting here is that Tillich takes over from article 2 "without faith [_Unglaube_]" and "with concupiscence," but passes silently over the phrase "without fear of God" and in its place introduces the concept of hubris or "pride" (_ST_ 2:47). Because he always speaks of the ground of being instead of God, he is probably uncomfortable with the phrase "without fear of God." Along with unbelief, that is, the lack of trust in God, Tillich lists hubris, which he interprets as the temptation of humans to make themselves existentially the center of their own selves and the world instead of having their center in God. Finally, he speaks of concupiscence, which he characterizes as the unbounded striving after knowledge, sex, and power.

Tillich distinguishes between original or hereditary sin and the subsequent "actual" sins. He rejects the view that through Adam's fall the entire human race has been corrupted so that we all live in estrangement and no one can escape sin.[12] He calls the supposed connection between the destiny of humanity and an entirely free act of Adam illogical and "absurd" because through a human being, Adam, freedom is imputed apart from destiny. One must view Adam instead as the essential human and as the one who symbolizes the transition from essence to existence. Original or hereditary sin is neither original nor hereditary, but is the universal destiny of estrangement that applies to every person: "Sin is a universal fact before it becomes an individual act." It is questionable, however, whether the same is meant here as what Augustine expressed when he spoke of humanity as a _massa perditionis,_ or depraved mass, a description with which Tillich agrees. Sin as a universal fact need not affect the individual in the way expressed by the concept of original sin. That gold is a valuable metal, for example, can also lay claim to being a universal fact. Yet this need not affect me as an individual when I neither purchase nor possess any object that is made from gold. Original sin as a universal fact, on the other hand, is understood as something hereditary that we cannot elude.

---

12. For the following see _ST_ 2:55f., quotation, 2:56.

According to Tillich, humans find themselves, along with their world, in a context of existential estrangement, unbelief, hubris, and concupiscence. "Each expression of the estranged state contradicts man's essential being, his potency for goodness. It contradicts the created structure of himself and his world and their interdependence. And self-contradiction drives toward self-destruction" (*ST* 2:59f.). Sin becomes "evil," as Tillich terms it, through its self-destructive consequences. Evil is the consequence of the state of sin and estrangement so that the doctrine of evil is derived from the doctrine of sin (*ST* 2:61). Through the state of estrangement humans contradict their essential self and destroy the structure of their being. This destruction results, then, in evil, in the structures of destruction. Because the individual exists within the polarity of freedom and destiny as well as of dynamic and form and individualization and participation, these structures are destroyed by estrangement.[13] Through hubris freedom is no longer related to destiny but to an indeterminate number of contingent objects. Thus freedom becomes caprice, and destiny degenerates into mechanical necessity. In a similar way the polarity of dynamic and form is destroyed so that dynamic without form becomes a formless search for self-transcendence, whereas form without dynamic is transformed into an oppressive, external law.

Individualization without participation becomes isolation in which humans become turned in upon themselves. We encounter the most isolated and lonely individuals in Western industrial society and encounter at the same time the loss of individuality that is becoming an increasingly frequent phenomenon in this society. Tillich summarizes his position in the following way: "Estranged from the ultimate power of being, man is determined by his finitude. He is given over to his natural fate. He came from nothing, and he returns to nothing. He is under the domination of death and is driven by the anxiety of having to die. This, in fact, is the first answer to the question about the relation of sin and death" (*ST* 2:66). Humans are left in this world with the inevitability of death and the angst of not-being, which leads to the fear of death. The angst for not-being is present in all finite creatures. Human beings, therefore, have wandered from dreamlike innocence into alienation from God and estrangement from their own existence and are increasingly threatened with self-destruction. Tillich is in

---

13. For this and the following see *ST* 2:62–66.

agreement with Martin Luther's assessment of the bondage of the will when this attests to the human inability to break out of the state of estrangement. "In spite of the power of his infinite freedom,...[man] is unable to achieve the reunion with God" (*ST* 2:79). Only God, who in Jesus Christ relinquishes essence for existence and overcomes the latter, can lead human beings back to God's own self and to true humanness.

Tillich paints a picture of a humanity that has failed itself and God and is thus caught in the clutches of its own failure so that it is choked by the noose that it has thrown around its own neck. Evil is not rooted in God nor in any antigod but alone in humanity itself, which has misused and continues to misuse its freedom. Even when Tillich frequently speaks of the demonic, he does not thereby indicate any antigodly power external to the structures of existence. According to Tillich, the symbol of the demonic represents "antidivine forces in individual and social life" (*ST* 3:102). Tillich can speak of the demonic self-elevation of one nation over others or the demonic persecution of Christians. Powers, however, that strive against God and, so to speak, seek to force his abdication are not thereby mentioned. The demonic remains limited to the level of that which is existence bound. In Tillich's thought evil, and whatever stands behind it, is a part of human existence that includes nature within its context. It is no longer this power that always only denies, but ultimately humans themselves who in their power or powerlessness deny themselves and their existence.

The Self-Centeredness of Humanity • Pannenberg

Already in his brief anthropology, *What Is Man?* Pannenberg (1928–) writes: "Where the ego falls in contrast with openness to the world—which happens, for example, through the greed that is enslaved to the things of the world—then the ego comes to be closed off toward God and thereby toward its own human destiny. This state of being closed up within itself is the essence of sin."[14] In his comprehensive and definitive *Anthropology in Theological Perspective,* Pannenberg takes up a concept from Helmuth Pless-

---

14. Wolfhart Pannenberg, *What Is Man? Contemporary Anthropology in Theological Perspective,* trans. Duane Priebe (Philadelphia: Fortress Press, 1970), 68.

ner and speaks of the exocentricity of human beings in contrast to a centered position with its dependence upon a here and now.[15] By use of the term "exocentricity" Pannenberg points to the fact that for human beings the center of their expressions of life lies not only in themselves but at the same time outside of themselves. This means that the human being displays a typical openness toward the world and toward God. In humans themselves there exists a tension between a centered position and an exocentricity that leads to a breach in the relationship of humans with their own selves, to an inner conflict (80f.). While normally the ego, which seeks its identity within itself, stands in tension with an exocentric self-transcendence, that is, with the search of the self outside of its own self, it sets itself against this external relationship so that everything becomes a means to the self-assertion of the ego (85). This leads to a distorted ego-constitution that Pannenberg equates with sin. Thus it is no surprise that Pannenberg affirms the Augustinian interpretation of human sinfulness as concupiscence (90f.).

Sinful desire, which arises from the human relationship to the world, can, according to Pannenberg, be designated by the Augustinian concept *superbia,* or pride, the false self-glorification and egocentricity of humanity that produces a turning away from God and a turning toward one's own self (93f.). Pannenberg sees this reflected in the actual life experience of human beings. The distortion of human behavior does not begin with a conscious turning away from God, but rather the estrangement from God takes place in various and often barely noticeable ways as distortions of our relationship to the world and to our own selves. Now, however, the centrality that culminates in ego-centeredness has become an existential structural moment of humanity. We each experience our own selves as the center of our individual world.[16] Pannenberg questions, then, how one can avoid viewing human nature as such as sinful. If one accepts the Augustinian analysis of sin and understands it as unrestrained love of self and concupiscence, then the natural life of human beings is sinful. Yet Pannenberg cautions that one must not characterize human nature in its essence as sinful, but rather only in the sense of the conditions of its existence by means of which human nature alters its natural living conditions. On the

---

15. See Wolfhart Pannenberg, *Anthropology in Theological Perspective,* trans. M. O'Connell (Philadelphia: Westminster, 1985), 37.

16. For this and the following see Pannenberg, *Anthropology,* 105–10.

one hand, sin is willed by human beings, yet, on the other hand, it is rooted within the natural conditions of human existence. This unity of the two aspects, as Pannenberg points out, has not always been recognized by theology.

Pannenberg raises the additional question of why one speaks of sin only in regard to human beings if humanity shares an ego-centeredness with other life-forms that are also guided in their behavior by an ego-center. For Pannenberg the answer is to be found in the fact that only in the case of humans is their own identity made a central theme for their behavior. Humans are aware of their own self and find this self-awareness to be both a gift and a challenge. While animals live in an environment without feeling a tension between this environment and their ego, humans remain open to the world around them and exist in a relationship of tension with it. Thus arises the possibility and actuality of a distortion between ego-centricity and exocentricity. The result is the responsibility of humans for their sinful behavior, for sin does not come upon them as an alien force to which they are helplessly handed over. It is much more the case that the concept of sin is inseparably bound with the ideas of accountability and guilt. Responsibility, however, can be taken up only when humans accept their actions as their own and assume liability for them. Thus Pannenberg can say in regard to human sinfulness that humans are of such a character that they

> can find pleasure in what is objectively evil (not only in itself but even for themselves). The observation that such is the case need not stir others to moral outrage. Such a reaction has its place, of course, especially when the structures of social life are being endangered. But those who realize that a failure to achieve the good is always a failure of the self as well will feel sadness more than anything else. In addition, there is little they can do to bring about a change. Good advice is of little avail in such cases, since deception with regard to the good is not simply an intellectual matter. The bondage of the will calls, therefore, for a liberation and, in the radical case, for a redemption that will establish the will's identity anew. (118f.)

Pannenberg speaks of a bondage of the will that, on the one hand, rules out the possibility that humans can once again find their own way back to the original balance of tension between exocentricity and ego-determination, and, on the other hand, encompasses the recognition that human beings follow willingly the path of evil. The bondage of the will, according to Pannenberg, has left intact the ability to choose, but it has reduced the scope of this ability and points toward a structure of motivation that precedes the decisions and actions of the individual and that is the cause of the failure of the human self. This structure, which always restricts human beings in that they are never able to reach high and wide enough, is called by Pannenberg original sin. For Pannenberg it is clear that human beings do not become sinners first through their actions and the imitation of the evil actions of others but that they are already sinners before they commit a single action of their own. This absoluteness of original sin leaves no place for human uprightness.

While Pannenberg accepts the traditional doctrine of original sin, he does not view Adam as the historical forebear of humanity through whom original sin is passed on to us. Rather, Adam is to be seen in Judaic and Pauline tradition as "the prototype of all human beings, as their embodiment, as the Human Being pure and simple. In every individual, Adam's journey from sin to death is repeated as in a copy" (122). Pannenberg notes, however, that the doctrine of original sin came under increasing disrepute within Protestantism and that in its place one spoke of a kingdom of sin or evil (125). Concerning this criticism from Pannenberg it should be noted that behind the concept of a kingdom of sin or evil lay a protest against an excessive individualization of the idea of original sin. This is especially evident in the thought of Walter Rauschenbusch.

For Pannenberg it is important to demonstrate the empirical universality of sin. He contends that the universality of sin as such is just as much illumined in light of the revelation of human destiny through the law as it is through the crucified and resurrected Christ.[17] What is shown here in regard to content can likewise be empirically demonstrated, even if not specifically under the name sin. A hint in this direction is seen by Pannenberg in the universality of death. Even the content of sin comes to light in the universality of concupiscence as a distinguishing feature of human behavior. One no longer needs the historical personage of Adam because the universality of sin can be empirically demonstrated. Already Augustine, however, following Paul, recognized that concupiscence and its consequences were empirically discernible as

---

17. For this and the following see Pannenberg, *Anthropology,* 138–42.

universal actualities. How then does Pannenberg formulate this empirical proof today? First, he follows Tillich, who maintained that sin led to the self-destruction of human beings. In this way Tillich had sought to demonstrate that the attempt of humans to ground their self-centered existence in their own selves, by which means they make themselves the center of their own world, produces precisely the opposite effect leading to the loss of their own self and to the failure of self-integration. He saw sickness, for example, as the dissolution of self-integration. There exists, therefore, a connection between sin and death in the collapse of the self-integration that is indispensable for the fulfillment of human life.

Regarding the empirical proof of the universality of sin Pannenberg argues from the phenomenon of aggression.[18] He points to angst as motif for aggressive behavior in which angst participates in the experience of the ego in the process of the development of the self. As a result of angst the ego can be thrown back upon itself, so that it clings to its own finiteness and loses itself. This clinging and losing express themselves in the form of aggression or depression. In both cases a failure of willpower occurs as well as a breakdown in the formation and preservation of an independent and genuine ego. While angst is the basic form in which sin manifests itself in human self-consciousness, "(destructive) aggression ... [as well as] flight [and] depression are also to be seen as expressions of human sinfulness." Pannenberg concludes his considerations by commenting that "if we understand the doctrine of sin as functioning in the context of a still unfinished process which has human identity as its goal, we will not misinterpret this doctrine as a product of aggression turned inward. The consciousness of the failure of the self—that is, of sin—is a necessary phase in the process whereby human beings are liberated to become themselves" (152).

Sin, therefore, is seen to have a positive side. Despite the immense discussion with tradition, especially with Augustine, Pannenberg cannot completely avoid an idealistic understanding of sin. It is thus no surprise that the concept of the kingdom of evil

---

18. For the following see Pannenberg, *Anthropology,* 142–51. The English version of the following quotation, which is found on p. 150, translates the German phrase "sowohl die (destruktive) Aggression als auch Flucht und Depression" inaccurately and somewhat amusingly as "both (destructive) aggression and flight depression."

is, as it were, passed over. Sin and its evil consequences always revolve around the ego in the thought of Pannenberg. A societal component of evil is hardly mentioned. One must certainly agree with Pannenberg that sin is self-denial before the reality of God and is also a denial of the potential openness of human beings to the world and to God. Yet this narrowing of the concepts of sin and evil must be elucidated with much more clarity in regard to its consequences for human society and for the entire creation. At this point liberation theology has chosen to follow an entirely different path that too, however, unless it is understood as a corrective, produces a one-sided view.

Sinful Social Structures • Liberation Theology

In liberation theology, and we will treat here specifically Latin American liberation theology, sin and evil are only implicit themes. A similar approach is to be found in feminist liberation theology and African-American liberation theology. An exception to this trend is Juan Luis Segundo. The last volume of his five-volume work, *A Theology for Artisans of a New Humanity*, bears the title *Evolution and Guilt*. Yet in Segundo one can find only an implicit connection to liberation theology. He emphasizes, for example, that a value, when it really shall be such, must be available in abundance and spread throughout a population or society.[19] When human values are not justly distributed within a specific country, the dominant class declares its own values as normative. They do not intend to share these norms with others, but rather quite the opposite. They elevate their own values to the status of norms because they already possess them as well as the means to control the mechanisms of justice. What is right and wrong, good and evil, however, has a chance of being implemented only when a broad agreement exists as to what these concepts mean.

When Segundo describes sin from the biblical perspective, he primarily relies upon the Gospel of John. There we learn that Jesus has come in order to overcome and take away the sin of the world (John 1:29).[20] This sin is not a free act but rather a condition of bondage from which Christ liberates. Liberation is therefore not a

---

19. See Juan Luis Segundo, *A Theology for Artisans of a New Humanity,* vol. 5: *Evolution and Guilt,* trans. John Drury (Maryknoll, N.Y.: Orbis, 1974), 40.

20. For the following see Segundo, *A Theology,* 5:52, 54.

theory but a matter of praxis. But why then does the entire god-less world stand under the power of evil (1 John 5:19)? From whence does this structural deficiency or this determinism come that turns the world into an antigodly entity? By way of answer to this question Segundo refers to a social mechanism that is essentially conservative. From the comment in 1 John 4:5, "They are from the world; therefore what they say is from the world, and the world listens to them," Segundo deduces that the powers that rule the world, in a maliciously circular argument, reject all that is new. A conservative ideology suppresses all other possible interpretations through a circular argumentation by means of which everything is already decided and predetermined.

In Segundo's description we discover, although he does not say so explicitly, a portrayal of Latin American societal reality as it is characterized by most liberation theologians. Thus Gustavo Gutiérrez writes: "But in the liberation approach sin is not considered as an individual, private, or merely interior reality—asserted just enough to necessitate a 'spiritual' redemption which does not challenge the order in which we live. Sin is regarded as a social, historical fact, the absence of brotherhood and love in relationships among men, the breach of friendship with God and with other men, and, therefore, an interior, personal fracture. When it is considered in this way, the collective dimensions of sin are rediscovered."[21] Sin, according to Gutiérrez, is clearly to be seen in structures of oppression, in the exploitation of one person by another, and in the conquest and enslavement of nations, races, and social classes. Sin is a fundamental alienation and the root of all injustice and exploitation. Yet one does not encounter sin directly as such but only in concrete examples of alienation. It is impossible, however, to recognize the concrete manifestations of sin without understanding how they came about.

Sin necessitates a radical liberation, including political liberation. By participating in the historical process of liberation one can demonstrate the fundamental alienation that is present in each individual case. This radical liberation, however, is not something that we ourselves earn, but it is rather a gift brought to us by Christ. Through his death and resurrection he has liberated human beings from sin and all its consequences as well as from all op-

---

21. Gustavo Gutiérrez, *A Theology of Liberation,* trans. and ed. Caridad Inda and John Eagleson (Maryknoll, N.Y.: Orbis, 1973), 175.

pression and injustice. This liberation, which Christ has made possible through his own destiny, is realized through the progress and growth of the kingdom of God. "The growth of the Kingdom is a process which occurs historically *in* liberation" (177). Although it is a liberating event, the growth of the kingdom of God cannot be equated with its coming; neither is it our entire redemption. Rather, it is a historical realization of the kingdom and thus announces its consummation.

Sin, as a rupture of the friendship with God and other persons, is in the biblical view, according to Gutiérrez, the ultimate cause of the poverty, injustice, and oppression in which humans live.[22] By designating sin as the ultimate cause of these conditions, Gutiérrez in no way intends to bring into question the structural grounds and objective determinants that have led to these conditions. He wishes to point out, however, that these things have not come about coincidentally. Behind the unjust structures a personal or collective will or force bears responsibility for the present situation, a will or force that rejects God and neighbor. Thus a societal transformation, regardless how radical, cannot automatically achieve the suppression of everything evil. How then can this sinful "will" be stopped that expresses itself in sinful or evil constellations of poverty, injustice, and oppression? To begin with Gutiérrez points to the death and resurrection of Jesus Christ as facilitating the kingdom of God and the overcoming of sin, for God has, through God's own self, taken away sin and announced the beginning of a new era.

For Gutiérrez, however, the church is also important. Because evil has been sanctioned by society, its removal can only be achieved societally. Thus he welcomes the fact that the church has now declared its solidarity with the Latin American situation rather than elevating itself above this situation. The church is attempting to accept responsibility for the injustice that it has supported through its solidarity with the establishment and its silence about the evil that resulted from this arrangement (108). Because God himself in the fullness of time sent Christ into the world to liberate all people from bondage to which they had been subjected by sin, it is now necessary to point to sinful injustice and oppression and to declare that the rejection of peace, which is furthered by social, political, economic, and cultural inequality, is an offense

---

22. For this and the following see Gutiérrez, *A Theology*, 35.

against God. The church in Latin America must make its presence felt in a new way and must prophetically label as sin the serious injustices that are overall present in that context. Through the denunciation of social injustice the church will at the same time make known its intention to distance itself from the existing structures of injustice (117f.).

The church must separate itself from the state so that it can free itself from this compromising relationship and be able to fulfill its own mission and to rely upon the strength of its Lord rather than upon earthly power. The prophetic task of the church is at the same time constructive and critical. The church must point to elements within the process of liberation that lead to greater humanness and justice, while at the same time rejecting those elements that continue to produce injustice and oppression. Liberation theology, therefore, recognizes the fundamental human sinfulness that expresses itself in unjust structures. It also realizes that a fundamental transformation is possible only because God has taken up the forgiving and transforming initiative in Jesus Christ. It remains, however, unclear how one should relate the activity of establishing a just society to the values of the kingdom of God. Will the kingdom of God be confused here with revolution? Gutiérrez rejects this suggestion when it arises accusingly from the context of a comfortable, establishment Christianity. Yet he has himself no simple answer and admits that the Latin American church does not speak with a single voice on the process of liberation.[23]

One must concede the possibility that genuine societal change does not originate with the church but is borne by other forces. One must also admit that liberation, revolution, and the advance of the kingdom of God are often viewed as parallel developments. However, when it is possible to live a Christian existence in a world that is characterized and threatened by evil, then this existence must not be allowed to atrophy into a matter of private religiosity but must shine forth in the world and in society. To the extent that liberation theology has recognized the societal roots and structure of evil and has responded with an active call for liberation from these structures, it has freed us from the privatization of evil and recovered salvation for society.

---

23. For this and the following see Gutiérrez, *A Theology,* 133ff.

Evil as Unavoidable Phenomenon • Process Theology

North American process theology, which is founded principally upon the work of the British-American mathematician and philosopher Alfred North Whitehead (1861–1947) and the American philosopher Charles Hartshorne and is especially propagated by the Center for Process Studies in Claremont, California, deals with the question of evil primarily with a view toward theodicy. The question raised here is how evil fits into a universe that is governed by a good God.

David Ray Griffin, at the very beginning of his considerations in *God, Power, and Evil: A Process Theodicy,* presents the following "formal statement of the problem of evil":

1. God is a perfect reality. (Definition)

2. A perfect reality is an omnipotent being. (By definition)

3. An omnipotent being could unilaterally bring about an actual world without any genuine evil. (By definition)

4. A perfect reality is a morally perfect being. (By definition)

5. A morally perfect being would want to bring about an actual world without any genuine evil. (By definition)

6. If there is genuine evil in the world, then there is no God. (Logical conclusion from 1 through 5)

7. There is genuine evil in the world. (Factual statement)

8. Therefore, there is no God. (Logical conclusion from 6 and 7)[24]

Griffin, of course, is not willing to accept the conclusion of his theses that there is no God if genuine evil is found to exist in the world. For him the problem appears to be rooted in our traditional conception of God. In our Western conception one has usually, according to Griffin, understood God as either controlling or being able to control every detail of the events of our world (17). This appeared to belong to the nature of God because he could not be God if he did not possess this power. The logical conclusion of this conception was that nothing happened in the world unless God either caused it or at least permitted it, despite the fact

---

24. David Ray Griffin, *God, Power, and Evil: A Process Theodicy* (Philadelphia: Westminster, 1976), 9.

that he had the power to prevent it. If God is so almighty that he determines every occurrence, then he is responsible for everything evil.[25] A God, however, who compels and always enforces his will is a despotic God, such as is prevalent in Judaism, Christianity, and Islam, and also gives rise to despotic human beings. This criticism of the conception of God was already brought into sharp focus by Whitehead. According to Griffin, however, this traditional view of God does not correspond to the biblical testimony of the Judeo-Christian tradition.

The biblical testimony suggests the rejection of either thesis 2 ("A perfect reality is an omnipotent being") or thesis 3 ("An omnipotent being could unilaterally bring about an actual world without any genuine evil").[26] Thus for Griffin process theology and its view of evil do not contradict the biblical tradition. In Griffin's view, God is not able to fully control every occurrence in the world (275). The reason for this is not to be found in God's weakness or imperfection, but rather in the view of God that is distinctive of process theology. Process theology maintains that "God's power is persuasive, not controlling" (276). Thus in an important sense God is responsible for the evil in the world, but, in Griffin's view, he cannot be indicted or held accountable for evil. The potential for genuine evil is grounded in the metaphysical, that is, necessary, features of the world. The willing or permitting of evil is not determined by the divine will but rests ultimately upon the essential being of God and the world.

The world, as process theology in the tradition of Whitehead has claimed, is not created out of nothing, but creation means rather "the creation of order out of chaos" (279). There is thus a real world that stands over against God and upon which his purposes are brought to bear. God, however, does not possess a monopoly of power, for the actual world necessarily contains potent actualities through which a certain amount of self-determination and influence upon the future are effected. Thus God cannot fully control the becoming within each actuality because every actuality will always in part be determined by that which has preceded it as well as through its own inherent potency. Evil can, for instance, arise out of this potency without

---

25. See in this regard Dalton DeVere Baldwin, "A Whiteheadian Solution to the Problem of Evil" (Ph.D. diss., Claremont Graduate School, 1975), 314f., who takes up this thesis of Whitehead as his own.

26. Griffin, *God,* 53.

corresponding to divine intention. Genuine evil is described as disharmony, as when, for example, varying elements of an experience conflict with one another so that there is a feeling of a mutual destruction, or when bodily pain or mental evil such as sorrow, fear, or dislike is produced (282). This is intrinsic to the structure of reality. It is also argued in this connection that sometimes morally responsible freedom turns consciously from its goal and introduces genuine evil.[27]

If one asks why such an evil will exists, one is told that voluntary love without morally responsible freedom is not possible. The freedom to decide in a morally responsible manner must always contain an alternative, otherwise it is not genuine freedom. Thus the possibility of evil as a worse alternative is necessarily presupposed. One is reminded here of Augustine, who also maintained that evil was necessary as a contrast to good so that good could distinguish itself from it. In Augustine's thought, however, this is presented only as a possibility in order to make the existence of evil plausible. In process theology, on the other hand, the necessity of evil constitutes a fundamental assumption about the structure of reality. Behind this view lies Whitehead's dipolar conception of God, who both precedes and follows. God is "preceding" in his eternal aim and "following" in the power of his persuasion and in the process character of all genuine being. Whitehead "shows how evil arises without making God responsible for any evil which cannot be justified. Excess evil which cannot be justified results from the wrong use of responsible freedom."[28] Thus God is freed from the suspicion of being unjust. Also, in this view evil does not detract from the divinity of God. Yet how is the structure of evil itself to be viewed?

Although process theology seldom reflects on the structure of evil, Marjorie Hewitt Suchocki takes up this theme in her well-informed dissertation. She writes: "The world, in its freedom, transcends God, even as God in his freedom transcends the world. But in this transcendence the world becomes truly responsible for its good and its evil. The metaphysical structure within which good or evil relationships take place is one which must pronounce the individual occasion itself as good.... The relationships which must develop in the interrelated community of being are the arena of rel-

---

27. For this and the following see Baldwin, "Whiteheadian Solution," 317.
28. Baldwin, "Whiteheadian Solution," ii, in his summary of his work.

ative good and evil. But given this structure of interrelationships, no evil is ever final: the structure is ultimately redemptive."[29] This does not mean that evil is not real, but rather that it anticipates its transformation. Evil will be overcome either already before the end of time or at the very least in the eschaton. Through God's providence the power of evil is already broken. Hence evil stands under the influence of grace that extends itself into the whole world so that the world might be redeemed. "God is the future of the world in every fresh moment; as the future of the world he is sheerly grace."

One is here reminded of the triumph of grace in the theology of Karl Barth. Similar to Barth, the activity of evil is relatively faint, and it has lost its God-opposing and destructive dynamic. It is a part of the evolutionary process that finally ends within this process when all things find their completion in God. Is this optimism, however, justified? Evil continues within our world without any signs of weariness. In light of its persistent wickedness evil will not enter into any kind of pact with good and is not ready for any transformation. It is certainly correct that God is not an omnipotent despot who determines every minute detail. It is, however, the conviction of the biblical documents that God not only has compassion and steadfastly desires to move everything toward his goal but also judges and punishes evildoers. Despite the many correct perspectives of process theology one cannot escape the suspicion that it has been neatly outlined in theory on a drawing board but often overlooks the living reality of this world.

The Inclusiveness of Evil • Feminist Perspectives

We have already seen that liberation theology claims that those in power elevate their own values to the status of norms in order to

---

29. For this and the following quotation see Marjorie Hewitt Suchocki, "The Correlation between Good and Evil" (Ph.D. diss., Claremont Graduate School, 1974), 249f. In a revised version of her dissertation, *The End of Evil: Process Eschatology in Historical Context* (Albany: SUNY Press, 1988), esp. 154, she once again emphasizes that our finite existence reveals a fundamental ambiguity in which good and evil are intertwined with one another and that this ambiguity produces evil as well as redemption. Thus redemption as the triumph of good over evil is seen as a historical process. Evil as a destructive power, which is not only active in this process but also opposes it, is not, however, taken into account.

dominate others. From this vantage point, it is only a small step for women, in their struggle to attain equality with men, to question as well that which has, usually by men, been set as the standard for right or wrong. Valerie Saiving, in a landmark article in 1960, questioned whether the traditional norms of good and evil apply to everyone. She claimed:

> The temptations of woman *as woman* are not the same as the temptations of man *as man,* and the specifically feminine forms of sin—"feminine" not because they are confined to women or because women are incapable of sinning in other ways, but because they are outgrowths of the basic feminine character structure—have a quality which can never be encompassed by such terms as "pride" and "will-to-power." They are better suggested by such items as triviality, distractibility, and diffuseness; lack of an organizing center of focus; dependence on others for one's own self-definition; ... in short, underdevelopment or negation of the self.[30]

Judith Plaskow, in her doctoral dissertation, "Sex, Sin, and Grace: Women's Experience and the Theologies of Reinhold Niebuhr and Paul Tillich," examined this claim in detail. Having analyzed Reinhold Niebuhr's and Paul Tillich's doctrines of sin and grace, she concluded that "although the two men claimed to speak to and from universal human experience in formulating those theologies, in fact, ... neither of them addresses the situation of women in Western society."[31] For instance, when Tillich wants to demonstrate the actualization of estrangement, he uses examples of unbelief, hubris, and concupiscence, thereby translating "hubris" as "self-elevation." Yet these characteristics, according to Plaskow, are more likely to be associated with men than with women in Western society (see 236). Similarly, when Niebuhr talks about the religious dimension of sin, he defines it as man's rebellion against God, his effort to usurp the place of God. Again, Niebuhr fails to convey with this definition the nature of women's sin and actually turns it into virtue, because for women self-centeredness is not sin, but " *'women's sin' is precisely the failure to turn toward*

---

30. Valerie Saiving, "The Human Situation: A Feminine View" (1960), in *Womanspirit Rising: A Feminist Reader in Religion,* ed. Carol P. Christ and Judith Plaskow (New York: Harper, 1979), 37.

31. Judith Ellen Plaskow, "Sex, Sin, and Grace: Women's Experience and the Theologies of Reinhold Niebuhr and Paul Tillich" (Ph.D. diss., Yale University, 1975), 234.

the self" (238). The failure of women is to take responsibility for
their own self-actualization.

It is, however, not only the problem of sin that is seen from a
limiting male perspective. Behind this there looms a one-sided conception of God. Plaskow, therefore, raises the following questions:
"Are the images of God as male and as person inseparably related?
Does the image of God as male person necessarily involve a hierarchical model of the divine/human relation? Does a hierarchical
model require that sin be defined as pride, and grace as judgment
and obedience?" (268). A male image of God leads to a male image
of sin and of that which is evil and therefore excludes women
from that kind of experience. Plaskow finds another problem with
Niebuhr and Tillich, namely, that they speak of sin "in almost exclusively individual terms" (269). Yet women's sins, the way they
treat themselves, are a product of social experience. "Through
consciousness raising, women become aware of both the social
context of sin and their own collusion with it" (275). The behavior of women is imposed by society and up to recently has been
largely accepted by women and not challenged. Plaskow, however,
recognizes that her own experience as a woman comes from the
perspective of a white, Western, middle-class woman (281).

Plaskow is certainly correct that male theologians, such as Niebuhr and Tillich, reflect on evil from their own societal perspective.
In this way, their perspective is limited by their own makeup
and by the influence of society on them. Yet can one really call
"the failure to take responsibility for self-actualization" a "sin"
when such behavior has hardly been actively destructive of others?
The same, however, cannot be said of what has been characterized by Plaskow and others as "male pride."[32] Plaskow's claims
seem to border on a position that Patricia Wilson-Kastner asso-
ciates with that of radical feminism. According to her, "Radical
feminists have insisted that male and female humanism is indeed
radically different.... Women are fundamentally good, they insist,
though women are the victims of male oppression."[33] Yet before
we associate Plaskow with representatives of this position, we
should listen to her own admission that she argues from a white,
middle-class, female context.

---

32. This question is rightly posed by Daphne Hampson, *Theology and
Feminism* (Oxford: Basil Blackwell, 1990), 123.

33. Patricia Wilson-Kastner, *Faith, Feminism, and the Christ* (Philadelphia:
Fortress Press, 1983), 55.

Susan Thistlethwaite has observed that white feminist theology often finds process theology, and its ancestor in faith, Protestant liberalism, quite congenial. "Many aspects of process theology make sense to white, middle-class women."[34] While no black female theologian has so far chosen a process perspective for her work, white feminist theologians claim that "feminism and [the] process God have commonalities both in their respective critiques of the classical tradition and their basic presuppositions."[35] The traditional worldview is seen as inadequate by both. "The classical tradition's way of conceiving self, world, and God are clearly dualistically defined and hierarchically patterned." This worldview draws dichotomies such as mind–body, spirit–nature, God–evil, being–becoming, subject–object, and activity–passivity. In each of these sets, one is given priority over the other and considered to be more valuable. Feminists add to this also the male–female dualism and the association of male with being superior. Both feminism and process thought come together in striving for a holistic worldview emphasizing becoming instead of being and relatedness and interdependence instead of self-completeness and independence. They assign limited active and passive power to all subjects and the interdependence of all things. "No subject is considered to be absolutely dependent or independent" (209). God is no longer conceived of as absolutely superior to everything else. The same kind of power is being attributed to God and to creatures; "the difference between the two is merely quantitative" (214). Thereby the traditional connotations of power, those of domination and control, are avoided. But God is not simply a human fabrication. Because "God is unfathomable mystery, the vastness of God's glory and holiness and power is too great for the human mind to grasp" (231). Therefore, all our concepts of God are human creations, and we should seek the best constructions that are coherent and religiously viable for the honor of God and for promoting the welfare of creatures. In classical liberal fashion we find omitted here the fact that God disclosed God's self both to the Israelite community and ultimately to all of humanity in the human form of Jesus of Nazareth. If one acknowledges God's self-disclosure, the issue of

34. Susan Brooks Thistlethwaite, *Sex, Race, and God: Christian Feminism in Black and White* (New York: Crossroad, 1989), 87.

35. See Anna Case-Winters, *God's Power: Traditional Understandings and Contemporary Challenges* (Louisville: Westminster, 1990), 205, for this and the following quote.

reconceptualizing God may be more difficult than some feminist theologians and proponents of process theology have envisioned.

Rosemary Radford Ruether is one of the few feminist theologians who explicitly reflects on the phenomenon of evil and in so doing picks up the dichotomy of good and evil, albeit with some significant modifications. She claims that some feminists feel that this dichotomy should be rejected because it denotes the "evil" side as "female." Therefore, "sexism is the underlying social foundation of the good-evil ideology."[36] According to Ruether, feminism claims that a most basic expression of the human community, the relationship between men and women, has been distorted through all known history. It has been turned into an oppressive relationship that has victimized women and turned men into tyrants. The relationship between male and female has been transformed into a dualism of superiority and inferiority. Ruether claims that this is "fundamentally a male ideology and has served two purposes: the support for male identity as normative humanity and the justification of servile roles for women. However much women may be socialized into these myths of female inferiority and evil and are induced to collaborate with them, women are neither their originators nor their primary perpetuators" (165). This means that women were simply drawn into this without having been able to extricate themselves from their lot. Once sexism is recognized as wrong, evil, and sinful, it brings about the total collapse of the myth of female evil. "Once a breach in the wall of sexist ideology and deep realization of woman is made, the entire ideological and social superstructure built up over thousands of years of sexism and justification of sexism is open to question. Every aspect of male privilege loses its authority as natural and divine right and is re-evaluated as sin and evil" (173).

The fundamental problem with sexism, according to Ruether, lies in the fact that it is based upon a distorted relationality. There can be no I-Thou relationship where there is no authentic self that is allowed to stand over against and respond to another. The basic humanity of both men and women is fundamentally truncated when the one has no access to public power and skills whereas the other controls all power and resources. Consequently, the male regresses in those areas in which he depends on the woman to serve

36. Rosemary Radford Ruether, *Sexism and God-Talk: Toward a Feminist Theology* (Boston: Beacon, 1983), 160.

him, while the woman is helpless in the public realm to which she is denied access. Ruether realizes that sexism leads to "a disproportionate stigmatization of males as responsible for evil and the consequent exculpation of women. Sin becomes something that males alone have done. Women have only been victims."[37] While she concedes that no male as an individual is expected to carry the total burden of guilt for sexism, because both males and females have been shaped by a preexisting system of male privilege and female subordination, females are at present in a better position in regard to being accountable for evil. "Their opportunities to do evil have been generally limited to the subsystem relationships within this overall monopoly of power and privilege by the male ruling class." This means that women can be accomplices to evil just as much as men if given the opportunity. They can be "racist, classist, self-hating, manipulative toward dominant males, dominating toward children." This admission by Ruether is quite revealing. According to her own analysis, this would mean that at present the domination and exploitation of one class of people by another, primarily females by males, must certainly be termed as evil and sinful. Once true emancipation and interdependence between men and women has been achieved, both will exhibit the same capacity for evil. When we now return to Plaskow's analysis of the shortcomings of such male descriptions of evil as exhibited by Tillich and Niebuhr, we must affirm that her criticism is correct when understood in the present context of latent or overt sexism. Tillich and Niebuhr were not, or did not want to be, cognizant of the present situation. Yet their analysis is correct when we go beyond the present lopsided arrangement and consider that which is at the heart of every human being, the capacity for evil.

Rosemary Ruether correctly points out "that the Genesis 3 story of the Fall of Adam through Eve does not become a normative story of the origins of evil in the Hebrew Bible."[38] Because the liberation of Israel from Egyptian bondage and the covenant at Mount Sinai is the key to Israel's identity, "the greatest evil, therefore, is the deliberate choice to reject this emancipation from Egyptian bondage, to long to be back in the land of slavery and idolatry." As the story of the golden calf tells us, evil is first

---

37. Ruether, *Sexism*, 180, for this and the two following quotes.

38. For this and the following two quotes see Rosemary Radford Ruether, *Womanguides: Readings toward a Feminist Theology* (Boston: Beacon, 1985), 82.

equated with an apostasy from God whereby the Israelites reject their own liberation. According to Ruether, this suggests for feminist theology that "sin is a fear of freedom, a longing for the security of bondage." According to Ruether, sin is similar to what Martin Heidegger called "inauthentic existence," that is to say, not wanting to live for yourself but living like everybody else. While Christians are certainly called to live their lives in responsibility before God, guided by the liberating word of the gospel and not tied to the law, Ruether's interpretation does justice neither to the story of the golden calf nor to the immense perversity of evil. The story of the golden calf does not show just the perverse longing for the fleshpots of Egypt but also the introduction of gods of one's own making and the rejection of the one living God. Susanne Heine rightly cautions: "With the prohibition against images the biblical tradition also rejects all attempts to gain control of God as an 'object' that can be manipulated and to claim him for all possible interests."[39] While Ruether's interpretation of evil is certainly a needed perspective coming from feminist theology, it dare not obliterate the fact that God is a God neither of feminism nor of male domination, but one who calls to judgment both feminists and male chauvinists if they forsake loyalty to God in the pursuit of a mistaken loyalty to themselves.

We could continue our consideration of contemporary approaches to the problem of evil, adducing many more representative positions. Pierre Teilhard de Chardin (1881–1955), for example, speaks in a fashion similar to process theology of the various trials and errors through which the process of evolution advances unstoppably toward its fulfillment in Christ. For Teilhard evil shows itself in evolutionary blind alleys, as in the phenomena of death and suffering, from which the process of evolution breaks off in order to develop further in other directions.[40] Or we could turn to a psychoanalyst like M. Scott Peck, who has rediscovered the reality of the satanic in his psychoanalytical praxis.[41] Yet these would only be variations of positions that we have already

---

39. Susanne Heine, *Matriarchs, Goddesses, and Images of God: A Critique of Feminist Theology,* trans. John Bowden (Minneapolis: Augsburg, 1989), 34.

40. See Pierre Teilhard de Chardin, "Reflections on Original Sin," in *Christianity and Evolution,* trans. René Hague (New York: Harcourt Brace Jovanovich, 1971), 187–98, esp. 196.

41. M. Scott Peck, *People of the Lie: The Hope for Healing Human Evil* (New York: Simon and Schuster, 1983), 37f.

outlined. We bring to an end here our sketch of contemporary discussions, but in a concluding excursus will examine the treatment of the problem of evil outside of a Christian context, an area that, in our ever-shrinking world, demands increasing attention.

EXCURSUS: THE TREATMENT OF EVIL OUTSIDE THE CHRISTIAN CONTEXT

In his book *The Symbolism of Evil,* Paul Ricoeur classified the various myths about the origin and effects of evil into four general paradigm groups.[42]

1. The first of these that he lists is the creation drama, which is vividly portrayed in the Sumerian and Akkadian theological myths and also in the theogonies of Homer and Hesiod. The origin of the evil that befalls human beings is encompassed within the great story of a final victory of order over chaos in the collective generation of the gods, the cosmos, and humanity. Evil precedes human beings, who find it already present and in whom it lives further. Evil belongs, therefore, to the origin of all things. At the genesis of the present world it had to be overcome, yet it contributed to the condition of the present world. The order of our world is thus continually threatened by evil.

2. A second paradigm group introduces the concept of a "fall" of humanity. A tragic view of existence shows itself here in which both humans and the gods participate in evil. A heroic figure, one who possessed higher qualities than we do, commits a serious mistake that causes their fall. The pride of this tragic hero is the cause as well as the effect of the wickedness that belongs to the level of the divine. Ricoeur sees this embodied especially in the myth of Prometheus.

3. The third paradigm group is illustrated by the Archaic-Orphic myths that find their continuation in Platonism and Neoplatonism. One could characterize this group as the myth of the soul in exile that is imprisoned in a foreign body. Life appears as punishment, perhaps also as the result of an act committed in a

---

42. See Paul Ricoeur, *The Symbolism of Evil,* trans. E. Buchanan (New York: Harper, 1967), 175–305, and also see the brief summary in Paul Ricoeur, "Evil," in *ER* 5:201–4.

previous life. Evil is here identified with incarnation and often also, as in Eastern myths, with reincarnation.

4. Finally, Ricoeur presents the biblical "myth of Paradise lost." In contrast to the three preceding paradigm groups Ricoeur shows that here the creation is viewed as good and even very good and humans alone initiate evil, even when they succumb to a temptation. Significant here is that the tempter is a creature like the humans and that evil is assessed ethically because it arises out of an act of disobedience. Thus the myth of Adam is a pure anthropological myth that points to the same nature from which all succeeding generations emerge.

In regard to the Eastern religions of Hinduism and Buddhism, Ricoeur's fourfold division would certainly be helpful. One is confronted there, however, with such a diversity of deities and demons and with gods who are supposedly good but prove to be worse that what one might expect, and supposedly evil demons who ultimately turn out to be good, that in principle no uniform classification can do justice to this reality.[43] A short summary can at the most highlight some of the phenomena encountered.

Hinduism and Buddhism

In Hinduism our conceptualization, shaped largely through Christianity, by and large fails us. It is difficult there to precisely determine what is good and what is evil. The Brahmanic literature contains wonderful moral sayings concerning selflessness and restraint, yet the most popular gods, such as Vishnu and Shiva, do not allow themselves to be identified with any moral law or principle.[44] They stand above morality, and even the god of philosophy transcends good and evil. The goal of a philosophical saint consists not of choosing good and avoiding evil, but in coming closer to God by transcending both good and evil. Morality is certainly a means by which to live a happy life, but it does not arise out of obedience to a categorical imperative or the will of God. Of course morality also has the status of a cosmic law because evil deeds inevitably bring evil consequences upon one, either in this life or in the next. But one speaks in this regard not so much of a law but of the fact that humans want to be happy, and to this end morality is

---

43. See here the difficulty that Paul Ricoeur points to in "Evil," 204f.

44. See Charles Eliot, *Hinduism and Buddhism: An Historical Sketch* (1921) (London: Routledge and Kegan Paul, 1971), 1:lxxii.

a necessary, even if inadequate, preparation. Perhaps there is still something that transcends this life, yet this cannot be expressed by the concept of happiness (lxxvi).

In Hinduism, whether one considers it pantheistic or polytheistic, one has little interest in a personification of evil, for one refrains from explaining evil causally. "The Hindus think that it is possible and better for the soul to leave the vain show of the world and find peace in union with God. They are therefore not concerned to prove that the world is good, although they cannot explain why God allows it to exist" (lxxix). This world is primarily a world of suffering and imperfection, and it is not worth wasting a lot of thought upon. The seventh-century Tamil poet Appar summarized this perspective poignantly:

> Evil, all evil, my race, evil my qualities all,
> Great am I only in sin, evil is even my good.
> Evil my innermost self, foolish, avoiding the pure.
> Beast am I not, yet the ways of the beast I can never forsake.
> I can exhort with strong words, telling men what they should hate,
> Yet I can never give gifts, only to beg them I know.
> Ah! wretched man that I am, where unto came I to birth?[45]

This poem sounds much like an Old Testament psalm of lament, yet with a decisive difference: here there is no recognition that the person who is ensnared in evil and sin and who cannot do anything by his or her own power will finally be accepted by God. The only recourse is the urgent call to flee evil and the senselessness of this life because fulfillment of life on earth is not possible. There are other poems, however, by the same poet in which he confesses his belief in Shiva, the god who allows him to fear neither death nor hell. Here one could again point to a connection with the Old Testament. Yet the Old Testament believer stood firmly upon this earth and was rooted in this life. Old Testament believers certainly recognized evil and the injustice of this world, sometimes even almost to the point of despair, but they never gave up hope in a final justice and redemption. This world and the next are not held radically separate from one another in the Israelite faith but rather, as God's creation, are seen as a unity. Perhaps it is the doctrine of karma that makes it so difficult for Hindus to attribute anything positive to this world, for they are bound up in an endless chain of evil through human desires and sins. Whatever negative things

---

45. In Louis Renou, ed., *Hinduism* (New York: George Braziller, 1962), 198.

we do in this world will have consequences for us in the following world.

Buddhism begins precisely where Hinduism leaves off. Because one has recognized that in this life we are ensnared in an apparently unending chain of evil, Buddhism seeks to show us the way to escape from this dragnet of evil. When we look at Buddhism, however, we encounter a religion that, in principle, offers only a teaching, yet which has seldom existed in pure form but has rather taken on characteristics of a folk religion. Additionally, in Mara, Buddhism has a figure that, so to speak, personifies evil. One says of Buddha that he discovered that when we understand the world in its entirety as it really is, we can free ourselves from it and no longer be attached to anything. "To perceive evil as evil is the first instruction. Then perceiving evil as evil, be repelled by it, be cleansed, be freed from it; this is the second instruction."[46] Early Buddhism refrained from teaching a determinism of the human will. It recognized the hard reality of human wickedness but also taught that we have the power to make moral decisions.

The first step of humans in freeing themselves from their predicament consists in the recognition of the evil nature of their actions.[47] Next comes a sense of guilt followed by a confession of wrongdoing and finally the restoration of a condition of goodness. Thus in the Buddhist scriptures one finds many reports of confession of sin. In Buddhist monastic communities a list of moral errors is read publicly every two weeks, and each monk is expected at this time to admit his guilt. If he refuses to do this, then he is additionally guilty of consciously lying. If one, however, admits one's sin, one receives forgiveness and consolation. Thus it is important to recognize and confess evil as evil.

For evil or guilt various terms are used. *Papa* characterizes evil in a broad sense, mostly with a view to moral guilt. *Akusala* is that which is neither correct nor good. *Vajja* indicates that which should be avoided as error or sin. *Apunna* is that which is neither useful nor virtuous, and, finally, *Aparadha* indicates an offense.[48] Alongside of the reflective analysis of evil and the possibilities of responding to it, the Buddhist narratives also know of a concrete

---

46. So Thomas Berry, "The Problem of Moral Evil and Guilt in Early Buddhism," in *Concilium: Moral Evil under Challenge,* ed. Johannes B. Metz (New York: Herder and Herder, 1970), 131.

47. For this and the following see Berry, "The Problem," 131f.

48. The preceding list is adapted from Berry, "The Problem," 130f.

figure, Mara, who, as the incarnation of passion, angst, doubt, and self-delusion, seeks to lead the Buddhist astray from the right path. Mara, whom one can describe as a god, is first of all a deva or lord in the sensual realm and is the chief opponent of Buddha and his followers.[49] Mara, which means "death," can also be called Antaka (the end), Papima (the evil one), or Kanha (the dark one). Already during the life of Buddha, Mara sought to lead him astray from the correct path, especially as Buddha experienced his crucial enlightenment on the true nature of the world, and Mara was later decisively involved in moving Buddha to abandon this life.

Mara still seeks to lead the followers of Buddha astray from the right path through worldly pleasures or to intimidate them through self-doubt. Mara also has daughters who are named Passion, Desire, and Discontent and sons who bear the names Confusion, Pride, and Merriment. Along with his offspring, Mara is the incarnation of everything that a genuine Buddhist should avoid. He is not restricted to a certain area, but his kingdom extends throughout the entire world so that one is never free in this world from the fear of birth, death, and the continuous chain of reincarnation.[50] Mara holds the majority of humans under his spell. He will try everything to lead the followers of Buddha astray from the path of enlightenment and from right perception, knowledge, and action. Thus he is called the great confuser of humanity. Despite the fundamentally evil character of Mara, the early Buddhists believed that the Buddha and other wise ones would overcome Mara and his kingdom of death so that someday even the evil one would become a believer following the right path.

The story finally ends with a universal homecoming of all, for right thought and right action will extend themselves universally. Similar to the way in which Buddhism teaches how we can live in peace with other persons and nature, it also seeks to come to terms with evil and convert it to the good. One finds, however, little mention of the depth of our entanglement in this world, as is consistently portrayed in Judeo-Christian belief. Evil is indeed a phenomenon that one must approach with constant awareness, yet one is not helplessly delivered over to evil. In Buddhism this optimistic view of humanity is a precondition for the way of salvation,

49. For this and the following see Nancy E. Auer Falk, "Mara," in *ER* 9:187f.
50. For this and the following see James W. Boyd, *Satan and Mara: Christian and Buddhist Symbols of Evil* (Leiden: E. J. Brill, 1975), 129f.

for how can one reach Nirvana, the complete detachment from everything, if one cannot escape the clutches of this world? Judeo-Christian anthropology, in contrast, is essentially more pessimistic and yet also more realistic. It recognizes that evil is not gradually retreating from this world. If one can speak of any change at all, evil appears to take on evermore menacing dimensions. The one refuge, therefore, is the grace of God. Yet God does not lift one out of this world but rather transforms this world into a new one. Even human beings who put their trust in God and seek to live in God's grace are included in this process of transformation.

Islam

The view of evil in Islam is conspicuously marked by Old and New Testament influences. These influences show themselves even in a common vocabulary. In the Old Testament *chattat* indicates sin against God (Lev. 5:1), a word that appears in the Qur'an in the sense of mistake as *khatia* (Sura 33:5). The distinction between forgivable and unforgivable sins (1 John 5:16ff.) is to be found in Islam as well as in Christianity, with varying lists, however, of what is understood to fall under these respective categories.[51]

Although Allah's determining will dominates, there are many indications in the Qur'an that humans are responsible for their own actions. Thus we read in Sura 4:145f.: "The hypocrites shall be cast into the lowest depths of the Fire: there shall be none to help them. But to those who repent and amend their ways, who hold fast to Allah and are sincere in their devotion to Allah—they shall be numbered with the faithful, and the faithful shall be richly rewarded by Allah." Although the human heart tends toward evil (Sura 12:53), human beings are capable of changing their ways and will be held accountable for their behavior.

The relationship between the behavior of human beings and the reaction of Allah is often comparable to a reciprocal give and take. Yet the tradition emphasizes the sovereignty of God.[52] God forgives the serious sins of those whom he will and likewise punishes for no sin those whom he will; that is, he forgives and punishes according to his discretion. This sovereignty is grounded upon the fact that Allah has purchased the faithful, and they are his property

---

51. J. Windrow Sweetman, *Islam and Christian Theology: A Study of the Interpretation of Theological Ideas in the Two Religions*, pt. 1, vol. 2 (London: Lutterworth, 1947), 195f. and 201.

52. For this and the following quotation see Sweetman, *Islam*, 199.

(Sura 9:111). If one recognizes oneself as belonging to Allah, one receives the garden (paradise) as reward: "They will fight for the cause of Allah, slay and be slain. Such is the true promise which he has made them in the Torah, the Gospel and the Koran." They are completely given over to Allah and must even, if necessary, sacrifice their lives for him. This is justified in the Qur'an with reference to the Jewish and Christian traditions. One must note concerning this justification, however, that in these traditions human beings are in a close relationship with God but are never considered to be his slaves. In the Old Testament view members of the people of God are those who live in obedience to God and refrain from evil, that is, they do nothing that conflicts with God's benevolent will. In the New Testament it is especially emphasized that the gospel is something liberating. The individual is no longer enslaved but is rather a free child of God who is, however, encouraged to live in voluntary obedience to God.

Also, under what is understood in Islam as sin one recognizes once again similarities with the Christian tradition. Intrinsic to sin are pride and self-determining arrogance.[53] The primary example for this evil behavior is to be found in Iblis (Satan), who refused to bow down before Adam as Allah had commanded him. It is a sign of his disobedience and pride that he does not carry out the command of Allah (Sura 2:34). Satan then seduces Adam and Eve so that they fall from their state of innocence. Yet Adam did not willingly take this fatal step, for he was seduced. He regrets his transgression and is immediately forgiven by Allah (Sura 2:36-39).[54] Thus one finds no mention in the Qur'an of an original sin that is passed on to others. Adam's fall brought mortality only to himself because it was the sin of a single individual. "Man was created weak" (Sura 4:28), is how the Qur'an puts it. Humans are not sinful but rather weak and fall into sin and evil. But in his grace Allah brings them onto the right path. Thus evil is not viewed as a threatening fate but as something that basically cannot affect humans.

The view that humans are sinners who delight in evil and continuously turn away from God and toward what is ungodly is seldom emphasized in the Qur'an. Human beings are moral crea-

---

53. See Sweetman, *Islam*, 202, and André LaCocque, "Sin and Guilt," in *ER* 13:331.
54. Sweetman, *Islam*, 186.

tures and are fully responsible for their behavior. However, they sin occasionally, and for this they are rightly punished. Yet they are capable of choosing the good and securing for themselves the reward of Allah. The fact remains largely hidden that behind all of this stands the unmerited goodness of Allah, from whom humans have no right to expect anything. Seen from the Christian perspective, the Muslim understanding of sin and human freedom is essentially Pelagian.

Chapter 9

The Structures of Evil

At the conclusion of this book we attempt to shed light upon the structures of evil cognizant of the findings and positions that we have already examined. We want to determine what one can describe as evil within a Christian framework and what is evil even beyond this framework. Four points here are especially worthy of notice. First, it is necessary to explore the extent of evil so that we know where evil is to be located. Second, we speak of humanity that, as we have seen, is touched directly by evil. In light of the threat from evil we need to ask to what extent human beings are able to fulfill their destiny of living in a just and humane way. Third, we must also ask whether evil can simply be identified with something structural or material, or whether it also has personal characteristics. Finally, the question must be raised concerning the end of evil: Will evil always be with us? Is evil gradually retreating? Or will evil always exist as a counterpart to good? One could, of course, raise still other questions or examine additional structures. Yet it is one of the limitations of being human that whatever we attempt, our efforts must necessarily remain fragmentary.

The Extent of Evil

Evil extends itself wherever good is not present in its fullness, be it through a deficiency of good (*privatio boni*) or through a suppression of good. Evil is present in nature in the form of natural evil. In the human realm we encounter moral evil, and in the divine realm that which is totally antigodly. Because human behavior is subject to genetic and physical influences, one cannot strictly distinguish between natural and moral evil. The genetic and structural intertwining of the individual with other humans leads us to interrelational and social components of moral evil.

Especially in the case of natural occurrences it is not always possible to identify an event or a condition as unequivocally good or evil. The coming together of the waters of the Red Sea, for example, was evil for the Egyptians but not for the Israelites. Hence so-called natural disasters usually first need a personal interpretation in order to be perceived as evil. Biological phenomena are similarly ambiguous. Death is a natural phenomenon associated with aging. Yet it can also be experienced as punishment for human sinfulness. We cannot define evil in an objective and universally binding manner, but must rather recognize evil as such from the perspective of a specific view of the whole of reality. Evil is absurd and senseless in the natural as well as in the moral and metaphysical realms. When, for example, the tower of Siloah collapses and buries humans beneath its rubble, their lives are ended in a senseless way because human beings, according to the biblical understanding, have been created to enjoy God throughout a long and normal life. Every sudden, early death and every impairment caused through illness is viewed as senseless and evil. But this does not yet address the question of the origin of evil as the cause of adversity. On the one hand, it can come from God as punishment because certain individuals have related wrongly to God, that is, sinned. But, on the other hand, evil can be caused by wicked or antigodly powers, as the causes of sickness in the case of many of the miracles of Jesus demonstrate.

When we view moral evil as it manifests itself in human actions, it will at the same time be labeled theologically as sinful because it stands in opposition to that which is expected from human beings from the perspective of God's will. For this, however, no evil action need occur, rather, even an intention or will that tends toward a certain direction can be labeled as evil. Moral evil can work against nature, as for instance in the misuse of God's creation, a behavior that would today be labeled as ecologically reprehensible. It can be directed toward other persons, that is, evil in the interpersonal realm, or it can be directed toward the self when a person acts in a self-destructive manner. These intentions and behavioral patterns are understood theologically as sinful because they are planned or carried out in disregard to God's intentions or even in direct denial of God's will. Morally evil behavior is always at the same time sin against God. One cannot behave sinfully or in an evil manner against nature or against one's own self without at the same time sinning against God because such action also violates the ultimate context of meaning in which one lives.

Moral evil cannot be objectively or definitively defined but can only be comprehended and judged on the basis of a specific view of reality. The Ten Commandments, for example, as guidelines for morally irreproachable behavior, are interpreted differently in the Old Testament than in the Sermon on the Mount and yet still differently in Luther's exposition of the Ten Commandments. This does not, however, lead to a relativizing of moral evil because the Ten Commandments possess an unchanging validity as an expression of the will of God and thus of that which is good and which stands in opposition to evil. Nevertheless, the intention of that which is addressed by this divine will must be understood anew in each situation. This results in distinctions of meaning but not in a conflict of meaning. Within even the most diverse life sciences a binding code of behavior is repeatedly discovered and is affirmed by these various disciplines. Yet this behavioral code must be reinterpreted in each new situation in order for it to be able to instruct human behavior in the requirements for the furtherance and preservation of life. Here we could include, for instance, what Wolfgang Wickler and other behavioral researchers have termed the biology of the Ten Commandments and what, in another form, is meant by the theological concept of natural law.

In the context of nature as well as in the area of moral behavior we have found it necessary to introduce the concept of God in order to be able to enunciate the concept of evil. God, however, is not a positive foil against which evil becomes visible in its life-threatening essence. Evil is directed much more against God's self. Human pride and arrogance always want to replace the creator with the created and to remove God as the sole point of orientation. Evil is ultimately an assault against God through which that which is created is declared autonomous and humanity only values itself. Hence the horizon of an ultimate meaning is lost that unites and transcends all human beings. The human community is threatened with dissolution into rivaling individuals, all of whom wish to have their own limited horizons recognized as universally valid, thereby denying others the same rights and viewing them as virtually nonexistent. This leads either to an introverted isolation of individuals or to a battle of everyone against everyone else. In both cases the result is life-threatening excesses and a manifestation of evil. The rebellion against God caused by human pride is ultimately turned against humans themselves, who become their own worst enemies. How, then, can humans live in the face of this evil that they themselves seem to have caused?

Humanity in the Face of Evil

If evil extends itself from the natural realm to God and is only describable in opposition and in contrast to God as that which is perfectly good, then one must agree with Augustine and Luther that there is no neutral territory between good and evil, between God and Satan. The human being lives under the influence either of good or of evil. Yet this diagnosis does not appear to do justice to the reality of human existence. Good and evil motives are mixed together in most of our actions or exist alongside of one another. A purely evil human being is just as much an artificial construct as a human being who is purely good. This recognition leads often to the claim that humans can choose freely between good and evil and can turn from evil toward the good if they only set their minds to it. But when Freud, for example, attributes a life and a death drive to humans, he does not yet say anything concerning the context in which the duality of the life and the death drives is unfolded. Paul, too, admits that Christians do not always prove themselves to be followers of Christ. Yet knowing this he does not deny that they are still Christians. Conversely, Augustine spoke of the virtues of the pagans and at the same time described them as splendid vices, interpreting these within the context of paganism.

Humans are always free insofar as they can choose between good and evil within the context of the freedom granted them by their genetic dispositions and psychosocial influences. The extent of this freedom may be greater for one than it is for another, but it is never completely absent, for in that case, the human person would be reduced to a completely determined, nonhuman existence. Within the context of their respective freedom humans are responsible for their (evil) deeds. And even beyond the confines of their freedom they remain responsible, for as rational beings they are capable, at least in principle, of recognizing the boundaries of their freedom and of assessing its predetermining factors. When, for example, someone is genetically disposed toward heart disease because the person's mother suffered from clogging of the coronary vessels, yet nevertheless does not stay properly fit but instead regularly eats fatty foods, such conduct can be called not only un-wise but also evil. A restriction of the freedom of choice, therefore, does not diminish one's accountability.

But what of the evil that comes upon humans like an overpow-ering fate, even when they take their own responsibility seriously? What do we say when someone who led a healthy life is diagnosed with an inoperable cancer that will cause death within six months? Or what of the evil that is already distributed at birth to someone who, for instance, because of a mother's drug abuse comes into the world severely genetically damaged? In such cases we cannot speak of the responsibility or of the guilt of the one who is struck by evil. At the most we could speak of the guilt or evil of a previ-ous generation, for instance of the drug-addicted mother, or in our contemporary generation, of the guilt of a company that produces cancer-causing materials and passes them into the food chain. The evil that is inflicted upon some innocent person is then the result of the evil actions of others to which he or she is subjected usu-ally without his or her consent. Such evil causal connections can at the most illustrate the perversion of humanity, but they cannot liberate the victims from the consequences of evil or make these consequences more acceptable to them.

Evil exists and strikes one person while it passes over others who seem to exhibit more affinity for evil in the decisions they make. This mystery has bewildered and dejected humans since at least the Old Testament story of Job, and they have not to this day found a solution to it. According to the Gospel of John, not even Jesus was able to directly answer the question why a certain man had been born blind. Yet he rejected the simple action-consequence connection. The sins of the man born blind or those of his parents are in Jesus' view insufficient for explaining why this particular man was afflicted in this way. The attempt of a theodicy, that is, the justification of God in the face of evil, must always remain in-complete and questionable.[1] To introduce a self-limitation of God, as it is most persuasively attempted in process theology, a theodicy must bear the weight of the question of why God, if he is truly God, limits himself in his actions.

---

1. John Hick, *Evil and the God of Love* (New York: Harper, 1966), 397f., can, for example, also give no answer as to the why of the Nazi crimes. He must limit himself to declaring that despite these crimes God's loving will reaches its eschatological goal. Despite his efforts, Hick is unable to offer a plausible theodicy.

The question of the meaning of evil is unanswerable from the very beginning because evil cannot have a meaning but is basically senseless because it contradicts the meaning of all existence, which is to glorify and honor God. An adequate answer is also elusive to the question of why many people do not escape evil's influence although they and other well-intentioned people diligently seek to do so, while others remain in God's sphere of influence despite being threatened by great evil. Even Augustine's response that we have all earned nothing but death and thus every lifting out of evil's realm of influence is an unearned act of grace does not remove the mystery of why some people persist in one of the two realms instead of moving to the other.

And what of the so-called hereditary or original sin into which we are all born? Is it similar to a mysterious fate or an evil alignment of genes? If the latter were the case, then one could conceivably overcome it by means of a yet to be discovered "prenatal gene therapy." Yet we are confronted neither with an inescapable, mysterious fate nor with a hereditary genetic misalignment. The concept of original sin is an expression of the simple fact that humans do not live in isolation but are always born into a community or context in which they mature, and from which they receive decisive impulses. As the various religions show, human society, and each of its parts, is characterized by a fundamental estrangement from its ultimate point of reference. We are all born into a sphere of alienation from God. Through various means, religious and otherwise, humanity seeks to overcome this evil constellation.

Among the various religions there is agreement on the basic fact of our estrangement from that which is good. Disputed, however, is the question of the valuation and overcoming of this estrangement. According to the Jewish and Christian understanding, the sphere of estrangement or evil is so strong that one cannot simply label it as illusory or unreal and thus escape from it. Even the recognition of the nature of things and of the interconnectedness of our existence helps us at the most to better cope with existence but not to escape from this evil sphere. The summoning of our energies and trying to lead morally impeccable lives do not change our lot, for we do not find ourselves on an island but are continually surrounded by sinful individuals who influence us. A decisive change can occur only when God himself takes the initiative. This idea of a divine initiative is already prefigured in the Old Testament covenant concept and finds its fulfillment in the new covenant in Jesus Christ.

If the evil sphere proves to be so extensive and serious, can we really be held accountable for belonging to it? The answer to this question is to be found within the history of humans themselves who speak of high moral ideals and often realize these in an exemplary way, but who fall again and again into the worst barbarism and self-destructive evil. This holds true for the individual as much as for humanity as a whole. For this reason the church has stressed that even "saints" only have a chance to break free from the spell of evil because God has graciously sanctified them. Humans are not the authors of their fortune but of their misfortune. If humans are so strongly held under the spell of evil, then we must inquire as to how such evil is to be understood.

The Personification of Evil

When we speak of a personification of evil, we do not wish to return to a kind of polydemonism that came to have disastrous effects in the medieval church and that led to witch-hunts and mass neuroses. At least since Rudolf Bultmann's essay on demythologization it has become clear that we cannot believe in the New Testament world of spirits and demons and at the same time enjoy all the technological "achievements" of the thoroughly enlightened twentieth century that have been made possible by human inventiveness and rational planning. At the same time we do not dare close our eyes to the fact that the irrational, demonic, and esoteric are rapidly gaining influence among people of all walks of life. Already in 1979, for instance, it was found that in the United States thirty-two million people followed astrology and a further seventeen million experimented with esoteric religions. Since then these numbers have increased substantially. In Europe the situation is not very different. In Germany, which is far from atypical in this regard, there is hardly a bookstore to be found without a section on esoteric and paranormal materials. Occultism is already familiar to German school children, and Satanism is not restricted to California.

The concept of evil, which was central to religious thought for millennia, has almost completely disappeared from the vocabulary of the human sciences that seek to describe the human situation.[2]

---

2. So M. Scott Peck, *People of the Lie* (New York: Simon and Schuster, 1983), 39f.

Psychologists and psychiatrists speak at the most about disease and its treatment, but they say little about egotism and guilt, "and certainly no one talks about sin!"[3] Sin even became taboo in theological circles so that one could only write of estrangement or of a falling short of one's own potential. Yet the times appear to be changing. Karl Menninger, the founder of the Menninger-Foundation in Topeka, Kansas, wrote in 1973 the book *Whatever Became of Sin?* He wanted to once again clearly name those things that are bad and evil and that require repentance. The psychiatrist M. Scott Peck, a student of Erich Fromm, today claims that the question concerning evil inevitably leads to the question of the devil, precisely as the issue of goodness leads to the question of God and creation.[4] "Humanity (and perhaps the entire universe) is locked into a titanic struggle between the forces of good and evil, between God and the devil. The battleground of this struggle is the individual human soul. The entire meaning of human life revolves around the battle. The only question of ultimate significance is whether the individual soul will be won by God or won by the devil."

Yet is it really necessary to personify evil? Is it not sufficient when one recognizes the penetrating power of evil? In this regard the philosopher of religion Frederick Sontag has written: "To personify the forces of evil in the Devil, or the powers of goodness in God, is not a falsification but a necessity, that is if we accept the crucial role of personality in all selection for existence or destruction."[5] None of those we have here cited comes out of evangelical circles from which one might reasonably expect such arguments to arise.

The basic consideration that has led to these statements is relatively simple. It has been recognized that the presupposition that evil cannot exist as an independent entity is questionable. Hence entirely new explanatory possibilities arise regarding the phenomenon of evil. From the perspective of human beings evil manifests itself in nature as well as in humanity. Psychoanalysis has already moved beyond humanity in its explanation of evil. Freud related the destructive forces within humanity to an ambivalent superego,

---

3. Karl Menninger, *Whatever Became of Sin?* (New York: Hawthorn, 1973), 228.

4. See Peck, *People*, 42; for the following quotation, 37.

5. Frederick Sontag, *The God of Evil: An Argument from the Existence of the Devil* (New York: Harper, 1970), 158.

and Jung, in a similar way, to archetypes and the shadow of the individual. The destructive tendencies of these phenomena were explained as arising from the memories of the individual or of humanity as a whole. When one wishes to remain within the confines of the objective reality of humanity and give no further explanation of the destructive forces, a constitutional atrophy of humanity would seem to be the tacit conclusion. Yet such an explanation was already rejected by Kant. One confronts here the mysterious nature of destructiveness while at the same time taking the good for granted. It is, however, interesting that the good is always traced back to God as its author so that the unity of its purpose can be preserved. When this is not done the inevitable result is the division and fragmentation of the good. Hence the good is to be understood as personal for it has its personal source in God, and in humanity it finds its personal recipient. But what, then, is the situation in regard to evil?

For the Judeo-Christian tradition it has always been clear that evil could not be God's equal. Rather, evil encounters its limits and limitation in God. Evil is therefore secondary to God. Yet this conclusion is often misunderstood as meaning that God must be either the author or at least the coauthor of evil. The story of the fall at the very beginning of the Old Testament canon, however, establishes that in a mysterious way evil came out of God's good creation. Precisely how it happened that evil denied its own origin and turned against the creator is not explained within the biblical writings. At the most one finds only extrabiblical speculations regarding this question. Although God was probably viewed in the beginning as the author of all things, both the good and the evil, this tension within God has rightly been abandoned and evil has been gradually excluded from God, because God was in danger of being perverted into a demonic power. The exclusion of evil from God is emphatically documented in the story of the fall. Analogous to our understanding of God, our conception of evil has also experienced an increasing differentiation between levels of evil and has led to a virtual hierarchy of evil spirits. Because it was the mission of Jesus to overcome evil, it is only natural that evil fought strenuously against him and opposed him from the first day of his mission to the last. This anti-Christian aspect of evil finds its logical continuation in the battle with the followers of Jesus and extends even to all persons who are born and live within evil's sphere of influence.

If the destructive forces of evil confronted us as an impersonal "it," we would have no choice but to view them as a fate or destiny to which we are helplessly handed over and from which there is no escape. Yet this view of evil is deficient for at least two reasons. In order to demonstrate the first reason it is not necessary to call to mind the extremes of black masses or of satanic cults whose followers, in pseudoreligious devotion, consciously dedicate themselves to the forces of evil. It suffices to look at the everyday behavior of human beings. Humans do not confront evil as an unalterable fate. Rather, they continually give themselves and others over to evil with a strangely destructive desire even though they realize that they should not do so and that in the end they will inflict harm upon themselves. Second, some of the characteristics of the phenomenon of aggression, as these have been examined by Konrad Lorenz for instance, likewise show that human beings are virtually addicted to evil. As the wave of interest in the occult and New Age reveals, humans yearn after powers that promise them the experience of a new wholeness. Humans then subject their "weak wills" willingly and with longing to these powers. Human beings, however, need not remain under the influence of these partly illusory, partly real and destructive powers of evil. The Christian faith testifies to the fact that it liberates human beings to their true selves and gives them genuine freedom and wholeness. Paul speaks of this when he says that we can become a new creation (Romans 6).

We are not confronted with an impersonal fate or destiny that we experience to be evil but rather with the influence of a will to which we subordinate our own will and from which we cannot escape through our own strength. We encounter evil as a threatening and overpowering opponent that desires to bring and keep us within its sphere of influence. A personal conception of these various destructive forces as *antigodly powers* emphasizes their manifoldness while at the same time taking into account their common purpose through which they always oppose the good, namely, God. With the term "antigodly powers" we avoid the potential misunderstanding that we are speaking here of Satan or the devil in a way analogous to myths and fairy tales. This would also make it clear that these powers are not to be located within humanity at either the individual or collective level but rather find their limits in God. Because God has a history with humanity, it is unlikely that these powers would not be included within this history. Therefore we must speak of the historicalness or the end of evil.

The End of Evil

Although the world as the creation of God is good, the eschatological "not yet" reminds us that the redemption brought about in and through Christ is not yet universal and self-evident. This fact is pointed to by a variety of natural occurrences that, as we know from the New Testament witness, will not become part of the new creation. One of these natural occurrences is the necessary death of one living organism so that other organisms can be preserved and fostered. We could describe these phenomena as "natural evil" in order to indicate that we are not speaking here of antigodly constellations but rather of occurrences that conform to the present form of the world. Yet we do not perceive the phenomenon of death as something natural but rather as something very much unnatural that we fear, deny, and continually attempt to avoid. Theologically, death and the necessity of dying can be interpreted as punishment for our sinfulness. From this negative phenomenon of the necessity of dying, however, we cannot refer univocally to its causation, that is, God or antigodly powers.[6] When something imperfect—that is not necessarily to say evil—is contained within God's natural activity, one cannot assume that evil will be ever more constrained within the program of history.

In the Christian tradition and its secularized variety the future of evil is interpreted in contradictory terms. Millenarian movements continue to appear and announce the imminent in-breaking of the thousand-year reign of Christ, an era in which evil will be completely removed from the picture. But these hopes have always been disappointed. Those representing the opposite tendency, who label certain religious or political figures as Antichrist in order to indicate that evil has reached its pinnacle, have fared no better.[7] Through the progression of history such analyses are continually relativized and often simply dismissed as wrong. Although in the course of history the human potential for good and evil has increased, as is to be seen in modern technological advances, one is

---

6. For a more detailed discussion see Hans Schwarz, *On the Way to the Future: A Christian View of Eschatology in the Light of Current Trends in Religion, Philosophy, and Science*, rev. ed. (Minneapolis: Augsburg, 1979), 196ff.

7. See Schwarz, *On the Way*, 254f.

not able to empirically determine that evil is either increasing or decreasing. If anything a sensitizing toward new areas in which humans are prone to evil is to be recognized, as can be seen, for example, in the increasing awareness in many countries of environmental problems. But even here human behavior is curiously inconsistent, for one finds it much easier to identify the mistakes and abuses of others than one's own.

In the biblical view, evil is not an enduring necessity needed as a moral backdrop for the good. As the biblical drama of redemption indicates, Satan has already fallen from heaven like a flash of lightning, and the old evil foe is already condemned, as Martin Luther wrote in "A Mighty Fortress Is Our God" (LBW 228). Whoever confesses Christ is already liberated from the sphere of evil. This fact is reiterated at every baptism when the stain of the old world is washed away and the baptized is marked—as with a branding iron—with the sign of the cross as belonging to God. The powers of darkness rule now only in a fractured way; they dare only continue to pursue their evil ways during the interim period between the coming of Jesus in Bethlehem and his coming in the parousia.

The well-known saying that Christians are at the same time saints and sinners (*simul justus et peccator*) points to the fact that Christians, although no longer within evil's sphere, must nevertheless live out their earthly existence under the conditions and within the context of evil. The Christian, who is continually tempted to wander off into a state of estrangement from God, commits evil deeds too. Luther, therefore, in his explanation of baptism in the Small Catechism emphasizes that the old Adam should be daily drowned through remorse and repentance and a new person must daily rise up who lives in purity eternally before God. The essential liberation from evil's sphere must every day be reappropriated and put into practice. Christians are in no better position, in this regard, than anyone else. They are not, as if by magic, immunized against evil so that it rolls off of them like water off an umbrella. Because through their God-centeredness Christians are able to recognize the good, they are also more keenly aware of evil. Their consciences are, so to speak, sensitized, and they perceive evil where others see only what is to them the normal affairs of the world. Christians find themselves placed within a greater arena of responsibility than others, for they are more aware of what or whom they must fight against and are more often challenged. When their inexplicable defeats bring them to the verge of despair (Romans 7), they can nonetheless take comfort in the fact that nothing can ultimately separate them from the love of God (Rom. 8:38f.). Their defeats and the victories of evil resemble rearguard actions that, although certainly to be taken seriously, no longer possess the sting of death and are unable to bring these persons eternally within evil's sphere.

When in the context of world history no visible progress against evil can be detected, is there at least progress in the lives of individual Christians? Making use of biblical imagery, Martin Luther pointed out in this regard that it is only to be expected that a good tree bear good fruit. This means that a person who has been liberated from the power of evil can achieve a sustained resistance against it. In this regard the Eastern Orthodox Church has introduced the concept of deification (*theosis*), in order to show that an increase of holiness and a decrease of evil can occur in human beings. This "sanctification," however, should be understood neither as a dynamic progression coupled with age nor as the success of one's own efforts to come continually closer to God. The "great saints" of the church always recognized how far removed they were from God and that every step along the way toward sanctification brought with it an increasing awareness of their own inadequacy and wickedness. The rift between the truly good God and humanity, that is, that which is created, can never be overcome upon this earth. For this the visible and universal conquest of evil is necessary when God will dwell among human beings and they will be his people and he will be their God (Rev. 21:3). But this remains an eschatological promise for which we wait and hope and that we can at the most experience proleptically in approximation.

We have seen within the context of our investigation how far the phenomenon of evil has branched out and in how many ways it manifests itself in this world. It has become clear to us that one cannot approach evil as if it were a relic of a previous developmental epoch of humanity. Evil remains among us as something very much alive and deeply threatening and destructive. Ultimately, evil is that which is antigodly; that is, it is that which experiences its limits and its rejection through God, the source of all that is good. It is through this God who has disclosed himself to us in the Judeo-Christian tradition that we can face up to evil in this world. Although we will not always be victorious, we need not fear that evil will devour us. God himself has set boundaries for evil that it cannot overstep.

Index of Ancient Texts

213

Index of Names

219

Index of Subjects

223